Redefining

Redefining the Self

Coming out as Lesbian

LAURA A. MARKOWE

Polity Press

First published in 1996 by Polity Press in association with Blackwell Publishers Ltd.

2 4 6 8 10 9 7 5 3 1

Editorial office:
Polity Press
65 Bridge Street
Cambridge CB2 1UR, UK

Marketing and production:
Blackwell Publishers Ltd
108 Cowley Road
Oxford OX4 1JF, UK

Published in the USA by
Blackwell Publishers Inc.
238 Main Street
Cambridge, MA 02142, USA

British Library Cataloguing-in-Publication Data

Markowe, Laura A.
Redefining the self: coming out as lesbian / Laura A. Markowe.
p. cm.
Includes bibliographical references and index.
ISBN 0–7456–1128–1 (hardcover : alk. paper). — ISBN 0–7456–1129–X (pbk. : alk. paper)
1. Lesbians. 2. Lesbians—Identity. 3. Coming out (Sexual orientation) I. Title.
HQ75.5.M37 1996 96–798
305.48'9664—dc20 CIP

A CIP catalogue record for this book is available from the British Library.

Typeset in 10½/12 pt Sabon by Photoprint, Torquay, Devon
Printed in Great Britain by T. J. Press (Padstow) Ltd., Padstow, Cornwall

This book is printed on acid-free paper.

Contents

Acknowledgements

Firstly, my thanks to all the women and men who participated in this study; and to all at the London School of Economics who helped me in different ways with the research. In particular, I am grateful to Jan Stockdale for advice, constructive criticism and support throughout.

Also, I would like to acknowledge award no. A00428624071 received from the Economic and Social Research Council.

While writing the book, I have appreciated help from friends. Especial thanks to Carol-Ann Hooper and Carolyn Whitehead for comments on draft chapters. Additionally, I thank colleagues at South Bank University for their support.

Finally, my thanks to my family, my mother especially, and to Jill Woollaston. Their background support and encouragement have been invaluable.

1

Context and issues

> . . . when I realized that I was sexually attracted to this particular woman . . . I felt absolutely terrible. I felt quite suicidal. I felt like walking into the sea . . . I felt panic stricken . . . and I felt quite excited and relieved in a way.
>
> (Emma, lesbian group)

> . . . the concept of liking someone of the same sex in that respect – in a sexual respect – is very foreign to me . . . it's a foreign land. I mean it's more foreign than going to a country you know nothing about . . .
>
> (Robert, heterosexual group)

Lesbians exist within a predominantly heterosexual society. Heterosexual relations structure societal notions of gender which reflect division and power inequalities between women and men. Our society reflects particular understandings of gender, as well as ideas on human nature and 'normality'. 'Coming out', both in terms of coming to identify oneself as lesbian, and in terms of telling others about oneself, takes place within this social context.

Heterosexuals' attitudes are a fundamental influence in shaping the social context within which coming out occurs. Therefore, it is essential to consider heterosexual perspectives on homosexuality, in addition to lesbians' perceptions and experiences of coming out, to understand the coming-out process.

This study is an attempt to investigate both 'coming out to self' and 'coming out to others'. Becoming aware of oneself as lesbian is a profound experience for the individual. Analysis of 'coming out', however, requires not just investigation at the individual, intrapsychic or interpersonal levels, but also an understanding of the issue at intergroup and societal levels.

A considerable amount of anecdotal material on coming out has been published in recent years. Research, however, has tended to focus on gay men rather than lesbians, and has tended to be

American rather than British. While some women develop awareness of themselves as lesbian within a political or radical feminist context, some have been more isolated from other lesbians. It is lesbian women from this latter group that form the focus of this study. The study aims to provide a systematic investigation of the coming-out process for these more isolated lesbians, by a lesbian, from a social-psychological perspective.

After looking at definitions, some issues and questions relating to coming out will be raised. This is followed by a brief summary of the background literature and theory relevant to the study. Finally, in this chapter, an outline of the book is presented.

Definitions

Coming out

Coming out has been defined in a variety of ways in previous studies. The working definition used here covers both 'coming out to self' – becoming aware of oneself as lesbian; and 'coming out to others' – disclosing this information to other people.

Lesbian

The term 'lesbian' has its origins in the association of the Greek island of Lesbos with the poet Sappho (*circa* 600 BC). References to the use of the term 'lesbian' (in the sense of referring to female homosexuality) provided by the *Oxford English Dictionary* (1989) date back to the last part of the nineteenth century. The dictionary definition of lesbian refers to women's homosexuality: 'Of a woman: homosexual, characterized by a sexual interest in other women. Also, of or pertaining to homosexual relations between women'.

This type of definition, focused only upon sex, provides a very limited view of lesbianism. Definition of the term 'lesbian' actually requires a broader, more complex basis, incorporating emotional, social and political aspects: issues that are to be developed and discussed in later chapters. For practical purposes, lesbian women participating in this study were simply women who defined themselves as lesbian or gay.

Homosexual

The *Oxford English Dictionary* (1989) defines 'homosexual' in terms of having a sexual propensity for one's own sex, and gives references to usage of the word dating back to the 1890s by, for example, Krafft-Ebing and Havelock Ellis.

Some people have used the term 'homosexual' for men only. However, 'homo-' is derived from the Greek *homos* meaning 'same', as opposed to 'hetero-', from the Greek *heteros* referring to 'other' (*Collins English Dictionary*, 1979). Within the text here, 'homosexual' is used to refer to both men and women, unless otherwise specified.

Gay

Popular use of the term 'gay' relating to homosexuality is relatively recent. It was associated in particular with gay liberation, a movement aimed at freeing homosexuals from discrimination, originating in the United States in the 1960s. The Gay Liberation Front began meeting in this country in London – at the London School of Economics – in 1970 (Weeks, 1977). As with the term 'homosexual', some use 'gay' to refer only to men. Here, it is used to refer to both women and men, unless gender is specified.

Although differences in origin and detailed meaning of the terms homosexual, gay and lesbian are recognized by the author, the terms are used synonymously within this book when describing lesbians, unless stated otherwise. Where the terms gay and homosexual have been used in previous studies, or by participants in this study, where possible, indication is given if usage was limited to males.

The coming-out process for lesbians: some issues and questions

Why is coming out of importance?

Previous studies (e.g. Sophie, 1985; de Monteflores and Schultz, 1978; Moses, 1978; Brooks, 1981), anecdotal material on coming out (e.g. Stewart-Park and Cassidy, 1977; Stanley and Wolfe, 1980; Penelope and Wolfe, 1989; Holmes, 1988; Hall Carpenter Archives, Lesbian Oral History Group, 1989), and pilot-study data (Markowe, 1985) have indicated that becoming aware of oneself as lesbian and disclosing this information to others often involves a complexity of dilemmas and issues to be resolved. It is rarely a simple, straightforward process. It may involve dealing with a variety of 'hazards' (Baetz, 1984), and may affect much of a gay person's everyday life (Durell, 1983). Reflecting the potentially problematic nature of coming out are studies that have found considerable levels of reported suicide attempts or suicidal thoughts (e.g. Trenchard and Warren, 1984; Bradford et al., 1994). At the individual and interpersonal levels, issues of coming out profoundly affect women's perceptions of self and their relations with family and friends. An understanding of the impact of coming to identify self as lesbian, and its effect on interpersonal relations, is important in order to identify possible problems, to generate ideas for the reduction of any such difficulties and, hence, to facilitate the process of coming out.

Taking a broader perspective, it will be argued that intra-psychic and interpersonal aspects of coming out may only be understood within the context of intergroup relations and the social/cultural context. From such a perspective, the issues of coming out may be seen as associated with, and as reflecting, fundamental aspects of notions of gender; relations between women and men in our society; power inequalities; and ideas on human nature, and 'normality'.

What happens during the coming-out process?

The coming-out process for lesbians is a complex process, that may broadly be divided into coming out to self, and coming out to others. Coming out to self, coming to define oneself as lesbian, has been considered in previous studies mainly from the perspective of stage theories (e.g. Cass, 1979; Chapman and Brannock, 1987). The pilot-study material raised questions of the appropriateness of viewing coming out to self in terms of linear stages. Positive and negative forces that may affect coming out to self and others were suggested.

When a woman has begun to think of herself as (possibly) lesbian, she may be in the position of considering making contact with other lesbians for the first time. She may also consider telling family or friends about herself. These decisions about coming out to others take place within the social context of a predominantly heterosexual society.

Importance of considering lesbian and *heterosexual perspectives*

Coming out needs to be interpreted at the societal and intergroup levels within the framework of the relationship of lesbianism to heterosexuality in our society; and at the interpersonal level by examining relations between lesbians and heterosexual people. It is suggested in this book that coming out as lesbian is only an issue within the context of a heterosexist society: a society that is predominantly heterosexual and in which there is oppression of homosexuality. In the same way as it may be perceived that an investigation of women needs to be understood within the broader context of gender relations (e.g. Hollway, 1989), it is suggested here that issues of coming out as lesbian may only be meaningfully interpreted within the context of the relationship between lesbianism and heterosexuality in our society. Thus coming out needs to be investigated taking into account this social context, and examining the heterosexual perspective as well as that of lesbians.

Gender issues

Homosexuality and heterosexuality need to be viewed from the perspective of societal notions of gender. These reflect fundamental inequalities between women and men in our society.

Early conceptualization of gender in terms of sex role may be seen as restricted. Later studies, however, have illuminated how gender may structure our thinking through cognitive schema (Bem, 1981); and how gender may more usefully be thought of in terms of negotiable boundaries (Condor, 1987). Further, assumptions of gender polarization, androcentrism and biological essentialism may be seen as embedded in our culture (Bem, 1993). From another perspective, there may be different social representations of gender (Duveen and Lloyd, 1987).

Rigid notions of gender division may be seen as serving to maintain the predominance of heterosexuality within our society. Coming out as lesbian needs to be understood within the context of gender inequalities; the function of heterosexuality in maintaining gender division; and differing conceptualizations of gender.

Comparison of coming out with other minority group or life experiences

Taking a broad view of the coming-out process, there are other minority group experiences, or life experiences, that have some similarities with the coming-out process for lesbians. An examination of similarities and differences between coming out and other minority group experiences or life events may serve to illuminate what is occurring during the coming-out process.

Notions of 'stigma' (Goffman, 1963; Jones et al., 1984) and coping with threatened identity (Breakwell, 1986) provide frameworks within which a variety of minority group or life experiences may be understood. Examples of such experiences described within these frameworks have ranged, in the case of stigma, from the physically handicapped to ex-mental patients, alcoholics or religious minority members; and from unemployment to sexually atypical employment, from the viewpoint of threatened identity. Coming out is to be examined from these perspectives in later chapters.

What would facilitate coming out?

Attempts to answer this question require consideration of issues at all levels, from intra-psychic through interpersonal and intergroup levels, to the cultural/ideological level. While coping mechanisms suggested, for example, in the threatened-identity model (Breakwell, 1986) may aid individuals at intra-psychic and interpersonal levels, and group support may play an important role, it may be that the crucial level for change is societal/cultural. Modifications in social representations to incorporate more flexible notions of gender and 'normality' may be essential for facilitating the coming-out process at intra-psychic and interpersonal levels.

Background

Areas that need consideration as background to understanding the coming-out process include lesbian identity; lesbian identity formation; the notion of coming out; heterosexuals' attitudes towards homosexuals, and stereotyping. Examination of these issues raises fundamental questions of conceptualization of gender; and relations between women and men in our society. Social-psychological perspectives of social identity theory (Tajfel, 1981) and social representations (Moscovici, 1984), as well as the notion of threatened identity (Breakwell, 1986), contribute to an understanding of coming out.

Lesbian identity and coming out

Previous studies concerned with lesbian identity have suggested that lesbians may be seen as 'homoemotional' rather than 'homosexual' (Wolff, 1973), and that there may be more than one lesbian identity (Ettorre, 1980; Kitzinger and Stainton Rogers, 1985). 'Lesbian existence' within the context of 'compulsory heterosexuality' was suggested by Rich (1981). Postmodernist thinking has focused on lesbian performance/behaviour rather than lesbian 'being' (e.g. Butler, 1991). These studies indicate lesbian identities may be seen as socially constructed.

In coming out to others, anecdotal material and findings of studies (e.g. Ponse, 1978; de Monteflores and Schultz, 1978; Moses, 1978) indicate the importance of considering non-disclosure as well as disclosure; and possible differences in the coming-out experiences of lesbians and gay men, and between younger and older gay people.

Coming out to family and coming out at work are two areas of particular importance, some lesbians telling family members and maybe coming out at work, and others taking the decision not to disclose this information (e.g. Trenchard and Warren, 1984; Taylor, 1986). Possible discrimination against the lesbian as a woman must be considered as well as that based on sexuality. In coming out at work, type of job and work environment are pertinent too.

Heterosexuals' attitudes and stereotyping

Attitudes towards homosexuality in Britain are still predominantly negative (e.g. Wellings et al., 1994). Such attitudes need to be understood within the historical and cultural context. Religion, for example, may have played an important underlying role in attitude formation (Coleman, 1980).

Many studies have attempted to construct scales to measure attitudes towards homosexuals (e.g. Herek, 1984a, 1988; Kite and Deaux, 1986). Conceptual and methodological problems of early studies have been highlighted by later studies.

Examples of issues investigated have been possible variations in attitudes towards homosexuals with sex or sex role of participant, or sex of target (e.g. Kite, 1984; Herek, 1988, 1994; Newman, 1989); and possible variation in attitudes towards homosexuals with beliefs about homosexuality as physiologically based, or determined by learning and personal choice (Aguero et al., 1984). A question raised is the possibility of changing attitudes towards homosexuality.

Stereotypes may affect interpersonal behaviour through, for example, self-fulfilling prophecies (Zanna and Pack, 1975; Jones et al., 1984). Studies of stereotyping of homosexuals have focused on sex role (e.g. Taylor, 1983), finding that lesbians tend to be perceived as similar to heterosexual men, and gay men as similar to heterosexual women. Measures of sex role have included the Bem Sex-Role Inventory (BSRI: Bem, 1974) and the Personal Attributes Questionnaire (PAQ: Spence et al., 1974, 1975).

A social-psychological perspective

A social-psychological analysis of coming out needs to be understood within the framework of issues of gender. Power differences related to gender are essential to consider. In coming out, whether to self or others, the lesbian must be seen as a woman, with all the implications being female has within our society.

Doise (1978, cited in Doise, 1984) has suggested different levels of analysis. The coming-out process requires examination from intergroup and societal perspectives, as well as on individual/interpersonal levels.

From the perspective of social identity theory, where social identity refers to the part of a person's self-concept deriving from group membership (Tajfel, 1981), or self-categorization theory (Turner et al., 1987), coming out may be seen in terms of salience of social categories (Oakes, 1987). This perspective incorporates notions of 'personal' and 'social' identity (Turner, 1982). Social identity as lesbian may be seen as becoming salient during the coming-out to self process. In coming out to others, social identity as lesbian is *made* salient.

Social representations may underlie lesbians' perceptions and experiences of coming out, and heterosexuals' attitudes towards homosexuals. Social representations have been defined by Moscovici and Hewstone (1983) in terms of cognitive matrices linking ideas, images etc., or as common-sense theories of aspects of society. Through social representations, scientific notions are transformed into common-sense knowledge. Social representations conventionalize and categorize persons or events, and are prescriptive (Moscovici, 1984). Attitudes may be considered as individual response dispositions based on collective representations (Jaspars and Fraser, 1984). Moscovici and Hewstone (1983) have suggested that social representations of human nature may underlie racialism. It is suggested here that such representations may underlie heterosexism too. In addition, social representations of gender (Duveen and Lloyd, 1987) are relevant to considering lesbians and coming out. Theories about the development of homosexuality, such as those based on a medical model, physiological explanations, or the psychoanalytic perspective, are likely to be reflected in relevant social representations, and may influence attitudes towards lesbians.

Attributions or 'common-sense explanations' (Hewstone, 1983) may influence the coming-out process on individual and social levels. Behaviour may be attributed to disposition or situation; or to internal or external factors. Biases in attribution include the 'fundamental attribution error' of a tendency to underestimate the effect of situational factors and overestimate the effect of dispositional factors (Ross, 1977); and actors attributing their actions to situation, while observers attribute the actions to disposition (Jones and Nisbett, 1972). Both these biases may occur when a lesbian tells a heterosexual person about herself.

Especially pertinent to coming out is the notion of social attribution (e.g. Deschamps, 1983), with attribution perceived as influenced by group memberships and social representations. Contributing towards an understanding of coming out at an intergroup level of analysis is the notion of social category memberships as dispositional attributions (Oakes, 1987). The societal perspective of attribution provides opportunity to consider the historical–temporal dimension (Hewstone, 1989a), which is of particular relevance in considering coming out. Attributions are likely to affect both coming out to self, and coming out to others.

There may be some similarities (as well as differences) between coming out and other minority group or life experiences relating to self-acceptance or self-disclosure. The notion of threat to identity (Breakwell, 1986) provides a general framework within which coming out and other experiences may be interpreted. Breakwell defined threat in terms of the identity processes of assimilation–accommodation and evaluation being unable to comply with the identity principles of continuity, distinctiveness and self-esteem. Threats may arise externally, or internally through conflict among the identity principles. Coping strategies may be at intra-psychic, interpersonal or intergroup levels. Choice of strategy is seen as determined by type of threat, social context, identity structure and cognitive resources.

Notions of self, self-presentation and self-disclosure all require consideration in an investigation of coming out. Mead's (1934) conceptualization of the self as originating and developing through social interaction provides a useful basis. A further perspective for considering coming out is the dramaturgical framework of Goffman (1959), with social interactions viewed as performances. Studies of self-disclosure generally (e.g. Jourard, 1971; Derlega et al., 1993) are relevant to understanding aspects of the coming-out process. Issues include the effects of non-disclosure, and self-disclosure in friendship formation.

The study

The study on which this book is based included interviews: with lesbians on their experiences of coming out; with heterosexual men and women on their attitudes towards lesbians and gay men; and with women on communication with friends and family.

Outline of book

'Coming out' may be considered from a variety of perspectives, including anthropological and historical, philosophical and political, sociological and psychological viewpoints. It is not possible within one book to begin to cover these diverse theoretical perspectives in the depth that each merits. Acknowledging these limitations, 'coming out' is presented within this book largely from a social-psychological perspective only. Incorporated into the study, however, and developed within the social-psychological framework, is an integral feminist perspective.

Having considered the main issues and context in this chapter, Chapter 2 begins with Clare's story. Clare is an imaginary lesbian, based on pilot interviews, who forms the basis for a reconceptualization of the coming-out process. In coming out to self, identification as lesbian is suggested to be based on strong emotional feelings directed towards women, together with awareness of lesbianism as an option, and a level of emotional acceptance of homosexuality. For coming out to others, initial circumstances, approaches taken in coming out, telling the other person, reactions and outcome, require investigation. Both coming out to self and others must be understood within the social context.

Chapter 3 provides part of the theoretical background. It is divided into two sections. The first part looks at some of the literature on lesbian identity and coming out. This includes focuses on the older lesbian, coming out to family, and coming out at work. Heterosexuals' attitudes towards lesbians are fundamental to an analysis of coming out. The second part of Chapter 3 looks at background literature concerned with attitudes towards homosexuality and stereotyping. Notions of sex role are examined, and possible implications of stereotyping are considered.

The social-psychological framework for the study is presented in Chapter 4. This includes issues of gender, social identity theory, social representations, and self-disclosure.

The first of the chapters focused on the findings of this study, Chapter 5, introduces the investigation, and discusses results relating to the social context of coming out. This includes coverage of stereotyping, perceptions of people's views about homosexuality, and perceptions of the portrayal of lesbians in the media.

Chapter 6 presents four case studies of women. The first three case studies in this chapter are of women who, like Clare the imaginary lesbian, have 'always' perceived themselves as lesbian. The fourth case study introduces a woman whose experiences were different. All the cases are described within the framework of Breakwell's model of coping with threatened identity.

In Chapter 7, the coming-out process, illustrated by a content analysis of the interview material, is described and discussed within the interpretational framework outlined in previous chapters. Areas of focus include, first, coming out to self; second, coming out to others (including to other lesbians, and to family and heterosexual friends); and, third, the interplay of influences in the coming-out process which includes a life-span perspective, and comparison with other minority group or life experiences, and general communication with family and friends.

Further case studies of women coming out are described in Chapter 8. These cases are representative of the lesbians who had some heterosexual background. Their coming-out experiences are contrasted with those of the 'always' lesbian women looked at in Chapter 6.

In Chapter 9, a brief look is taken at some issues of therapy for lesbians that are relevant to coming out.

Finally, in Chapter 10, the findings of the study are summarized; and implications concerning social-psychological theory, issues of gender, the contrast between lesbian and heterosexual perspectives, and facilitation of coming out are discussed. Conclusions relate to the centrality of emotional feelings in coming out to self; the emphasis on viewing coming out, whether to self or others, within the social context; and the need for change in social representations of gender and human nature.

2

A reconceptualization of coming out

An imaginary lesbian

Clare is an imaginary lesbian, a composite figure constructed from pilot-study data (from twenty participants), as well as something of my own experiences in coming out.

There are major differences between individuals' experiences of coming out, with, for example, some women having 'always' perceived themselves as lesbian, and others, leading a heterosexual life for many years before coming to define themselves as lesbian. Age and historical period differences may also exist. Clare, about forty years old in the mid 1980s, thus necessarily reflects the experiences of some women more than others, although an attempt has been made to illustrate something of other possible pathways that may be taken in the coming-out process. The diverse, sometimes contradictory, experiences described are all part of lesbians' accounts of coming out.

Clare

Clare feels that she has probably always been a lesbian. Although she had no label for her feelings until her teens or later, she recalled her first feelings of attraction towards women as a very young child. For some of her lesbian friends, such feelings may have begun some years later.

> In retrospect, I think I knew probably when I was very young – seven, eight . . .

She also recalled having felt 'different' from other girls. Possibly, she preferred boys' toys, or maybe even wanted to be a boy.

> I always had a sense of myself as not really fitting in.

> I remember when I was a child, I wanted to be a boy . . .

> As a child . . . I used to think of myself as a person rather than a girl.

> I was just never interested in playing with dolls, or games of 'mothers and fathers' . . .

As a child, Clare may have felt isolated, but equally, her childhood may have been a happy one.

From the age of maybe eleven or twelve, and especially during her teens, Clare was becoming more aware of her feelings towards girls or women, while friends were becoming interested in boys.

> I was never interested in boys, never, not for a minute.

Clare's feelings felt completely natural to her.

> I'd always had girlfriends, always knew what I was feeling, but I suppose it never particularly worried me or upset me, but I suppose I thought it was just me.

> When I had the crush on this . . . teacher, it was so natural, I just never never thought it was unnatural or abnormal . . .

She only began to think of such feelings as in any way unnatural with the beginnings of awareness of social disapproval.

> [I] don't think I knew the word lesbian then. I knew there was something slightly unnatural in having such strong feelings towards someone of the same sex.

It was around this time that Clare first started to become aware of words such as 'homosexual', 'lesbian' or 'queer'.

> When I first heard the word 'lesbian' . . . I knew there was something terribly wrong . . . it was used as an insult.

> [Lesbian]: it's a word I hate and abominate because of associations . . . when a girl.

> A friend at school used the word 'homosexual' – I went home and looked it up in the dictionary! . . . I began to wonder about myself . . . and worry . . .

> Then, they didn't say gay, lesbian or homosexual; they tended to say queer.

From this time onwards, on and off, Clare wondered if she really were a lesbian.

Clare's ideas about homosexuality were gradually forming, particularly through comments made by school friends, and articles she read in the newspapers. The former tended to portray homosexuality as something to be joked about; as a taboo subject only to be whispered about; or as something abhorrent and disgusting. From the press, Clare began to understand that homosexuality was regarded as some kind of sickness or immaturity, and that homosexuals were people likely to lead sad and lonely lives. Alongside such analysis, were reports of 'queer-bashing', physical attacks on homosexuals. There never seemed to be any suggestion at school that anyone in one's class might be lesbian, and similarly, in the newspapers, there seemed no indication that any of the paper's readers might be homosexual themselves.

> I felt strange thinking that there was nobody else in the world who felt like I did.

> The type of woman on television completely discourages you from coming out to yourself, let alone to other people.

Throughout this time Clare was experiencing considerable conflict of feelings. At times she felt there was no question that she was a lesbian, while at other times she felt unable to comprehend how she could be the type of person her school friends whispered and laughed about, and the newspapers described as so strange and unattractive. Maybe she was just going through 'a phase'. Clare felt isolated, frightened and different from everyone else.

> We're talking about a very long time ago. Feelings that came up and were too unbearable to think about or contemplate, and so were buried and reburied, and then rose again and again.

With all the societal and peer pressure towards heterosexual conformity, Clare might have taken a different pathway and become involved with boys during her teenage years.

> It really seemed like you had to go out with boys to be accepted at all, and so that's what I did after a while. I thought it was a terrible pity you couldn't go out with girls instead, but I just thought that was it, you couldn't.

> I was at a convent and I was very programmed into rights and wrongs, and oughts and shoulds, and I had a peer group who went into boys quite early, and it was enforced on me that this was the thing to do . . .

This heterosexual involvement might have lasted a comparatively short time, or might have led on to thoughts of marriage, or marriage itself, in spite of awareness of lesbian feelings.

> I was very frightened about it [feelings of attraction towards women], because it wasn't a path that I wanted to take. I wanted initially to take a very conventional path, marriage, early marriage and children, and lots of them.

> I sort of sat up all night before the wedding thinking I'm sure I'm a lesbian – what am I doing this for, but it seemed too late to get out of it really.

Marriage to a man would not necessarily reflect heterosexual rather than lesbian feelings.

> I never felt attracted to men. I always liked women.
> (a woman who married)

For Clare, there was already now, during her teens, a definite perception of herself as lesbian.

> I knew that it was definite. There was no way out. There was no choice.

In contrast to Clare, some other women did not come to perceive themselves as lesbian until a later age, after years of heterosexuality, and then it happened suddenly.

> It turned my world upside down. One minute I was one person, and the next minute, I didn't know who I was.

Clare, however, had not become involved with boys during her teens, and now felt that she needed very much to talk to someone about her feelings.

> When I was at home and didn't know anyone, it was horrible, because, I mean, you just couldn't really say what you felt, or how you felt . . .

> I felt desperately that I needed to talk to someone, but for various reasons, I just felt there was no one among my family or friends I could turn to . . . at the same time, I was terrified that people would find out about me being a lesbian – it was only some years later that I began to realize they'd actually only ever know if I chose to tell them.

Clare went through a period of feeling unable to talk to anyone about herself, of isolation and fear. For some lesbians this period may last only a short time. For others, it may last many years. Clare considered whom she might be able to discuss her feelings with. She thought of telling friends or family, but recalled what they had said in the past about homosexuality. She considered her work situation (school, job or career) and how openness about herself would affect her position. She thought about how telling one person might lead to others being told. Risks of the person not understanding, of them being upset, of rejection, and of job difficulties or loss, kept her silent. (For an older, married lesbian, there might also be the possibility of losing one's children.) Balanced against these risks for Clare were the strain and general effects of feeling unable to be open with anyone, of having to lie, directly, or by omission.

Clare eventually decided that she must attempt to contact other lesbians.

Coming out to other lesbians

For women like Clare – unlike maybe younger women who have approached lesbianism through feminist groups – initially contacting other lesbians was a daunting and major step in the coming-out process, requiring planning and positive action. What prompted Clare finally to take this step? It may have been new career circumstances; moving home, away from the family, or into a new neighbourhood; or perceptions of more positive attitudes towards homosexuality reflected in the media. Very importantly, some level of emotional acceptance of herself as lesbian was needed.

> I came to London when I was twenty-one because I knew that I wasn't going to meet other women who felt the same as I did – I still wasn't putting a name to it – where I lived. And even when I came to London, I didn't know what to look for. I didn't know of the existence of *Gay News*, or any clubs, or any publications, or any organizations, or Gay Switchboard – nothing at all.

> I read about Sappho [lesbian group] quite early on, and didn't dare go . . .

Clare was aware perhaps of some kind of lesbian stereotype, and was very unsure of what to expect in meeting lesbians for the first time.

> I think I always thought of lesbians as being old – ladies in sort of baggy trousers, thick shoes, probably walking dogs, short hair, anoraks, unattractive.

> I had the stereotype image in my head . . . Not the femme ones; I thought they were all the butch types.

> Well, I suppose one had been brainwashed into the idea that most gay women were pretty butch, that there wasn't any other kind of women, and so there was a certain amount of apprehension as to whether you were going to meet anybody with whom you had anything in common.

Having found a reference to Lesbian Line in a magazine, it took Clare three weeks to bring herself to dial the number.

> I rang up and asked for therapy or counselling, or something, and I asked them if there was a cure . . .

Clare's first meeting with other lesbians both contradicted and reinforced stereotypical images.

> I think the first shock was that they were ordinary people!

> A lot of them did fit the image I had.
>
> (Quotes from the same participant)

> Quite a butch scene . . .

Coming out to others

> I found it very difficult to tell other people, very, very difficult.

Why might Clare want to tell friends or family that she is a lesbian? Heterosexual people may suggest that it is not something that one should talk about to others, and point out that they do not tell people of their sexuality. This ignores the numerous indications of their sexual orientation ranging from chatting about boyfriends or husbands, to weddings and wedding rings, and the use of the title 'Mrs'. Clare, while not out to particular friends or family members could not convey that a girlfriend meant more to her than an ordinary friend. She had to deal with questions about boyfriends and her social life, and was under some pressure to find herself a husband. Unless she actually indicated in some way that she was lesbian, others assumed that she was heterosexual. This assumption of heterosexuality was a strain to deal with.

> I feel dishonest.

> I don't like lying . . . I kept finding myself very close to the point of having to tell lies almost, just to shut them up – cover up or whatever.

> I find it very difficult when they ask me, 'Why haven't you got any children,

> because you obviously like children?' I like children a lot, and I find it very embarrassing to explain why . . . I still find it difficult to say 'Well, because I'm gay, and because I believe that a child has a right to a father too'.

> I had to tell everyone immediately . . . particularly female friends because I was going through this guilt complex . . . I felt it was fairer on them to tell them.

> The more I come out, the more I relax, and the less guilty I feel.

> You just wanted that something extra, just to be able to have other friends that you could talk to, and be yourself with.

Coming out to heterosexual friends

Friends may appear easier to approach than family. Reactions, however, may vary, and women may feel cautious. Clare decided not to come out to certain friends.

> I've always been dubious about coming out to them . . . I'm frightened in case they won't accept – [I'm frightened] that the friendship is going to end.

> There are people that I feel really badly that do not know, and yet I don't think that I want to jeopardize a friendship by telling them.

> I was loath to confide . . . in heterosexual friends because I thought they wouldn't understand.

Clare may have tested the ground to find out people's attitudes towards homosexuality before attempting to tell them about herself. If she decided to come out to a friend, she could approach telling them about herself in different ways.

> I don't like having to make a grand statement. I prefer just to be honest about things, and sort of just talk about it in a natural way without feeling this pressure to say it all out of the blue, which is very difficult to do anyway . . . if there's an opportunity . . . if the subject comes up in some way, then it's easier just to bring it into the conversation, but actually having to tell people cold is very difficult.

Clare felt that some of her friends knew without her having to tell them, but the actual situation was not clear.

> On the whole they tend to say 'Oh, I'm glad you told me' or 'Why did you feel you had to tell me' or that they know anyway, or some people, you

know that they know, but you know also that they don't particularly want you to talk about it. So there's different reactions really, and often you get a different reaction to what you'd expect, which is the strange thing. And I think in the past I've sort of made the mistake of thinking that people know, or assuming people know because it seems obvious, and then something perhaps somebody else says makes me realize that they don't know, and it's people that I would assume would know that sometimes don't, and it's people you would least suspect to be thinking about it that actually do know. So when you tell people you often get different reactions to what you think.

A lot of people, I didn't really tell. I just thought that they would find out somehow because I had told other people, and somehow it would filter through. But it doesn't necessarily – people do keep confidences sometimes.

Some reactions were unexpectedly hostile, or not quite as anticipated.

Some people at my college stopped talking to me like that, and didn't speak to me for the next two years, not even to say hullo. I was quite hurt in a way and sort of . . . surprised . . . I knew that people didn't like lesbians very much, but I was surprised they were so up front about it.

My best friend wrote to me and said she was shocked and disgusted, and never wanted to hear from me again. Goodbye.

Telling people initially seemed to be easy, and reactions seemed to be favourable. I'm putting the emphasis on 'seemed to' because the reality is that as time progresses, I think I've discovered who are my real friends, those who've stayed with me as it were, or those who have actually not been able to take it on board.

My friends are a little bit funny about it.

Rejection is obviously extremely distressing. Clare's feelings about other responses varied.

I wanted her to be interested and ask me how it happened, and so we could have a sort of friendly chat [and she didn't want that at all – she couldn't cope with it].

It was quite a source of comfort . . . at the time . . . a sort of a measure of acceptance.

But there were benefits of coming out to friends:

I can talk to them quite honestly about how I feel.

Coming out to family

Telling parents about oneself is probably harder than dealing with friends, or brothers and sisters, and many lesbians choose not to come out to their parents.

> I find it difficult to tell people of that generation – I think because I feel they don't understand what it's all about.

> There's no point telling him because he won't understand.

> I don't really think it's worth putting them through the hassle unless it just has to come out.

> I don't really want to worry my father, because I'm quite sure that he would see it as a very insecure future . . .

Clare may feel that her parents possibly already know without her having to put it into words.

> I just thought that she must know, but she's eighty-seven so I didn't say anything to her.

> I don't think my mother needed to be told . . .

> They might have guessed, or they might not have done. It's not spoken about.

> I think she knows at one level, but whether she'd put a label 'lesbian' onto it, I don't know . . .

> Well, I've not come out to the family at all, I mean even though I have an idea that my mother knows, but she won't say anything, and neither will I . . . I should think my father would probably be hurt, and perhaps shocked. Perhaps my mother, with her perhaps having an idea . . . her first reaction would be, What would the neighbours think? . . . but she might understand – I don't know – but I don't really think I could actually come out to them at all . . . I might change my mind, but I don't really think so. I don't think I would want to actually now.

> I thought my mother had known for years, but when I actually told her, it turned out she'd had no idea about it.

If Clare does decide to tell her parents, this may improve her relationship with them. However, telling them may instead turn out not to fulfil Clare's expectations. For example, after a good initial reaction, Clare may find her parents then become reluctant to discuss the subject with her. Clare may even have to deal with more serious reactions including being told to leave home, or being forbidden to meet other lesbians.

> It was a shock to my mother and I had a very difficult time. She could not accept it.
>
> (A woman whose mother told her to leave the country)

Clare may be more likely to have told her brothers and sisters about herself than her parents. She considered it quite thoroughly before attempting to tell them. As with friends, Clare wished to be able to talk freely about herself, and reactions may vary.

> I'm closest to my sister, and I wanted to tell her for a long time, but I didn't know what her reaction was going to be – I'd heard of other people's families' reactions that sometimes had come as a surprise . . . and I didn't want to take the risk of not seeing my niece and nephew grow up, so I didn't tell them for a long time.

> I thought for a long time that it was ridiculous I hadn't told her . . . Because I couldn't talk about myself to her without coming out to her, we didn't really share so much.

> She totally accepted it, in so far as she doesn't say it's wrong, but she also would rather not talk about it.

Clare may feel it is unnecessary to come out.

> I don't particularly feel that there is anything to be gained by my revealing anything to the brothers and sisters-in-law. I think I'm probably frightened of doing it as well, but I can't see any positive gains.

Clare has not been involved with men at any stage, but many lesbians have had some heterosexual experience. If Clare had been one of those women who had married, and possibly had children, she would need to consider the question of coming out to husband and/or children.

> I don't think [my husband realizes] even now – or he may.

> My husband, as I discovered, reacted predictably initially . . . can I join in . . . how exciting . . . and then, as it became more evident that I was strongly attracted to women and likely to form a lasting relationship, his whole attitude changed, and he became – understandably in a way because

> I was still married – very withdrawn, and it was a very unhappy period of my life. I began to drink heavily, became alcoholic . . .

Children may react in a straightforward manner, or there may be hostility and confusion.

> I came across my daughter's diary once and read it . . . when she was fourteen, and she had written 'My mother is a lesbian – I don't know what to do', and this shocked me and really I didn't know that I had been that overt. I thought I had kept this hidden, as I strongly believe that your sexuality shouldn't be overt until your children are adult . . .

Coming out at work

Clare's concern about the possible effects of work colleagues or employers knowing that she is lesbian led her to decide not to tell anyone at work. She felt that it would damage her working relationship with her colleagues; that they might stop speaking to her, or refuse to work with her; or that she might even lose her job. In some areas, such as those where children are involved, Clare's position would be particularly sensitive. However, not being out meant that Clare had to evolve ways of dealing with tea-break talk about husbands and boyfriends, and situations in which the subject of homosexuality arose in conversation. These latter occasions are particularly difficult to deal with. Amongst lesbians, feelings about being out at work are likely to be mixed.

> [In nursing] I felt really worried that the other women would refuse to work with me.

> As a teacher, in secondary school education, I really did not feel it was very wise to start flaunting my sexuality around – so I spent a long time feeling very frightened about it – should I give it all up – it didn't seem to be an easy way to live at all.

> Nothing upsets parents like having a gay headmistress.

> I let it be too widely known and I regret it now, not because it stood in the way of anything, but . . . unless there's an opportunity to talk about it in a very positive way, there actually isn't a lot of point in telling any but your closest working friends.

> People can be cruel if they want to be . . . suppose somebody wants your job . . .

> [At work] sometimes if they said anything bad, I would feel terrible, and I'd feel, well, why can't I say something to defend . . .

> I don't not want to be out at work, but it's another thing to be out.

The women's movement

It was not until Clare's late twenties or early thirties that the feminist movement seemed to begin to play a part in her life.

> For some reason it played no part in my life in the seventies – I can't understand that, but I didn't know it was there really.

Clare may feel that the women's movement has played a positive part in her coming-out experiences, but some lesbians have rather mixed feelings about it.

> I suppose it's made it easier for women to actually be together and to actually not feel bad about enjoying other women's company, but, I mean, it's also had a strange effect, in that certainly in the early days it sort of split off gay women from feminists, and there's still that feeling. There's still a sort of division and a lot of mistrust, I suppose, of people who are political lesbians. So I don't know that it's made it easier for coming out.

> I have very ambivalent feelings about the women's movement and lesbianism, and the degree of raucous, radical, political lesbianism which I cannot feel for . . . There's still a lot of personal suffering I think attached to being lesbian, and I don't think they've begun to touch that.

> In some ways it's made it worse.

> Rather than being something I just happened to do behind a closed door which was nobody's business [the women's movement] did make [being a lesbian] into . . . much more of a way of life.

> [But] you couldn't say you were a lesbian, and it was very heterosexual.

Clare has accepted herself as lesbian, and come out into the lesbian community. She has perhaps come out to a few heterosexual friends, and to her sister, but not to her parents or work colleagues. She still has some mixed feelings, but basically feels increasingly positive about her lesbian identity. Coming out to herself was a difficult and isolating experience. Coming out to others, although hard to approach, has been, on the whole, a very positive experience.

Coming out as a process

Analysis of pilot-study data, including the lesbian interviews that contributed towards Clare's story; interviews with heterosexual men and women; interviews with women on self-disclosure; and stereotype investigations, forms the basis for the following reconceptualization of the coming-out process.

Coming out to self

Coming out to self is a process that may have its origins very early in life. It is seen as an interaction between a complexity of internal and external cues that may lead to an individual's eventual identification of self as lesbian. On a generalized level, primary emotional attachments with women rather than men, together with awareness of lesbianism as an option, as well as some degree of emotional acceptance of lesbianism, are seen as forming a basis for self-identification as lesbian.

It is not suggested that all women with this basis will identify as lesbians, but only that those women who do come to identify themselves as lesbian would probably have such a background. For some women other aspects, such as a political analysis or a physical relationship with another woman, may be important for self-definition as lesbian. However, it is suggested here that it is the emotional basis that is of major importance in leading to eventual self-identification as lesbian, a view consistent with Wolff's (1973) notion of 'homoemotionality', and Faderman's (1981) concept of 'romantic friendship'. Furthermore, emotion is seen as a social construct (e.g. Averill, 1985).

Coming out to others

To examine the process of coming out to others, it is necessary to consider the initial circumstances that may or may not lead to a decision to come out; approaches taken to coming out, and the lesbian telling the other person; perceptions of reactions which may change over time; and, finally, the modified circumstances, and associated satisfaction or dissatisfaction with the outcome.

A number of questions relate to each of the aspects mentioned. Considering the initial circumstances, why is the lesbian contemplating telling another person about herself and what does she hope to gain? She may wish to be able to talk freely with the other person, and not to have to lie or 'lead a double life'. She may need to relieve present isolation and possibly needs support. She probably hopes to improve her relationship with the person she is telling. At the same time, a lesbian is likely to be aware of possible risks in telling the other person. She may think the person might not understand, or might be upset, and she may anticipate possible rejection. Often, consideration of these latter issues predominates, and the woman decides not to come out.

If the woman moves further towards coming out, she may consider how best to approach telling another person, perhaps attempting first to test the ground. When a lesbian tells a heterosexual person about herself, personal understanding of what homosexuality means to each of the individuals concerned, their perceptions of societal attitudes and stereotypes, and their previous knowledge of and relationship with each other are all relevant.

The initial reaction of a heterosexual person is likely to include some degree of surprise or shock, as well as some ambivalence of feelings. Over a period of time, the general reaction may change.

The general outcome includes modification of circumstances for the lesbian, and some change in her relationship with the heterosexual person. Satisfaction with outcome depends partly on the extent to which the original reasons for coming out, both conscious and unconscious, have been met (e.g. need for acceptance or being able to talk more freely).

Further aspects of the coming-out process

Coming out to self

Although coming out to self may generally precede coming out to others, this is certainly not always the case. Counter-examples include a woman finding herself involved with another woman before she has consciously considered herself as lesbian; or another person thinking or suggesting to a woman that she may be lesbian before the woman has thought of this possibility herself.

Coming out to others

Is it possible to discern any order in disclosure of sexual orientation to others? For example, might friends tend to be told before family, or siblings before parents? Does the age of the lesbian on coming out to others affect who she might choose to tell first? Might a younger lesbian be more likely to attempt to tell her family about herself than an older woman? It is unlikely that any general order of disclosure will be found, since it will depend on particular circumstances, and on an individual's closeness to family or friends. However, given individual variations for some, there are probably some general ways of ordering coming out to others that may provide an easier pathway than other routes. For example, coming out to other lesbians before coming out to family or heterosexual friends would be likely to provide a background of support.

Coming out is a process that is unlikely to have a definable end-point. Since throughout life there are likely to be interactions with people newly met, the question of whether to disclose one's sexual orientation to new friends, acquaintances or work colleagues will probably arise again and again. However, for some women, at certain times in their lives, a position may be reached where they have come out to some of their family or friends and, feeling reasonably comfortable with their present circumstances, have decided that it is unnecessary for anyone else to be told.

The social perspective

Both coming out to self and coming out to others need to be examined from a social perspective, and cannot be understood simply in individual terms.

In our society, sex-role differentiation is evident in much of everyday life. Information may be processed in terms of gender schema (Bem, 1981). There may be a social representation of human nature that includes views on what a 'normal' person is, and why people are different (Moscovici and Hewstone, 1983), and this may underlie heterosexism. I suggest that it is only through the heterosexist nature of society, which has its foundations in gender division and inequality, as well as in the notions of 'normality' reflected in social representations of gender and human nature, that coming out as lesbian emerges as an issue.

Some basic questions

The imaginary lesbian raises a number of questions. What is lesbian identity and how does lesbian identity formation occur? What do we mean by 'coming out'? What does the process of coming out involve, particularly for women who are not directly involved with feminism? What are heterosexual people's attitudes towards homosexuality? Is there stereotyping of lesbians? How can women's experiences of coming out be explained from a social-psychological perspective? What would make the process of coming out easier? The following chapters address these questions. Furthermore, it will be argued that underlying all these questions is a fundamental issue: the predominant notions of gender and human nature/'normality' within our society.

3
Lesbian identity and attitudes towards homosexuality: the background

Lesbians' experiences of coming out must be interpreted within a historical and social context. Within this chapter we consider this context from two main perspectives. Firstly, we look at contributions from previous studies on lesbian identity and coming out. Secondly, we examine what previous studies have suggested about heterosexuals' attitudes towards homosexuality and stereotyping.

Lesbian identity and coming out

What is lesbian identity? Is there more than one type of lesbian identity? How would different lesbian identities relate to experiences of coming out? Generally, what do previous studies tell us about lesbian identity and coming out? It is suggested here that underlying the major issues are society's understanding of gender and, on a more general level, societal notions of human nature and 'normality'.

Some perspectives on lesbian identity

A historical view

Predominant notions of gender and 'normality' vary over time. The socio-historical context shapes how we think about and understand lesbian identity. Indeed, it has been argued that the history of sexuality is relatively modern. Halperin (1989) found modern-day understandings of sexuality relating to its autonomy and individuating function absent in the sexual experience of classical Athenians. D'Emilio (1983) suggested it was capitalism and wage labour, freeing individuals from the interdependent family unit, that allowed homosexual identities as opposed to homosexual behaviour to develop. However, we can trace some contemporary notions of identity back in time. Dollimore (1988) contrasted how the writers André Gide and Oscar Wilde perceived themselves. While Gide understood his homosexuality in terms of an authentic self, Wilde, a socialist, rejected notions of an essential self, viewing desire as a social product. Further, for Wilde individualism was bound up with transgressive desire which would produce cultural diversity and social progress. Dollimore related Wilde's notions to today's theoretical debates and postmodernist ideas.

Attempting to consider lesbians in history highlights fundamental questions of definition. What is a lesbian? Who may be described as lesbian? As will be seen, there are no simple answers to these questions. The Lesbian History Group (1989) indicated some of the problems arising in identifying women who lived in the past as lesbian: little explicit information available; suppression, omission or distortion of material, by historians or publishers, in order not to embarrass or alienate family or readers; and varying definitions of 'lesbian'.

Forms of lesbianism, however, have almost certainly existed throughout history, from the ancient civilizations of the past to the lesbians of today (Cavin, 1985; Duberman et al., 1989). Faderman (1981) suggested that lesbian identity may be traced back to the romantic friendships of the seventeenth, eighteenth and nineteenth centuries with origins in the Renaissance.

It is the dominant notions of gender and human nature, within a particular era, and specific to the particular culture, that have shaped what has been understood as lesbian identity within our society. The way in which lesbian identities challenge these dominant representations, and societal response to lesbianism, have varied considerably over time. This century, for example, has seen movement from the medicalization of lesbianism, to gay liberation, and radical feminist perspectives of lesbian identities, in both Britain and the United States.

Today's lesbians

Social and societal aspects are fundamental to understanding lesbian identity. McIntosh (1968), in suggesting homosexuality must be seen as a social role rather than a condition, pointed out that anthropological evidence indicated that in some societies the role does not exist and, in addition, that the role may vary in different societies. Richardson (1981a) proposed that lesbian identities be viewed as socially constructed and maintained through social interaction.

A variety of different notions of late twentieth-century lesbian identity have been suggested by empirical research. Wolff (1973) emphasized the emotional bias and suggested that for lesbians, the term 'homoemotional' might replace that of 'homosexual'.

The idea that there is more than one type of lesbian identity has been suggested in several different ways. Ettorre (1980) suggested there were two types of social lesbian: the 'sick, but not sorry' group who tend to accept traditional lesbian images, and the 'sorry, but not sick' group who challenge traditional images. Two basic types of lesbian identity were also discussed by Golden (1987), based on those of Ponse (1978). These were 'primary lesbians', who perceive themselves as having been different from an early age, without choice; and 'elective lesbians' who perceive their lesbian identity as a conscious choice. Thus, a basic contrast emerges between notions of 'born' lesbians and 'self-chosen' lesbians.

Kitzinger and Stainton Rogers (1985) suggested five lesbian identities. These included the 'personal fulfilment', the 'special person', the 'individualistic', the 'radical feminist' and the 'traditional' identities.

What kind of impact would different lesbian identities have on coming out? Let us consider this from the perspective of the challenges the different identities present to a predominantly heterosexual society. All lesbian identities present some challenge to heterosexual society's general notions of human nature and gender. However, different lesbian identities present their challenge with varying intensity and focus. For example, Wolff's (1973) homoemotionality challenges dominant notions of human nature with its direction of emotions towards the same sex rather than the opposite sex, but, to some extent, fits in with predominant ideas on gender – i.e. that women are perceived as emotional. Ettorre's (1980) 'sorry, but not sick' group presents a more direct challenge to heterosexual society's notions than her 'sick, but not sorry' group. Similarly, Kitzinger and Stainton Rogers's (1985) radical feminist identity presents a different kind of challenge to heterosexual notions than the other identities their study suggested. Their 'personal fulfilment', 'special person' and 'individualistic' lesbian identities may be seen as corresponding more closely with the predominant notions of gender and human nature in our society, and would thus present less of a challenge to societal representations.

Lesbians are also members of other groups and their identities must be understood within the context of these other group memberships. Lesbians, as women, experience stress as members of a double minority (Brooks, 1981). Some lesbians are also members of other minority groups and may experience further oppression relating to these group memberships, both within a lesbian community and outside. Black lesbians, for example, form an important part of our lesbian communities (Mason-John and Khambatta, 1993; Mason-John, 1995). Sexuality and sexual identity may be conceptualized differently in non-Western cultures, and this has implications for ethnic minority group members assuming gay/lesbian identities (Chan, 1995). Disabled lesbians are a further example of a group of women whose identity as lesbian needs to be understood within the context of another group membership (Appleby, 1994).

Lesbian communities influence identity. Krieger (1982) discussed how the individual lesbian's sense of self may be both affirmed and challenged in the lesbian community. Weitz (1984) investigated development of lesbian group identity, as illustrated by the American lesbian periodical *The Ladder*, between 1956 and 1972. From initial strong ties with the male homosexual community, reflection of the medical model, and attempts at integration into general society, there was development to rejection of negative identity, and active fighting against discrimination. Finally, there was radical redefinition in the early 1970s and new ties with women's liberation.

Lesbian communities must be understood as dynamic and continuously evolving. They provide women with a social context for their lesbian identity that both contrasts with, and reflects, the dominant notions of gender and human nature of the larger society.

Radical feminist views

Radical feminist perspectives illuminate the impact of societal constructions upon our understanding of sexuality. Rich (1981) was concerned with 'The bias of compulsory heterosexuality, through which lesbian experience is perceived on a scale ranging from deviant to abhorrent, or simply rendered invisible . . . ' (p. 4). She suggested the assumption of female heterosexuality is remarkable: 'it is an enormous assumption to have glided so silently into the foundations of our thought' (Rich, 1981, p. 9). Moreover, she suggested, there is a need to recognize and study heterosexuality as a political institution. Kitzinger (1987) also emphasized how both heterosexuality and lesbianism must be seen as political constructions.

Radical feminist lesbians and more traditional lesbians perceive their lesbian identity differently. A political lesbian has been defined by the Leeds Revolutionary Feminist Group as a 'women-identified woman' who is not sexually available to men (Onlywomen Press, 1981). For some, a radical feminist identity involves separatism (Hoagland and Penelope, 1988). Jeffreys (1993) emphasized the difference between 'lesbian feminists' and 'lesbians who are also feminists' (p. xi). For the former, lesbianism and feminism are integral, but for the latter, they are separate.

Wittig (1992) has argued that a lesbian 'is *not* a woman, either economically, or politically, or ideologically' (p. 108). She suggested that women are not a 'natural' group: rather they form a class – a political and economic category. Further, it is a relationship of servitude towards a man that makes a woman.

Queer theory and postmodernist perspectives

> Queer is a form of resistance, a refusal of labels, pathologies and moralities. It is defined more by what it is against than what it is for.
>
> (McIntosh, 1993, p. 31)

Confrontational, anti-assimilationist, and favouring direct action, including civil disobedience, queer activism emerged from the oppressive context experienced by lesbians and gay men during the late 1980s. It provided an opportunity for gay men and lesbians to work together. Formal groupings of queer activists were represented in the United States by Queer Nation, formed in 1990, and in the United Kingdom by OutRage, formed soon after (Smyth, 1992; Berlant and Freeman, 1993).

Queer theory is based on deconstruction. Social constructionist theorizing of lesbians and gay men diverged from each other, with gender a central issue for lesbian theorists, but not for gay men. Queer theory may be seen as a development of male gay theorizing, which contributes a focus on sex and sexual transgression (McIntosh, 1993).

Sedgwick (1990) suggested that conceptualization of homosexuality reflects sexual and gender definition. The sexual definition may be minoritizing (e.g. gay identity/essentialist) or universalizing (e.g. social constructionist/'lesbian continuum'). The gender definition related to inversion (e.g. androgyny) or separatism (e.g. lesbian separatist).

A poststructuralist perspective may illuminate theoretical issues. For example, Weedon (1987) developed a feminist poststructuralist framework based on theoretical ideas from Derrida, Althusser, Lacan, Kristeva and Foucault. The framework incorporated notions of language and subjectivity, discourse and power, and psychoanalysis. Such a perspective is useful 'as a way of conceptualizing the relationship between language, social institutions and individual consciousness which focuses on how power is exercised and on the possibilities of change' (Weedon, 1987, p. 19).

Seidman (1993) viewed postmodernist perspectives in gay thinking as originating from the reactions of those who were marginalized by the emphasis on a unitary identity through race, bisexuality or non-conventional sexuality. Postmodernist ideas have focused on lesbianism as behaviour/performance, arguing against notions of 'being' lesbian (e.g. Butler, 1991; Phelan, 1993). Phelan (1993) focused on 'becoming' lesbian rather than 'coming out', perceiving the latter as implying discovery instead of construction and choice; and emphasized the need for politics.

How useful are such perspectives? Seidman (1993, p. 135) has suggested:

> In its critique of identity politics as normalizing and exclusionary, in its disruption of an illusory unity that masks difference and domination, in forcing us to view identities as political artifices, poststructuralism is valuable. To the extent, however, that poststructural critique edges toward an anti-identity or postidentity standpoint, to the extent that it folds into a politics of the disruptive gesture, it lacks coherence.

While it is theoretically illuminating to consider lesbianism in postmodernist/poststructuralist terms, on a more practical level, it seems less useful to argue that lesbian identity does not exist. From a psychological perspective, lesbian identity permits some kind of stability and continuity in relations with others. It also facilitates social and political organization. Within our society, we all assume a variety of identities/roles (e.g. relating to gender, occupation, ethnic/religious origin). These vary in permanence, status and importance, but all contribute in differing degree to our perceptions of self and the way we relate to others. It would seem most useful, therefore, to focus on construction of identity, and its basis in a social notion of self.

Furthermore, lesbian identity needs to be understood within the context of dominant social representations of gender and human nature. Different lesbian identities present varying challenges to societal notions of gender and 'normality'. It is this that has an impact on women's experiences of coming out.

Lesbian identity formation

The formation of lesbian identity takes place within the social context of predominant representations of gender and human nature. For some women, this context would have been positively modified by contact with feminist groups or feminist thinking. For many other women, the direct influence of feminism would be considerably less, and the social context within which they form their lesbian identity would be dominated by the representations of the larger heterosexual society. Within this latter grouping in particular, would be the women who were likely to experience most isolation during the formation of their lesbian identity. The women directly involved with feminism would be more likely to be exposed to an environment that has created new positive meanings for lesbian identity, and an understanding of lesbianism that challenges society's dominant notions of gender and human nature. This section looks at studies which have attempted to describe the process of lesbian identity formation and raises some questions about validity.

The earliest studies concerning homosexual identity formation focused on male homosexuality. Whether or not a woman is directly involved in feminist activities, as a woman, her identity development as lesbian would vary from a man's experience of development of gay male identity. Women's and men's experiences generally must differ in any society where men form the dominant group. However, there is some value in considering studies on gay men's identity formation, since there may be some common features in gay male and lesbian identity development, and differences or contrasts may serve to illuminate the lesbian identity formation process.

Dank (1971) provided an early study of gay men. He pointed out

> the development of a homosexual identity is dependent on the meanings that the actor attaches to the concepts of homosexual and homosexuality, and that these meanings are directly related to the meanings that are available in his immediate environment; and the meanings that are available in his immediate environment are related to the meanings that are allowed to circulate in the wider society.
>
> (Dank, 1971, p. 195)

Formation of gay/lesbian identity has tended to be investigated from the perspective of attempting to discern and define the stages that constitute the process. An early model, designed to be specifically applicable to homosexuals of both sexes, was that of Cass (1979). She suggested six stages. These included stage 1 of identity confusion, after which, where it has been accepted by the person that she or he may be homosexual, there is a stage of identity comparison, which may develop towards stage 3, that of identity tolerance. This in turn may lead to the fourth stage of identity acceptance, which may lead to stage 5, identity pride, from which stage 6, identity synthesis may finally be reached.

A number of other studies focusing upon lesbian identity formation or development have followed (e.g. Gramick, 1984; Lewis, 1984; Sophie, 1985; Elliott, 1985; Chapman and Brannock, 1987; Schneider, 1989). Further studies have also been concerned with both lesbian and gay male development (e.g. Troiden, 1989; Herdt, 1989).

Major questions that must be asked about studies on lesbian identity formation include whether individual development actually proceeds in sequence through linear stages; the extent to which the samples are representative; and whether there are important differences between gay male and lesbian development.

For many women, lesbian identity formation probably does not follow a linear progression. Kahn (1991) distinguished different patterns of identity development, some women reporting never having identified as heterosexual, and others who did report heterosexual identification; some women knowing they were different from a very early age and others not questioning their identity until later; some women progressing through stages without missing any out, and others skipping some stages. Rust (1993) suggested replacing the linear stage developmental model with a social constructionist model. Identity formation would be conceptualized 'as an ongoing dynamic process of describing one's social location within a changing social context' (Rust, 1993, p. 74).

Studies that present mean ages for occurrences such as feeling 'different'/cognitive awareness/physical attraction, without providing measures of variability, unfortunately suggest a linearity in identity development that may well not exist.

Most studies can contribute something towards our understanding of lesbian identity formation, but caution is needed in generalizing from them. For example, Cass (1979) developed her model from her clinical work. Lesbians from a clinical setting cannot be seen as generally representative. Sophie (1985) based her study on volunteers in response to an article, and a campus newspaper advertisement asking for women confused about their sexuality or going through changes regarding sexuality. The sample size was fourteen. Any generalization must be inappropriate where there has been this kind of bias in sample selection.

Furthermore, as already noted, women directly involved with feminism would be likely to have different experiences from those of more isolated women.

What differences have been suggested between the identity development of lesbians and that of gay men? Herdt (1989, p. 26) noted that 'Males tend more often to define themselves as gay in contexts of same-sex erotic contact, whereas females experience their lesbian feelings in situations of romantic love and emotional attachment'. Cass (1990) described how lesbian identity formation is more likely to have been stimulated by emotional or social events than sexual. Indeed, some lesbians today live in romantic but asexual relationships: 'Boston marriages' (Rothblum and Brehony, 1993). Differences between men's and women's experiences, with the male emphasis on physical sex, and the female emphasis on emotion/love, may be seen as arising from differences in gender-role socialization and different societal expectations for women and men (Troiden, 1989; Cass, 1990; Blumstein and Schwartz, 1990).

Brown (1995) reviewed biological, psychodynamic and 'stage' models of lesbian identity development. She suggested there is a need to develop a model with a 'biopsychosocial' framework, so that interaction with 'physical and emotional environmental contexts' (p. 19) may be understood. Brown criticized present models for not accounting for the diversity of lesbian experience and for their cultural limitations.

Overall, development of lesbian identity must be seen in relation to the context of the dominant representations of gender and human nature within a society. An examination of ageing and the older lesbian illustrates this further.

The older lesbian

Lesbian identity cannot be viewed as static. Apart from any changes that may occur during the ageing process itself, there are historical time variations relating to notions of gender, sexuality and human nature in general. These have a crucial impact upon lesbian identities. For example, there has been an obvious change from the notions of lesbian identity influenced by the sexologists during the early part of this century to some of the lesbian identities of today. If we consider more recent history too, there have been changes. Contrasting the 1950s with the 1970s, we are aware of changes in the position of women within our societies and changes in attitudes towards sexuality. A woman whose perception of self as lesbian was beginning to form during the 1950s, with its more restrictive notions of sexuality, would almost certainly view her lesbian identity differently from a woman, perhaps born during the 1960s, who came to perceive herself as lesbian during the 1970s. As social and societal representations relating to gender, sexuality and human nature change, notions of lesbian identity vary.

To what extent can any differences between older and younger lesbians be attributed to either development or socio-historic period? Kimmel (1978) looked at gay adult development from the point of view of Levinson's developmental stages. He considered the relationship between developmental data and historical events, concluding differences between older and younger gay men did exist, but that their origins were unclear. The differences could have arisen from either ageing itself or historical period differences. Adelman (1990) found a relationship between adjustment to ageing and sequence of events in early gay development. However, she attributed the trends shown to socio-historical factors, and suggested differences to younger gays are generational rather than developmental.

The image of the older lesbian provided by research during the last ten years has been essentially positive. Berger (1984) found the stereotype of the isolated and depressed older homosexual to be inaccurate, and Raphael and Robinson (1980) looking particularly at lesbians' love and friendship patterns, concluded that their sample represented positive role models. Kehoe (1986) found the older lesbian to be a survivor and a balanced personality. Neild and Pearson (1992), introducing accounts from older lesbians in Britain collected for a television programme, commented on both the joy and the sadness of the women's lives.

Many older lesbians' lives surely do reflect positive images. However, it must be pointed out that women who participate in research studies are unlikely to be representative of lesbians more generally. Friend (1990) suggested that it tended to be the 'affirmative' gay and lesbian people that are represented in research literature rather than the 'stereotypic' or 'passing'. The 'affirmative' were described by Friend as self-accepting, psychologically well adjusted, and as having reconstructed the meaning of being gay/lesbian into something positive. Cruikshank (1990) cautioned that those who participated in studies are likely to be the most robust, with a political consciousness. Generally, researchers would be less likely to reach more isolated lesbians.

Lesbian identity formation and maintenance is fundamentally interlinked with 'coming out', a process that affects all aspects of life as lesbian.

Coming out

Definitions

'Coming out', firstly, in the sense of becoming aware of oneself as lesbian, and secondly, in the sense of disclosing this information to other people, is of fundamental importance to lesbian existence. The term 'coming out' has been defined and used in different ways in previous literature.

A definition that encompassed notions of both coming out to self and coming out to others was put forward by Hodges and Hutter (1977, p. 13) who suggested: 'The phrase coming out, as used by gay people, has three meanings: to acknowledge one's homosexuality to oneself; to reveal oneself as homosexual to other gay people; and lastly, to declare one's homosexuality to everyone and anyone'.

The working definition chosen here, like that of Hodges and Hutter, includes both the process leading to self-identification as lesbian/gay, and also the revealing of oneself to others as lesbian/gay.

An initial picture of coming out

Coming out, both to self and to others, has been described in strikingly negative terms. For example:

> During the realization process, she may have to deal with a loss in self-confidence, self-hatred, physical illness, nervous breakdown, alcoholism, marriage attempts, realization of wasted years of trying to be someone she isn't, numerous therapy sessions, and suicide attempts. This is euphemistically called coming out to yourself.
>
> (Baetz, 1984, p. 46)

Baetz (1984) suggested a more accurate description for this process might be in terms of a major battle against a culturally constructed, internal invisible enemy.

An equally clear image of what 'coming out to others' may involve was provided by Stewart-Park and Cassidy (1977, p. 1):

> When we come out of the closet – that is admit publicly that we are lesbians – it's rather like out of the frying pan into the fire. None of us enjoys living in the closet. It implies first that we are ashamed of our sexuality; secondly it isolates us from each other; and thirdly, it makes it difficult to have an honest relationship with anyone. Once we come out, we risk losing our jobs, our friends, the relationships we have with our families; and if we have children we risk losing them.

Different aspects of 'coming out to others' were described by Baetz (1984) in terms of crossroads with particular hazards. In this way, she looked at coming out to family, and coming out at school or work. Baetz suggested each decision-making crossroad a lesbian meets concerns not just a personal choice but involves culturally constructed impediments to pursuing a lesbian lifestyle.

Why should coming out involve a 'battle', 'risks' and 'hazards'? Are these realistic pictures of coming out? If so, what lies at the basis of such experiences? The answers to these questions are crucial as lesbian/gay identity may affect considerably wide-ranging aspects of life:

> People who identify as heterosexual have little idea how far identifying as gay affects our everyday lives. Every family gathering, every social occasion, every school outing, shop, office or factory tea-break, involves dodging or confronting questions about relationships or sexual conquests.
>
> (Durell, 1983, p. 14)

Some aspects of the coming-out process

The dilemma

Do I tell my mother, heterosexual friend or work colleague that I am a lesbian – or not? This fundamental dilemma of disclosure versus non-disclosure lies at the basis of the coming-out process. It is likely to be a dilemma experienced by both the more isolated lesbian, who functions mainly within heterosexual society, and the lesbian directly involved with feminism, although perhaps in varying ways. What kind of impact does this dilemma have upon the lives of lesbian women?

In order to conceal their homosexuality, Ponse (1978) suggested lesbians may employ strategies of 'passing' as heterosexual, restrict contact with heterosexuals, and separate the gay world from the outside (thus 'living a double life'). Moses (1978), looking at identity management, suggested the major determinant may be the extent of concern of identification as a lesbian when among heterosexuals. With greater concern, Moses suggested, situations were found more difficult and there was an increase in behaviour aimed at non-identification as a lesbian, and a decrease in risk-taking behaviour. Supporting Moses's findings, Franke and Leary (1991) found that the strongest predictor of openness was perception of how others felt about lesbians or gay men, and not self-acceptance of sexuality.

While a number of previous studies have focused investigation and discussion of coming out at the individual/interpersonal levels of analysis, an understanding of the intergroup and societal contexts as well is crucial for interpretation of the coming-out process. These different levels of analysis will be focused upon in later chapters. Together, the perspectives will illuminate the basis for the dilemma in coming out.

Age differences in coming out?

Are there differences between older and younger lesbians in experiences of coming out? Discussing the experiences of young gay and lesbian people growing up, Plummer (1989) described a context of assumptions of heterosexuality, and sexual stigma. He suggested the heterosexual assumption incorporates mechanisms including a 'hidden curriculum', absence of role models, peer group pressures and homophobic responses. Problems that may arise for young lesbian and gay people, Plummer suggested, include negative self-image; secrecy and isolation; access difficulties for meeting other gay people; and suicidal thoughts/suicide attempts. He suggested that by the early 1980s, however, it was becoming easier for young people to come out, with the growth of Gay Switchboard, and the emergence of gay youth organizations. Plummer emphasized the varieties of gay youth experience.

Differences between lesbians and gay men

Specific differences arise between lesbian and gay male experiences, some of which have already been mentioned. Sex-role factors, political and legal issues, and the existence of the women's movement all need consideration (De Monteflores and Schultz, 1978).

What is the thread that runs through all these different aspects of coming out? Why is there a dilemma over disclosing one's lesbian identity to significant others? What underlies the differences and similarities in the coming-out experiences of gay men and lesbians, and of older and younger lesbians? There can be no simple answers to these complex issues. However, the influence of societal conceptualizations of gender and human nature must provide a focus for investigation.

Coming out to family

Traditional images of the family reflect conventional notions of gender role. A daughter, sister or wife coming out as lesbian is challenging the foundation on which the traditional family unit is based: she is threatening the conventional gender-role expectations. It may be for this reason that coming out, or not, to family, telling one's parents, brothers or sisters, and possibly husband and children, that one is lesbian, or deciding not to, is likely to be among the most difficult coming-out decisions that a lesbian experiences.

In spite of the obvious importance of this area of 'coming out' for individual gay people, there have been comparatively few studies directly concerning it. The studies that have focused upon this area have tended to be American rather than British.

Parents are probably harder to deal with on this issue than siblings. As Baetz (1984, p. 45) presented the problem: 'How do you choose between possible disownment by your parents or a dwindling relationship riddled with half-truths, if those are your choices?' Gross (1978) mentioned how some clients reported most of their energies being directed towards their parents not discovering their secret (i.e. that they were homosexual).

Trenchard and Warren (1984) in their study involving gay and lesbian young people in the London area, found that over half of the sample were out to all their family, while about two-thirds had come out to at least one member of the family. Over a third of the lesbians classified their parents' initial reaction as good or reasonable, with the others perceiving their parents' reactions as indifferent, mixed or negative. Chapman and Brannock (1987), in a study of lesbians in the United States, reported that two-thirds of their sample indicated that their families knew of their lesbianism: the other women were divided between those who were out to some family members but not all, and those whose families did not know. Under a third of the women reported their families accepted their lesbianism, and a similar proportion reported rejection.

Notions of gender role are a basic aspect of all family relationships, and it is towards these expectations that lesbianism constitutes a threat. However, one may speculate that the challenge presented by a woman coming out as lesbian to parents or to husband is greater than that presented by a woman coming out to brothers or sisters. Gender-role expectations may be more evident within a parent–daughter relationship, and certainly within a husband–wife relationship, than they are between siblings.

Some studies have specifically focused on issues related to parents. Muller (1987) interviewed both a sample of lesbians and gay men who were 'out' to a parent, and some parents, in a study in the United States. The study was from the perspective of being a mother of a gay son. Four types of relationship were described by Muller: loving denial, hostile recognition, resentful denial, and loving-open relationships.

Parents may go through a grieving period following disclosure. The major structural change in the family may trigger a mourning process (Zitter, 1987). Parents may go through five stages of grief similar to those associated with death by Kubler-Ross (1969) (Robinson et al., 1989).

The challenge presented to conventional notions of gender by lesbianism might be expected to display differences as well as similarities to the challenge or threat presented by male homosexuality. Men and women occupy very different positions within our society relating to role expectations and power. Lesbianism and male homosexuality thus have differing implications for the traditional family structure and conventional gender roles. Lesbians and gay men are therefore likely to have different experiences in coming out within the family context.

Muller (1987) found that lesbians seemed to have more difficult relationships with their parents than gay sons. Savin-Williams (1989) in a study of young gay men and lesbians, looked at parental influences on self-esteem from the 'reflected appraisals' perspective of Rosenberg (1979). This perspective suggests that people are influenced by others' attitudes towards them, and eventually perceive themselves as others view them. The model was supported more by the gay male data than by the lesbians' responses.

What is the position of the lesbian mother? While some lesbian mothers are still married, others may be divorced or separated, or have never married; and while some are living with a lesbian partner, others are not (Hanscombe and Forster, 1982). They are often viewed negatively by society e.g. as inappropriate mothers in the motherhood hierarchy (DiLapi, 1989). However, studies have generally indicated little difference between children of lesbians and children of heterosexual mothers (Green and Bozett, 1991). For example, similar social and personal development has been found (Patterson, 1994) and no difference in self-esteem (Huggins, 1989). There has been no evidence that lesbians' children are more likely to become gay/lesbian, or to show gender-identity confusion or cross-gender behaviour (Golombok and Fivush, 1994). Hanscombe and Forster (1982) found the children of lesbian mothers they spoke to 'shared an open attitude towards sexuality, love and parenting . . .' (p. 133). For the lesbian mother, like other lesbians, coming out only becomes an issue within the context of negative societal attitudes. The possible effect of such attitudes upon the children must obviously be the major concern, but present evidence, although limited, suggests any problems experienced are not affecting the children's general development.

Possible effects on a husband must also be considered. Buxton (1994) suggested major issues facing a straight spouse of a gay/lesbian partner included 'damage to their sexuality; negation of their concept of marriage; conflicting spousal and parental roles; destruction of their own self-concept; breakdown of trust and integrity; possible family break-up and disintegration of their belief system' (p. xix). Ultimately, however, she pointed out the crisis may be the start of a healing process. 'Respect for individual differences and rights, as well as the espousal of social responsibility by all members of society – gay, lesbian, bisexual and straight – is the ultimate goal' (Buxton, 1994, p. 317).

The decision to come out or not to parents, siblings and other family members has many practical implications for the lesbian. It can be seen, however, that in examining the issue of coming out to family, we must consider not only the interpersonal level of analysis, but beyond that, the larger social and societal context. Social representations relating to sexuality both create and reflect values, images, gender roles and attitudes towards sex, as well as notions of 'normality', all of which have an impact upon individual experiences of coming out to family.

Coming out at work

'One's private life has nothing to do with work and must be kept separate. A person's sexual orientation is irrelevant to the work situation.' Such assumptions may well be made, both implicitly and explicitly. However, there is increasing evidence that the reality of the working world is very different. Gender and sexuality have an impact within the work environment that cannot be ignored.

Hall (1989) suggested that unlike heterosexuals who exit from family roles when working in an organization, homosexuals are perceived as remaining in the affective realm. However, Schneider (1986) pointed out that sexual identity/behaviour is not confined to private life for either heterosexuals or homosexuals. Work and intimacy cannot be seen as distinct.

Experiences of lesbians at work must be seen as reflecting their status both as women and as lesbians. There is now much evidence of discrimination against women in the workforce ranging from limited opportunities and low pay (Lewis, 1992; Lonsdale, 1992) to sexual harassment (Stockdale, 1991). Taylor (1986, p. 26) suggested that 'Sexism and heterosexism are inextricably combined and make time spent at work an on-going battle'.

For the lesbian who is not out at work, others' assumptions of her heterosexuality may be hard to deal with. Rich (1981), in discussing MacKinnon's (1979) *Sexual Harassment of Working Women: A Case of Sex Discrimination*, noted that a specific difference between experiences of lesbians and homosexual men arose since

> A lesbian, closeted on her job because of heterosexist prejudice, is not simply forced into denying the truth of her outside relationships or private life; her job depends on her pretending to be not merely heterosexual but a heterosexual *woman*, in terms of dressing and playing the feminine, deferential role required of 'real' women.
>
> (Rich, 1981, p. 14)

What are the possible effects of hiding one's lesbian identity in the workplace? Hall (1989) described preoccupation with concealment, and heightened sensitivity towards the behaviour or attitudes of others. Non-disclosure, she suggested, may lead to anger or anxiety; inner conflicts created by being secretive; and sometimes, avoidance of heterosexual colleagues.

What are the implications of disclosing one's lesbian identity at work? Hall (1989) suggested that those who are thoroughly open at work are likely to forfeit their individuality: they may, as Goffman (1963) suggested be perceived as representatives of their category. There is evidence from both studies in the United States and in Britain of discrimination against lesbians at work (e.g. Levine and Leonard, 1984; Taylor, 1986).

The type of job a lesbian has may influence whether or not she chooses to come out at work, and the consequences of that decision. For example, working with children may be seen as particularly problematic. Olson (1987) carried out a survey of gay and lesbian teachers from different parts of the United States, and found sexual preference reported as a reason for leaving the profession.

Recent research has focused on other work areas that raise different issues for lesbians coming out: examples include the British police service (Burke, 1993), the medical profession (Rose, 1994), and psychology (Griffin and Zukas, 1993). Although there would obviously be a complexity of issues to consider, Burke (1993) and Rose (1994) found some indication of reduction of role conflict/stress on coming out.

Thus, the question of coming out at work is a practical concern for lesbians. Issues of gender and sexuality arise within the working environment, as within wider society.

Attitudes towards homosexuality and stereotyping

What impact do heterosexual people's attitudes towards homosexuality have on lesbian experiences of coming out? This question requires us to focus on the nature of attitudes towards homosexuality in our society. What do previous studies indicate with regard to the content and origins of these attitudes? Do they suggest that stereotypes of lesbians exist and, if so, how may these influence the coming-out process? These are the questions to be examined in this section.

Gay people's experiences of prejudice, discrimination and oppression have been described in a wide variety of sources. Such experiences are not isolated incidents. It is the everyday life of the gay/lesbian person that is seriously affected: at home, in school or at work (Galloway, 1983).

Some progress towards more open and positive attitudes to homosexuality has been made. Thirty years ago, in the United Kingdom, television and radio programmes specifically for lesbians and gay men did not exist. Job advertisements in national newspapers did not specify equal opportunities policies covering lesbians and gay men. There are examples of both of these now. Parallel developments have taken place in the United States. However, there have also been a variety of initiatives, in both countries, reflecting more positive attitudes, which ultimately have not been introduced, or have been fundamentally modified, in response to a backlash of opinion against the original ideas. So are attitudes towards homosexuality really becoming more positive or not? The situation needs further examination.

The general context: some current issues

A recent national survey in Britain found nearly 65 per cent of men and 59 per cent of women perceived sex between two women as mostly or always wrong (Wellings et al., 1994). Figures from surveys in the United States have suggested similarly negative patterns of disapproval of homosexuality. Michael et al. (1994) found nearly 65 per cent of their survey respondents perceived same-gender sex as always wrong.

Illustrations of the consequences of negative attitudes towards homosexuality are numerous and diverse. Recent examples include reactions to a British High Court ruling on lesbians as parents (*Guardian*, 30 June 1994; 2 July 1994), and UK Ministry of Defence dismissals of 260 lesbians and gay men from the armed forces since 1990 (*Guardian*, 5 August 1994).

Issues pertinent to the context of coming out during the 1980s, and of continuing relevance in the 1990s, include AIDS; publishing and media presentation of lesbianism; educational provision; and laws relating to homosexuality (in particular, in the United Kingdom, Section 28 of the Local Government Act, 1988).

AIDS (Acquired Immune Deficiency Syndrome), a new and fatal disease, occurs most frequently in the West among gay or bisexual men (Richardson, 1987b). Although lesbians are a low-risk group for AIDS, as Richardson pointed out, they tend to have been categorized with gay men. Indeed, almost two-thirds of respondents to the *British Social Attitudes Survey* (Jowell et al., 1990) perceived lesbians as greatly, or quite a lot, at risk from AIDS.

Overall during the 1980s, there was greater availability of literature about lesbians, and books relevant to lesbian or feminist issues, with the growth of women's publishing companies (e.g. Virago, The Women's Press). Now, there are even such books from mainstream publishers (e.g. *The Penguin Book of Lesbian Short Stories*, Reynolds, 1993).

However, the treatment of homosexuality by the press has often not been positive. Armitage et al. (1987) reported on a survey of over 250 newspapers and magazines monitored for lesbian/gay content. Treatment of homosexuality was generally negative with most publications displaying heterosexism.

In contrast, British television has begun to present more realistic images of lesbians. The series *Out on Tuesday*, first shown in 1989 was particularly influential, increasing general awareness of lesbian and gay issues (Hamer with Ashbrook, 1994). Media presentation of homosexuality obviously affects both lesbians' perceptions in coming out, and heterosexuals' attitudes.

Educational provision also affects coming out. Attempts have been made to analyse the situation for lesbians and gay persons in the British education system and make suggestions for school curriculum development (e.g. Gay Teachers' Group, 1987; Harris, 1990; Epstein, 1994; for the situation in the United States, see Fassinger, 1993). However, the picture is currently not positive for the implementation of ideas. Even the educational psychology services in this country have neglected gay and lesbian issues (Comely, 1991). Both reflecting and perpetuating negative attitudes towards homosexuality has been the introduction of legislation.

After much debate in both the House of Commons (e.g. Hansard, 15 December 1987 and 9 March 1988) and the House of Lords (e.g. Hansard, 16 and 17 February 1988), Parliament passed Section 28 of the Local Government Act, 1988, prohibiting local authorities from 'intentionally promoting homosexuality'. One of its key points was that schools should not teach that homosexuality was acceptable as 'a pretended family relationship'. As well as teaching, it was thought that the Section might affect gay and lesbian counselling services, provision of library books concerned with homosexuality, and the arts. Legally, it seems the effects may be less than was originally thought. Geoffrey Robertson, QC, in the *Guardian* newspaper (1 June 1988) suggested that Section 28's main effect may be as a symbol of prejudice. However, the Annual General Meeting of the National Council for Civil Liberties, 1988, condemned Section 28 as a direct threat to the civil liberties of lesbians and gay men.

Reinhold (1994) has illustrated how ideas on 'the family' and heterosexuality as normal/natural, as opposed to homosexuality as abnormal/unnatural, formed the background to the Section 28 debates. Further, she demonstrated how our ideas on gender link into this opposition of family and homosexuality.

How does the situation in the United Kingdom compare with that of other European countries? It has been suggested by Tatchell (1990) that the United Kingdom has more laws discriminating against homosexuality than any other country in Europe, and that more lesbians and gay men are prosecuted here under such laws than in other European countries. A cross-cultural study of attitudes towards homosexuality in England, Germany and Spain, by Jensen et al. (1988), found attitudes in all these countries were disapproving rather than approving. Attitudes and legislation do vary across Europe. Although negative in a number of countries, there are some exceptions, with Denmark and the Netherlands providing examples of positive approaches (see Tatchell, 1990, for details).

Many of these diverse examples of recent issues fail to reflect perceptions of homosexuality as in any way a 'normal' aspect of social life. While there have certainly been some encouraging developments, such as the emergence of feminist publishing companies, the general context remains largely negative.

The nature of attitudes towards homosexuality

Investigation of attitudes towards homosexuals has been approached from a variety of perspectives. Some studies have focused on the religious background. Some have taken psychological or sociological perspectives. A number of studies have attempted to construct scales for measurement of heterosexuals' attitudes towards homosexuals.

Some of the roots of attitudes towards homosexuality in Britain and the United States may be found in the cultural background of the Christian religion. Coleman (1980) suggested that the Christian attitude has been remarkably consistent through history with homosexual offences viewed as sinful and rigorously punished from the second century through to the end of the nineteenth century.

A variety of empirical studies have focused upon different aspects of attitudes towards homosexuality. Looking at some of these, we begin to see something of the influence of notions of human nature and 'normality', as well as the impact of issues of gender, upon attitudes towards homosexuality.

First, what evidence is there that ideas about human nature and 'normality' are involved in attitudes towards homosexuality?

Some studies have found factors that reflect homosexuality as unnatural. For example, Herek (1984a, p. 48) found a 'condemnation–tolerance' factor that included 'items that characterize homosexuality as unnatural, disgusting, perverse, and sinful; as a danger to society and requiring negative social sanctions; and as a source of personal anxiety to the individual respondent, consequently leading to avoidance of gay men and lesbians'. In Kitzinger's (1987) study, factors were found where lesbianism was regarded as unnatural from a 'scientific' point of view, and from a religious perspective.

Perceptions of threat may be considered to reflect reaction to something that departs from 'normality'. Leitner and Cado (1982) suggested that the greater the stress for the individual – implying greater change in construing of self – the more negative his or her attitudes towards homosexuality. Millham et al. (1976) found that a personal anxiety factor accounted for approximately half of the variance in describing female homosexuals. This factor covered items indicating anxiety, disgust or avoidance related to homosexuals.

Investigation of the functions that attitudes towards homosexuality serve illuminates the underlying importance of both shared notions of human nature/'normality', and ideas of gender. Early studies by MacDonald et al. (1973), and MacDonald and Games (1974), suggested that attitudes towards homosexuals may reflect a need to maintain a double standard between the sexes, with homosexuality condemned so as to reduce sex-role confusion. Herek (1984b) suggested attitudes may be experiential, defensive or symbolic. Experiential attitudes develop with generalizations based on a person's previous interaction with lesbians/gay men. Defensive attitudes arise from inner conflict or anxiety. Symbolic attitudes express abstract ideological concepts. Herek (1988) conceptualized psychological defensiveness in three ways: firstly, on a psychodynamic basis; secondly, insecurity with own gender identity was thought to be associated with conforming to gender role; and thirdly, insecurity was hypothesized to lead to exaggeration of difference between self and a gay person.

Functions of attitudes towards lesbians/gay men may be understood on individual and social or cultural levels. From a sociological perspective, attitudes towards homosexuality reflect stigmatization (Martin and Hetrick, 1988); and negative reactions towards lesbianism may be linked to its threat to male power, and men's fears of women's independence (Weitz, 1989). Weitz described how lesbians and other groups of women existing independently from men, such as spinsters, widows and nuns, may be subject to stigmatization and punishment.

These diverse functions underlying attitudes towards homosexuality, clearly display the influence of ideas about human nature/ 'normality' and gender division on attitudes.

Do heterosexuals' perceptions of the origins of homosexuality interact with their attitudes towards homosexuals? Aguero et al. (1984) found that individuals with negative affect and the belief that homosexuality was learned showed the greatest dislike of homosexuals. Individuals with negative affect and belief of homosexuality as genetic were found to avoid social situations where homosexuals were present. In a cross-national study in four societies (the Philippines, Arizona, Hawaii and Sweden), Ernulf et al. (1989) found those who believed homosexuals were 'born that way' were more tolerant of homosexuals than those who believed homosexuality was a choice or learned.

Generally, is there agreement or disagreement in attitudes towards homosexuality? Heath and McMahon (1991) looked at the distribution of *British Social Attitudes* survey responses on homosexual relations. They found there was polarization of views, with distinct peaks at the two extremes of the scale. Thus, 59 per cent perceived homosexual relations as always wrong, and a lower peak of 15 per cent perceived homosexual relations as not at all wrong, with a similar pattern appearing in previous *British Social Attitudes* surveys.

Some theoretical/methodological considerations

Aspects of some studies in this area raise theoretical or methodological questions. Areas of concern include definitions; neglect of the social context; and some statistical analyses.

For example, does the term 'homosexual' refer to men, women or both sexes? This has sometimes not been made clear. Black and Stevenson (1984) found that nearly three-quarters of male participants and over a third of female participants in their study reported that they had used the term 'homosexual' as primarily referring to males. In a survey on British social attitudes (Jowell et al., 1990), while almost three-quarters of the respondents reported understanding the term 'homosexual' as applying to either sex, one-quarter reported interpreting the term as applying to men only.

Further, it has been suggested by many that the term 'homophobia' is inappropriate because the phenomenon that it describes is not a phobia. Kitzinger (1987) has made the point that it is only possible to define prejudice against homosexuals within the context of particular ideological frameworks. For example, she described how attitudes perceived as 'favourable' from a liberal humanistic point of view, would be perceived in a different way from the perspective of traditional psychoanalysis.

Neglect of the social context in looking at attitudes towards homosexuality is a further issue. Although Plasek and Allard (1984) focused on studies concerned with male homosexuality, many of their criticisms are pertinent when considering research on attitudes towards lesbians. Attitudes towards homosexuality should not just be assumed to be stable in varying situations. Reactions towards homosexuality in group situations require consideration as well as those on an individual level. Further, in construction of questionnaires on attitudes towards homosexuality, 'the failure to base the instruments on grounded observations of social reality brings into question the findings of *all* existing studies' (Plasek and Allard, 1984, p. 32).

Statistical analyses must be appropriate and any limitations recognized. Examples where interpretation of findings require caution include the application of factor analysis to dichotomous data (as in Millham et al., 1976); the comparative lack of clarity in interpreting factors produced by oblique rotation (used, for example, in Herek, 1984a); and statistical problems inherent within techniques such as Q-methodology (used by Kitzinger, 1987; see Kerlinger, 1986).

Attitudes towards homosexuals, sex differences and sex role

Sex differences

Some previous studies have indicated sex differences in attitudes towards homosexuality, but the extent and nature of these differences are by no means clear. In a meta-analytic review of sex differences in attitudes toward homosexuals, Kite (1984) found a small effect indicating that men's attitudes towards homosexuals were more negative than women's attitudes. She suggested that this may be dependent on an interaction between sex of target (i.e. male or female homosexual) and sex of participant.

Recent studies have indicated that males express more negative attitudes than females (e.g. Wellings and Wadsworth, 1990), in particular, towards gay men (Herek, 1988). Generally, heterosexuals have tended to show more negative attitudes, or discomfort, towards same-sex gay people (Whitley, 1988; Herek, 1994; Gentry, 1987). However, Kite (1992) found that male participants' reactions to an individual were affected by attitude towards homosexuality (tolerant/intolerant) and the sexual orientation of the individual, but that there was little difference in reactions towards lesbians and gay men. Individual differences towards homosexuality occur, and some inconsistencies in findings relating to reaction towards same-sex or opposite-sex gay persons may arise from context (Kite, 1994). Another study by Jensen et al. (1988) did not find sex to be a good predictor of attitudes. In a meta-analysis, Oliver and Hyde (1993) did not find gender differences in attitudes towards homosexuality. Reflecting on this last study, Whitley and Kite (1995) and Oliver and Hyde (1995) illustrated how use of different methodological criteria may influence findings.

Thus, overall the diversity of these findings may reflect methodological variables including sampling, and the different measures of attitudes towards homosexuality used. Socio-historical context would also have an impact.

The roots of any sex differences in attitudes towards homosexuality lie deep within societal conceptualizations of gender. They may reflect concern with maintaining gender difference; preserving clear boundaries between men and women, and between masculinity and femininity; and with supporting a social structure of heterosexuality.

Sex role

Sex role refers to qualities or behaviours expected to characterize males and females. There is some evidence that those with less traditional sex-role beliefs are more tolerant of homosexuality (Weinberger and Millham, 1979; Whitley, 1987; Herek, 1988), although there are some contradictory findings, such as males with more expressive traits tending to be more rejecting of homosexuals (Black and Stevenson, 1984). Sex-role attitudes may contribute differently to attitudes towards lesbians and/or gay men for males and females (Newman, 1989). However, the evidence as to the relative importance of sex-role attitudes for men and women is not yet clear, with some conflicting findings.

Overall, it seems that the precise relationship between attitudes, gender and sex role has yet to be determined.

Possibilities of changing attitudes

Could negative attitudes towards homosexuality be changed into more positive ones? Laner and Laner (1980) suggested that dislike of lesbians might be reduced through heterosexually defined conventionality of style. Many lesbians might quite reasonably object to such a solution, and whether it would work on a practical level is questionable. It is essential to consider the functions attitudes serve. Where defensive functions are involved, change in attitude through education or contact with gay/lesbian people is difficult (Larsen et al., 1980; Herek, 1984b, 1988).

An evaluation of intervention strategies designed to modify attitudes towards homosexuality, described in a number of previous studies, was carried out by Stevenson (1988). He concluded that education may change attitudes towards homosexuality, although the change may be limited in extent and duration. The specific qualities of presentations leading to greater tolerance in attitudes were, however, unclear.

Considering data from the series of *British Social Attitudes* surveys, broken down by birth cohort, Heath and McMahon (1991) concluded that age differences in attitudes to homosexuality appeared to be related to life-cycle rather than generational change. These findings indicated that the attitudes would be likely to persist.

Herek (1991) has suggested the institutional roots of anti-gay prejudice need to be attacked by, for example, bringing in anti-discrimination statutes. People being required to modify behaviour may lead to attitude change. Further, this would allow lesbians and gay men to disclose their sexual orientation: 'Coming out to heterosexuals is perhaps the most powerful strategy lesbians and gay men have available for attacking prejudice' (Herek, 1991, p. 78). Thus, Herek suggested coming out enables stereotypes to be refuted and social norms changed.

A recent phenomenon, originating in the United States, is that of 'outing', where there is public declaration by people within the gay community that some well-known or eminent person is gay or lesbian. Behind this is the idea that if such people were recognized as gay, it would ease the position for other gay people. Gross (1993) suggested that the argument in favour of outing was motivated firstly, by the costs of homophobia highlighted with the AIDS epidemic; secondly, by the gay liberation view of the importance of coming out, both politically and personally; and thirdly, by essentialist notions of gay identity, and assumptions of a lesbian and gay community. However, as has been pointed out by Puddephatt (1991), the general secretary of Liberty (formerly, NCCL), 'outing' infringes the fundamental civil liberty of the right to privacy, and is likely to contribute towards an 'atmosphere of fear and intimidation' (p. 17). 'Outing' raises serious moral questions. The issue may be debated from the perspectives of privacy and secrecy, dignity, 'truth' and trust, and politics (Mohr, 1992; Card, 1995). Although 'coming out' may well contribute towards more positive attitudes, for the reasons given by Puddephatt above, I suggest decisions to 'come out' must remain with individuals themselves: 'outing' is not, in general, an acceptable option.

Attitudes and attitude change continue to be a much researched area in social psychology (Olson and Zanna, 1993). Psychologists have been concerned with the nature and structure of attitudes, attitude formation and change, and the relationship between attitudes and behaviour. Attitude-change theories have included those that focus on simple affective processes; persuasion; the impact of behaviour; and social influence (Eagly and Chaiken, 1993). The complexity of ideas that have been suggested provide considerable scope for analysis of attitudes towards homosexuality. However, such analysis does need to be based firmly within a perspective that incorporates the social context.

In conclusion, it would seem that it may be possible to change attitudes towards lesbians/gay men, but the functions the attitudes are serving need to be considered, and different strategies for the different types of attitude are likely to be appropriate. While it is useful and perhaps most practical to consider changing attitudes on the individual level, for more fundamental and widespread change in attitudes towards homosexuality, we must focus upon societal notions of human nature and gender.

To summarize, themes that emerge from the findings in the literature relating to attitudes towards homosexuality are firstly, a general negativity; secondly, the underlying influence of notions of gender; and thirdly, often implicitly, ideas of homosexuality as something that is not 'normal'. Examination of previous studies indicates a complexity of pertinent issues, with evidence of underlying influences, that make simple explanations of attitudes towards homosexuality inappropriate.

Stereotyping

If stereotypes of lesbians exist, they may influence both coming out to self and coming out to others.

Definitions and the nature of stereotyping

Examining the witch-hunts in Europe from the fifteenth to the seventeenth centuries, Cohn (1976) provided a vivid description of how a stereotype may be formed, and the subsequent reluctance of people to question its validity. What is meant by stereotyping? Why do stereotypes persist, and can they be changed?

Allport (1954, p. 191) defined a stereotype as 'an exaggerated belief associated with a category'. It may be favourable or unfavourable and it serves to rationalize conduct towards the category. He perceived stereotypes functioning firstly as justificatory devices for accepting or rejecting groups, and secondly as selective or screening devices for simplicity of thinking and perception. He pointed out stereotypes may develop from sharpening facts and overgeneralization of facts, or they may be completely unsupported by facts. For Secord and Backman (1964), stereotyping is the 'action of assigning attributes to a person solely on the basis of the class or category to which he belongs' (p. 67). Tajfel (1981, p. 132) suggested that stereotypes 'introduce simplicity and order where there is complexity and nearly random variation'. Rigidity and resistance to contradictory information was suggested by Tajfel to be one of the most prominent features of hostile stereotypes.

Tajfel (1981) described individual and social functions of stereotyping. Individual functions included cognitive functions whereby stimuli are systematized or ordered through categorization, and defence or preservation of individual values, with stereotypes functioning to protect the existing system of social values. Social functions of stereotyping included creation and maintenance both of group ideologies and of differentiation between social groups.

A recent model of stereotyping based on self-categorization theory (Oakes et al., 1994), challenges some of the conventional conceptualization of stereotypes. Categorization is seen as an elaborative process, not one aimed at reduction of information. Further, rather than being rigid or fixed, Oakes et al. suggested stereotyping is characterized by variability and context dependence. They viewed stereotypes as varying with intergroup relations, context, and perceiver perspective. Underlying stereotypical judgements, they suggested, are political values that vary for different groups. Stereotypes produced by different groups can be equally valid.

Can stereotypes be changed with disconfirming evidence? For such change, Hewstone (1989b) suggested cognitive 'escape routes' such as discounting need to be cut off; the disconfirming information needs to be linked to typical members of the outgroup; the perceivers need to be highly motivated; and intergroup anxiety should be low.

Stereotyping of homosexuals

Previous literature indicates stereotypes of gay men and lesbians that reflect underlying perceptions relating to both (ab)normality and gender role.

In answer to the question 'What is deviant?', Simmons (1965) found homosexuals were mentioned by 49 per cent of the sample, and lesbians by 13 per cent. Ward (1979), in a factor analysis of trait data, found three interpretable factors: 'sinful lust', 'sensitive intellectual' and 'sick deviant', related differently to rejection of homosexuals. The 'sick deviant' was related to greater rejection. Page and Yee (1985) presented participants with items from the Broverman et al. (1970) rating scale, for description of a 'male homosexual', a 'lesbian', or a 'normal, healthy adult'. Lesbians were perceived significantly differently from the normal adult on approximately a quarter of the scales.

Focusing on gender, Kite and Deaux (1987) found evidence to support Freud's inversion model in which homosexuals are assumed to be similar to opposite-sex heterosexuals. Similarly, Taylor (1983), comparing stereotypes of male and female homosexuals with stereotypes of male and female non-homosexuals, found ratings supported a cross-gender hypothesis. Thus, overall, studies indicate the probability of a lesbian stereotype that reflects both abnormality and gender-role perceptions.

Now, we need to consider more closely what gender/sex role refers to; how it has been defined and measured; and its general relationship to homosexuality.

Sex role and sex-role stereotyping

Sex role

It may seem useful to make a distinction between 'sex', the biological division of male and female; and 'gender', the socially constructed notions of femininity and masculinity (e.g. see Deaux, 1985). However, in practice, this is problematic. Many previous studies have used the terms interchangeably. Furthermore, the possibility of interaction between biology and environment may make it inappropriate to make the distinction (see Kitzinger, 1994).

A simple definition of the term 'sex role' is provided by Howells (1986, p. 268) who suggested it refers to 'those behaviours understood or expected to characterize males and females within a society'.

Measurement of sex role

Instruments designed to measure masculinity–femininity or sex-role stereotypes include the Bem Sex-Role Inventory (BSRI: Bem, 1974), and the Personal Attributes Questionnaire (PAQ: Spence et al., 1975). The BSRI includes independent masculinity and femininity scales each consisting of twenty personality characteristics selected on the basis of sex-typed social desirability. PAQ items describing behaviour traits form male-valued, female-valued and sex-specific subscales, determined according to stereotypic pole and ratings of ideal male/female. Categories of masculine, feminine, androgynous and undifferentiated are produced such that androgynous individuals score high on both masculinity and femininity, and the undifferentiated score low on both.

The notion of psychological androgyny has come to be seen as conceptually limited. Masculinity and femininity are complex social constructions. Fundamental questions are raised in attempting to measure such constructs. What are these instruments actually measuring? Are they measuring instrumental and expressive traits rather than sex role? In focusing upon sex categories, are we perhaps reinforcing unhelpful and unnecessary social constructions of gender difference?

Further perspectives on sex-role stereotyping

What are the problems in conceptualization of sex-role stereotyping, and are there more useful perspectives that can be taken on gender?

Firstly, sex-role investigations incorporate the assumption of the existence of masculinity and femininity. These constructs are imposed upon the participants in the sex-role studies, and hence reflected in the findings of the research (Condor, 1987; Bem, 1993).

Secondly, sex stereotypes tend to be regarded as cross-situational, and the particular social context in which they have arisen is overlooked (Condor, 1987). Self-descriptions on the BSRI have been found to vary with social role. Thus Uleman and Weston (1986) found parental role instructions, in contrast to standard instructions, resulted in a greater number of androgynous mothers and feminine fathers; and student-role instructions led to an increased number of undifferentiated women, and a decreased number of androgynous men and women.

Alternative perspectives on gender may provide a more useful viewpoint than that of sex-role categorization and androgyny. Proposing gender-schema theory, Bem (1981) suggested society teaches children a network of sex-related associations that may become a cognitive schema, with the male–female dichotomy perceived as relevant to most aspects of life.

Developing her theory of gender schematicity, Bem (1993)

suggested there are three gender lenses within the culture: gender polarization, androcentrism and biological essentialism. These hidden assumptions about sex and gender are located within cultural discourse, social institutions and individual psyches. This type of analysis clearly provides a potentially more useful and meaningful basis for understanding gender than the early notions of masculinity/femininity.

Gerson and Peiss (1985) suggested a conceptual framework for analysis of gender relations in terms of boundaries, negotiation and domination, and consciousness. Condor (1987) has looked at gender boundaries as an alternative to the sex-category approach. In contrast to the sex category, the gender boundary is not necessarily static, as boundaries may be crossed and negotiated. This reconceptualization would emphasize 'that sex categorizations are socially constructed and reconstructed in everyday life' (Condor, 1987, p. 55). Since negotiation is involved, aspects of power may be considered. Such an approach, Condor suggested, allows for changes in social representations of 'male' and 'female'.

The notion of sex/gender role is complex. It may be interpreted in a number of ways, and attempts to study or measure it need to take into account problems of definition, and limitations of conceptualization. However, sex-role variations are of fundamental importance in considering homosexuality.

Sex role and homosexuality

A number of studies have suggested a link between homosexuality and sex role. For example, Bell et al. (1981) found childhood gender nonconformity to be strongly associated with development of homosexuality for both men and women. However, caution is needed in interpreting any such links. Ross (1983, p. 3) concluded 'homosexuality and deviant social sex role are not necessary or sufficient causes of one another'.

Within lesbian communities, 'butch–femme' role-playing reflects association of sex role and homosexuality. This involves lesbians assuming either a masculine ('butch') role or a feminine ('femme') role. It has never been general among lesbians, but occurred among some up to the 1960s, and there has been a revival of it by some women during the 1980s (Jeffreys, 1989, 1993; Ardill and O'Sullivan, 1990). Jeffreys (1989) pointed out that while in the 1950s and 1960s, role-playing was a survival strategy, now it needs to be seen as a dangerous political development, the polarity of male–female being based on that of dominance and submission.

Perceptions of association of homosexuality with sex-role inversion reflect the general pervasiveness of gender distinctions within our society.

Implications of stereotyping

It is the effect stereotyping may have on interpersonal behaviour that makes it so important to consider in relation to coming out. Women may well hold stereotypes themselves in the early stages of coming to identify as lesbian (Lewis, 1984). Stereotyping may continue to affect homosexuals who have become part of the homosexual community, since there may be feedback between stereotypes and actual behaviour (Ward, 1979).

A number of empirical studies illustrate the possible implications of stereotyping on interpersonal behaviour. Farina et al. (1968) carried out an experiment involving pairs of male participants, one of each pair of the experimental groups having been led to believe that he was perceived by the other either as someone who had experienced mental illness, or as a homosexual, although all partners had actually been presented with a control-group life history describing 'a pretty normal person'. Both conversation and performance on a task were found to be influenced by belief that one is viewed as stigmatized, and effect on behaviour was independent of the actions of the other person.

Through interpersonal, self-fulfilling prophecies, stereotypes may affect behaviour. Zanna and Pack (1975) found that self-presentation conformed to perceived sex-role expectations. Snyder et al. (1977) found targets unknowingly perceived as physically attractive came to behave in a friendlier, more likeable manner than those perceived as unattractive. When Snyder and Uranowitz (1978) presented participants with a case history of a woman, followed later for some with the information that she was living a lesbian lifestyle or a heterosexual lifestyle, their findings suggested interaction between stereotypes and memory of facts. Jenks (1986) demonstrated that people perceived as deviant regarding a specific trait or characteristic may then be perceived as deviant regarding other characteristics, supporting the notion of a master status theory. He found homosexuals and atheists were perceived as having had less education, as being of lower social class, as using drugs more often, and being in greater need of counselling, than Republicans and

Catholics. In Olson's (1987) study of gay and lesbian teachers the majority of participants reported experiencing effects of stereotyping. Having to lead a double life was mentioned most frequently.

A useful framework for looking at the possible effects of stereotypes in the coming-out situation is provided by the work of Jones et al. (1984) on the role of stereotypes in 'marked' relationships. They used the term 'mark' as a 'generic term for perceived or inferred conditions of deviation from a prototype or norm that *might* initiate the stigmatizing process' (Jones et al., 1984, p. 8). Hence, the person bearing a discrediting mark is 'markable' and may become a 'marked' person. A 'marker' is the person who perceives or infers the mark. Discussing the role of stereotypes in marked relationships, Jones et al. looked at determinants of the impact of false beliefs and considered factors that determine when false beliefs will be confirmed or disconfirmed. Issues suggested as relevant included whether or not there is interaction between belief holder and target person; ease/difficulty of disconfirming particular types of traits; the perceived cost to the belief holder; the target person's power and motivation in disconfirming false beliefs, and his or her perceived costs and rewards.

There is a further question of importance in considering both stereotyping of homosexuals, and the coming-out situation: that is, are people generally able to detect the sexual orientation of a person where they have not been specifically informed? Berger et al. (1987) found groups based on gender and sexual preference unable to identify sexual orientation above chance levels, although some individuals, referred to as 'hitters', did exceed chance levels of detection.

These studies have mainly illustrated some of the implications of stereotyping on an individual/interpersonal level. However, stereotyping must also be viewed from intergroup and cultural perspectives. Weitz (1989) suggested cultural stereotypes make it less likely lesbianism will be perceived in terms of an alternative lifestyle, and in this way may serve to reduce the threat of lesbianism to male power. Intergroup/societal level implications are to be examined further in the next chapter.

The coming-out process takes place within the context of heterosexual attitudes towards homosexuals and stereotyping within society. We have traced underlying themes in the literature in this area relating to notions of 'normality' and gender. These require further investigation. The issues looked at in this section are relevant to all lesbians' experiences of coming out within predominantly heterosexual societies. For those lesbians who are more isolated from other lesbians, the effects of heterosexual attitudes towards homosexuality, and stereotyping, are particularly pertinent.

Having considered some aspects of lesbian identity and coming out, as well as attitudes towards homosexuality, we are ready to begin constructing a social-psychological framework for interpretation of the coming-out process.

4

A social-psychological framework for coming out

Coming out needs to be examined within an essentially *social*-psychological perspective. It is suggested that coming out only arises as a concern within the context of a heterosexist society, and that heterosexism may be seen as rooted in gender division and inequalities, and social representations of human nature. This chapter begins with a look at issues of gender, and then focuses on social identity theory and social representations relevant to coming out. Finally, self-disclosure issues are considered. These different perspectives cover the range of levels of analysis from the intergroup and societal, to the individual and interpersonal.

Lesbians as women: some issues of gender

It has been seen that sex role may be important in the stereotyping of homosexuals. The issue of gender has further, more profound relevance to the understanding of homosexuality and coming out. Our language, our culture and our institutions, our everyday interactions with each other, our perceptions and interpretations of our environment, our social constructions of reality, are all founded upon a basis of gender division; and essentially, within our society, notions of gender are closely bound with heterosexual relations. The concept of gender pervades our social world, and heterosexuality is an integral aspect of this. There is also power inequality between women and men. Women's position in society is socially, culturally and economically different from that of men.

Gender and heterosexuality

The link between notions of gender and heterosexuality is fundamental. Bem (1981) discussed how the development of gender-based schematic processing may be fostered by heterosexuality, which facilitates generalizing the sexes to be different. In a development of these ideas, Bem (1993) perceived the three lenses of gender – gender polarization, androcentrism and biological essentialism – as forming the basis for oppression of lesbians and gay men. In particular, gender polarization operates by defining mutually exclusive scripts for being male and female, and also by defining those deviating from the scripts as problematic: 'as unnatural or immoral from a religious perspective or as biologically anomalous or psychologically pathological from a scientific perspective' (Bem, 1993, p. 81). Further, gender polarization may be seen as interacting with individual psyches 'to make homosexuality the quintessential threat to one's status as a man or a woman', such that a homosexual impulse becomes 'an irreversible threat to normality' (Bem, 1993, p. 165).

Sexual orientation was also seen as fundamental to perceptions of gender identity by Spence and Sawin (1985). They suggested that in assessment of masculinity or femininity, heterosexual men and women are likely to give particular weight to physical characteristics and sexual orientation:

> [Homosexuals] may have particular difficulties in reconciling their sense of maleness or femaleness with their contradiction of what society at large considers a major (if not *the* major) consequence of appropriate gender identification.
>
> (Spence and Sawin, 1985, p. 62)

Taking a psychoanalytic perspective, Stoller suggested that homosexuality may be seen as a 'threat to one's sense of core gender identity, of existence, of being' (Stoller, 1975, p. 296).

While there has been little theoretical analysis of heterosexuality until recently (see Wilkinson and Kitzinger, 1993), an examination of its implications contributes towards a deeper understanding of lesbianism. The association between gender, heterosexuality and power inequalities is fundamental.

Power and gender

Power differences between men and women operate at a number of different levels affecting many aspects of women's lives. The three lenses of gender, androcentrism, biological essentialism and gender polarization, may be seen as reproducing male power through discourses and social institutions as well as individual internalization (Bem, 1993). Let us consider some examples of inequalities between women and men.

Gender inequalities may be seen as permeating social interaction through perhaps the most fundamental aspect of social life: language. Graddol and Swann (1989) illustrated how there are parallels in language of the unequal value applied to women's and men's social roles.

Considering gender differences on another level, certain personality qualities or characteristics have tended to be regarded as 'masculine' (e.g. independence, assertiveness, autonomy), while others have tended to be regarded as 'feminine' (e.g. dependence, passivity, sensitivity, caring for others), and socialization encourages the development of different patterns of behaviour in boys and girls in preparation for adult roles (Williams, 1987). Looking at men and women in terms of dominance and subordination, Miller (1986) suggested that women have been treated as the subordinate group, and characteristics associated with women have come to be defined as weaknesses. Miller suggested that such characteristics (e.g. vulnerability and emotion) may be perceived instead in terms of strengths. However, Breakwell (1990) pointed out that feminist responses to stereotyping, either suggesting women should adopt instrumentality rather than expressiveness, or suggesting a re-evaluation of expressiveness, both make a fundamental error in dealing with stereotypes as if their reflection of women is true. This is compounded, as Breakwell described, by the additional problem arising from use of a stereotype, of describing women as a homogeneous group.

Analysis of the construct of emotion provides a further perspective. It has been suggested that in certain circumstances women may appear more emotional than men (e.g. LaFrance and Banaji, 1992). However, rather than considering emotion in individual terms, it may be viewed more usefully as a socially constructed, cultural product, applied differently to women and men, and reflecting power differences (Shields, 1987; Crawford et al., 1992).

Women's position generally within society may be seen as reflecting power differences. Differences between males and females in the areas of education and employment (e.g. Oakley, 1981b; Griffin, 1985; Spender and Sarah, 1988; Wilson, 1991) reflect this power differential. Women tend to be concentrated in different types of employment from men, and their occupations are often perceived as of lower status to those of men; where both men and women work within the same occupations, men tend to occupy the higher positions; and overall, women's earnings are substantially less than men's in this country (Oakley, 1981b; Firth-Cozens and West, 1991; Lonsdale, 1992). Further, sexual harassment at work most frequently concerns male behaviour towards women (Stockdale, 1991). Gender must be seen as an integral aspect of organizational life, reflecting the power relations of the wider society (Cassell and Walsh, 1993). From a variety of perspectives women may be seen as occupying the position of a subordinate group in our society.

Women within our society have generally been expected to assume the roles of wife and mother. Other ways of living have been considered less desirable, although today there are more different options for women than there used to be (Williams, 1987). However, there is still considerable societal pressure for women to conform to traditional roles. Violating others' expectations of sex-role behaviour creates role conflict and is a source of stress (Frieze et al., 1978). Related to societal approval of women in the traditional roles of wife and mother, is societal disapproval of the spinster. Discussing male and female ageing, Sontag (1979, p. 466) noted 'For men there is no destiny equivalent to the humiliating condition of being an old maid, a spinster'. Jeffreys (1985) provided an examination of the spinster's position between 1880 and 1930. She pointed out that 'Any attack on the spinster is inevitably an attack on the lesbian' (Jeffreys, 1985, p. 100). Societal encouragement of the traditional women's roles of wife and mother, and disapproval of the role of spinster may particularly affect feelings and experiences in coming out to self.

It has been suggested by Giddens (1992) that emotional and sexual equality in relationships (the 'pure relationship') could potentially form the basis of democratization of personal life.

At present, heterosexual relations incorporate power inequalities between women and men. Rich (1981) discussed lesbian existence in the context of male power and 'compulsory heterosexuality'. In the radical feminist approach described by Kitzinger (1987), heterosexuality is seen as central to women's oppression. Lesbianism is perceived as 'fundamentally a political statement representing the bonding of women against male supremacy' (Kitzinger, 1987, p. vii). Jeffreys (1990) took this notion further. Examining the 'sexual revolution' of the 1960s, Jeffreys presented her perspective of its meaning and consequences for women. She developed particular understandings of 'heterosexuality' and 'homosexuality' which incorporate notions of power differences and equality respectively, and are not necessarily linked to the gender of those in the relationship. Thus, Jeffreys suggested 'heterosexual desire' may be seen in terms of eroticizing power difference, while 'homosexual desire' eroticizes equality. Like Kitzinger, Jeffreys viewed heterosexuality 'as a political institution through which male dominance is organised and maintained' (Jeffreys, 1990, p. 3).

In attempting to understand the coming-out process, lesbians must be considered as women within a society in which there exist fundamental differences in the positions of men and women.

Gender and psychological theory

Much psychological research and theory has tended to neglect gender issues. Feminist criticism of mainstream social science research has been related to its content, ideology, theory and methodology (Wilkinson, 1986). Wilkinson described how mainstream social science research is seen as failing to specify underlying assumptions, and incorporating male values rather than being value-free. She suggested mainstream research may be seen by feminists as ahistorical, or acultural, and as removing issues from the context of the real world. The importance of considering psychological research on gender within the social context (e.g. see Spence, 1993), and taking into account power relations as well as the underlying value system in studying the psychology of women (Nicolson, 1993), cannot be over-emphasized.

Some useful ideas on the conceptualization of gender have already been looked at (e.g. Bem, 1981, 1993; and Condor, 1987 – see Chapter 3). Some other studies have suggested ways of taking gender into account in psychological theory.

For example, Deaux and Major (1987) suggested an interactive model of gender-related behaviour focused on display rather than acquisition of gender-linked behaviours. Gender behaviour was perceived as taking place within the context of social interaction.

Gilligan (1982) described how femininity may be seen as defined through attachment, while masculinity is defined through separation, and how descriptions of relationships progressing towards a maturity of interdependence have been omitted from work on adult development. More recently, Brown and Gilligan (1992) have focused upon adolescence as a time of disconnection for girls. However, criticisms of Gilligan's work have included the question of whether the developmental process described is gender-specific, and the difficulty of testing her ideas empirically (Breakwell, 1994); as well as neglect of culture (Haste, 1994).

Gender may also be viewed within the context of social or widespread beliefs (Breakwell, 1990). Social beliefs, Breakwell suggested, may be seen as both determined by the social structure, and as influencing cognition and behaviour on the individual level.

Haste (1993) perceived the metaphor of dualism and polarity as having been central to our understanding of gender. Based on this, masculinity and femininity are seen as polarities, and women are perceived in terms of 'otherness', since femininity is viewed as the negation of masculinity. Haste, taking a cultural feminist viewpoint, argued for an authentic perspective on female experience. She suggested, however, that for change to occur, there must be change in the underlying metaphors of gender, and the principles of dualism must be challenged.

There has been much debate recently both 'for' and 'against' sex-difference research (e.g. see Kitzinger, 1994; Eagly, 1995). Eagly (1995) suggested psychological research indicates some sex differences in behaviour. Although aware of some dangers in misuse of such knowledge, she pointed out the information may be used beneficially for women and for men. Buss (1995) suggested sex differences are found where there have been different adaptive problems for men and women in human evolutionary history. Hyde and Plant (1995) pointed out gender differences vary in size across different behaviour and that a considerable proportion (25 per cent) are close to zero.

Rather than focusing on difference/no difference issues, Hare-Mustin and Marecek (1990) suggested taking a postmodernist perspective on gender. Constructivism and deconstruction imply 'that the social context shapes knowledge, and that meanings are historically situated and constructed and reconstructed through the medium of language' (Hare-Mustin and Marecek, 1990, p. 25). Meanings are seen as negotiated, and associations between power and meaning are examined. Further, Hare-Mustin and Marecek described how deconstruction (based on the ideas of Derrida) considers meanings of words relative to their differences from other words, and focuses on 'gaps, inconsistencies, and contradictions' (p. 47). Thus, for Hare-Mustin and Marecek (1990, p. 56) 'Postmodernism accepts multiplicity, randomness, incoherence, indeterminacy, and paradox, which positivist paradigms are designed to exclude'.

These studies indicate the importance of considering gender when looking at issues of development and communication. By focusing on gender here, the intention is not to reinforce notions of sex difference, but to draw attention to the pervasive nature of socially constructed gender divisions within our society, and the power imbalances these incorporate. It is essential to examine the coming-out process for lesbians within a framework that takes gender into account. These issues of gender, heterosexuality, and power difference form the background for the social-psychological framework presented here for the coming-out process for lesbians.

Social identity

Coming out both to self and others may usefully be considered within the context of social identity theory (Tajfel 1981, 1982a,

1982b) or self-categorization theory (Turner et al., 1987). These provide both intergroup and intragroup perspectives, and links with social representations and attribution theory.

Social identity theory

Tajfel (1981) defined a group in terms of 'a cognitive entity that is meaningful to the individual at a particular point of time' (p. 254). Such a group does not imply 'a face-to-face relationship' between people (Tajfel, 1981), but may be considered rather as a psychological group (Turner, 1982).

Social identity is defined as 'that *part* of an individual's self-concept which derives from his knowledge of his membership of a social group (or groups) together with the value and emotional significance attached to that membership' (Tajfel, 1981, p. 255). Salience of group membership, and comparisons made with other groups are important aspects of Tajfel's theory.

Turner (1982) suggested a conceptualization of the self-concept as largely composed of the hypothetical cognitive structures of social and personal identity. The most basic assumptions of Turner et al.'s (1987) self-categorization theory defined the self-concept in terms of cognitive representations available to an individual, suggested there are multiple concepts of self, and that their functioning is situation-specific. Cognitive representations of the self may take the form of self-categorizations. 'Depersonalization' – a process of 'self-stereotyping' – was seen as a change to the social level of identity from the personal level.

Further, Turner et al.'s (1987) self-categorization theory made the assumption that it is through comparisons with members of the next-higher-level self-category that self-categorizations become salient. Categorization and comparison are seen as interdependent.

Oakes (1987) related Bruner's (1957) theories of perception to salience and the functioning of social categorizations. Bruner perceived 'accessibility' and 'fit' determining categorization. 'Accessibility' applies to the relative readiness of a particular category to become activated. 'Fit' refers to how well stimulus characteristics match category specifications. Factors determining relative accessibility may include importance of that group membership to a person's self-definition, as well as the attached value or emotional significance. Fit is defined in terms of the extent to which observed similarities and differences between people are seen as correlating with stereotypical division into social categories.

Consequences of group membership, Tajfel (1981) suggested,

include individuals tending to wish to belong to groups that contribute positively towards identity; and tending to leave groups which do not, unless there are 'objective' reasons making this impossible, or leaving would conflict with values relating to acceptable self-image. Two possible solutions, suggested by Tajfel, where there is difficulty regarding leaving a group, are reinterpretation of a group's features so that they may be perceived as justified or acceptable; and/or social action to lead to a change in the situation.

The social identity approach incorporates a notion of power differences. Thus, Hogg and Abrams (1988, p. 14) emphasized that from this perspective '*society comprises social categories which stand in power and status relations to one another*'. Tajfel (1981) suggested that comparisons may be based on the perceived illegitimacy of the relationship between groups. Thus, 'the perceived *illegitimacy* of an existing relationship in status, power, domination or any other differential implies the development of *some* dimensions of comparability' (Tajfel, 1981, p. 266). For example, comparisons may be based simply on the notion that 'all people are equal'.

Gender and social identity

Basic theorizing on social identity (e.g. Tajfel, 1981; Turner, 1982) has tended to neglect the possible impact of gender. Studies of social identity theory within the context of gender have suggested that the theory may be seen as 'agentic' as opposed to 'communal' (Williams, 1984); as neglecting emotion (Skevington, 1989); and as ahistorical (Condor, 1989). Many social identities have been found rather than a single social identity of women (Skevington and Baker, 1989).

Coming out as lesbian from a social identity perspective

Coming out to self

Definition of a group in terms of a psychological grouping rather than necessarily involving actual person-to-person contact is pertinent. Many women may define themselves as possibly lesbian before meeting other lesbians.

From the perspective of salience of social categorizations, as defined by Oakes, becoming aware of self as lesbian would be seen as a function of the interaction between 'accessibility' or the readiness of the category of lesbians to become activated, and the 'fit' between perception of self and the perceived categorical specifications of lesbians. Accessibility would depend not only upon awareness of the existence of lesbians, but also upon emotional significance of the categorization. Fit would be related to the match between self-perceptions and any stereotypical notions of lesbianism. Negative stereotypical perceptions of lesbians would decrease perceptions of fit of self with social category characteristics.

In coming out to self, the social category of lesbians becomes psychologically salient. Although the distinction between 'personal identity' and 'social identity' may be useful, 'personal identity' needs to be viewed as fundamentally social. Rather than viewing coming out to self in terms of 'depersonalization', the process may be viewed as moving from one level of social identity in which group membership as lesbian is not salient, to another level, in which this categorization has become salient.

Initially, as a woman becomes aware of herself as possibly homosexual, the group of lesbians may be perceived negatively. Conflicting or ambivalent feelings on group membership would be likely. On the one hand, belonging to the group may not be viewed as contributing positively towards identity. On the other hand, a woman may perceive herself as having no choice: leaving the group on a psychological level is 'objectively' impossible. With defining of self as lesbian, women's perceptions of the category of lesbians would become more positive: 'where some social category contributes to defining the self, the need for positive self-esteem should motivate a desire to evaluate that category positively' (Turner, 1982, p. 33).

A woman's social identification as lesbian would interact with her identification as a woman, and with her other group memberships, e.g. ethnic/class/occupational. Further, women as a group would be likely to be used for comparisons.

Lesbian communities

Within the context of a predominantly heterosexual society, lesbians form a negatively valued group. Initial coming out into a lesbian community would be approached with ambivalence. Once contact was made with other group members, positive reinforcement for lesbian identity would occur through interdependence, including interpersonal attraction and satisfaction of needs, a feature of psychological group membership. Further, perceptions of shared threat may enhance group cohesiveness where interpersonal relations are negative (Turner, 1984). Depersonalization (Turner et al., 1987) would occur where women coming out into a lesbian community emphasized social identity over personal identity, and conformed to the stereotype of lesbians.

If groups based on women reflect communal rather than agentic social identity (Williams, 1984; Skevington, 1989), and greater positive affect (Skevington, 1989), then lesbian communities may reflect these qualities. Ingroup and outgroup perspectives may differ here.

'The lesbian community' cannot be regarded as a homogeneous grouping, which adds complexity to considering the issues involved. For example, Kristiansen (1990) found that while gay movement lesbians may have an intragroup relationship with gay men, feminist lesbians may relate to gay men in an intergroup manner.

Coming out to others

In the situation of a lesbian coming out to another person, social identity as lesbian would be *made* salient. One possible scenario is that the lesbian has come to perceive her social identity as basically positive. Social identity as lesbian may be perceived as largely negative by the heterosexual person, and possibly threatening to the distinctiveness of heterosexuality (and/or gender roles). Further, for the heterosexual person, the lesbian's social identity may be completely unexpected, and may during the coming-out communication become salient to the exclusion of previous perceptions of the lesbian's personal identity.

Stereotypical notions will be pertinent. Based on a study of perceptions of male homosexuality, within a social identity theory framework, Abrams et al. (1989) found an interaction between label (homosexual/heterosexual) and stereotype trait information. Viss and Burn (1992) found that self-perceptions of lesbians, based on ratings of stereotypical adjectives, differed from heterosexuals' perceptions of lesbians as a group.

The main comparison group for lesbians would be likely to be that of women generally, the next more inclusive, and positively valued group. Lesbians probably make comparisons with other women, regarding a variety of issues, and affecting coming out in different ways.

A societal perspective: social representations

Background and theory

A historical study of sexuality by Foucault (1979), taking a societal perspective, has suggested that contrary to the notion of 'an age of repression', during the last three hundred years, there has been 'a discursive explosion' around the issue of sex.

> What is peculiar to modern societies, in fact, is not that they consigned sex to a shadow existence, but that they dedicated themselves to speaking of it *ad infinitum*, while exploiting it as *the* secret.
>
> (Foucault, 1979, p. 35)

Foucault described how sex in the West became linked with the ritual of confession and the discourse of science; and discussed the underlying power relations involved. To understand the coming-out process, we need to consider historical and cultural context. The notion of social representations provides a social-psychological perspective that allows this.

Social representations have been described by Moscovici and Hewstone (1983) as 'cognitive matrices co-ordinating ideas, words, images and perceptions that are all interlinked. They are common-sense "theories" about key aspects of society' (p. 115). Common-sense knowledge is seen as accepted by 'everyone' and based on shared traditions: 'Common sense comprises the images, mental connections and metaphors that are used and talked about by everyone when trying to explain familiar problems or predict their outcome' (Moscovici and Hewstone, 1983, p. 103).

Moscovici (1984) described social representations as having two roles. Firstly, they conventionalize persons, events or objects, and locate them in a category; and secondly, they are prescriptive. He suggested their purpose is to make the unfamiliar, familiar. Scientific notions are seen as becoming transformed into the common-sense knowledge of lay people or 'amateur scientists' (Moscovici and Hewstone, 1983). Psychoanalysis was used by Moscovici (1984) as an example of a social representation.

Social functions of representations include allowing communication between individuals or groups; guiding social action; and socialization of individuals (Moscovici and Hewstone, 1983).

Social representations theory, while focusing on the collective, has provided a less adequate explanation of the role of the individual. Purkhardt (1993) suggested shifting from the Cartesian to the Hegelian paradigm, allowing the social individual and social reality to be understood within 'an organism–environment–culture system'.

Social representations may be linked with other psychological concepts or perspectives, allowing a focus on shared, collective properties. Jaspars and Fraser (1984) suggested considering attitudes in terms of individual response dispositions that are based on collective representations. Attribution theory is another area where links have been suggested (e.g. Deschamps, 1983; Hewstone, 1989a).

Attribution has been defined by Hewstone (1983) in terms of 'common-sense explanation' and 'how and why ordinary people explain events' (p. 2). The theory is concerned with attribution of behaviour to disposition or situation; to internal or external factors. Early studies (e.g. Heider, 1958; Jones and Davis, 1965; Kelley, 1967) were focused upon the individual. More recent work has shown that the theory may be interpreted additionally within intergroup and societal frameworks. It is these more social levels of attribution theory that contribute most to understanding the coming-out process:

> in a great number of situations we do not attribute to another personal or intrinsic qualities reflecting individual intentions, but rather characteristics of the group to which s/he belongs or to which s/he has been assigned. This is done as a function of the respective positions which the categories occupy and the relations between groups.
>
> (Deschamps, 1983, p. 232)

Deschamps's (1983) ideas link attribution with social categorization and social representations. Hewstone and Jaspars (1982) suggested incorporating the notion of actor–observer differences/ingroup–outgroup differences into social attribution theory; and further, that self-attributions may be made on the basis of social category membership. Oakes (1987) suggested that under certain conditions attributions will be produced relating to '"*persons" (people) as social category members* rather than to personality (or external factors), i.e., a qualitatively distinct type (or level) of person attribution' (p. 135). Thus, social attribution links attribution, intergroup relations and social representations.

Which social representations may be seen as relating to the coming-out process? There is some lack of clarity and agreement on what constitutes a social representation, and how common they are. However, social representations of human nature (Moscovici and Hewstone, 1983), and gender (Duveen and Lloyd, 1987), are particularly pertinent to considering coming out as lesbian.

Gender and social representations

Duveen and Lloyd (1987) suggested that with additional elaboration of the concept, it is appropriate to analyse gender as a social representation. Comparing gender with Moscovici's social representation of psychoanalysis, Duveen and Lloyd (1987) pointed out some contrasts. Gender pervades society whilst the domain of psychoanalysis is bounded. Further, while social representations of gender imply compulsory classification, those of psychoanalysis may be seen as voluntary.

Competing representations of gender were suggested by Duveen and Lloyd (1987). Based on research in schools, they suggested that it cannot be assumed that social representations of gender will be the same in different classrooms. They suggested there is re-construction of gender identities with progressive internalization of social representations. When these representations have been established, they may form the basis for children to anchor further representations of social life. (See Duveen and Lloyd, 1986, and Lloyd and Duveen, 1992, for elaboration of their ideas on social gender identity.)

Homosexuality and social representations

Underlying stereotypes, attributions and attitudes relating to lesbians, there may be social representations of human nature and gender. A discussion of racialism by Moscovici and Hewstone (1983) provides a possible parallel for considering social representations relevant to sexuality and heterosexism. Moscovici and Hewstone suggested that searching beyond stereotypes, attitudes and actions relating to racialism, a representation of human nature may be discovered. This was seen as consisting of biological, psychological and religious elements, with views, for example, on what a 'normal' individual is, and why people are different. It would seem likely that just as racialism may be seen as corresponding to such a representation, heterosexism (or, more generally, notions of sexuality) may be seen as corresponding to a similar social representation.

If social representations underlie attitudes, stereotypes and actions, this has implications for possibilities of attitude change and dealing with prejudice (Moscovici and Hewstone, 1983; Moscovici, 1984; Jaspars and Fraser, 1984). An understanding of the underlying representations, and differences between representations held by different groups of people is therefore important in considering attitudes towards homosexuality.

Theories of development of homosexuality

During the last century a number of theories on the origins and development of homosexuality have been suggested. These have included psychoanalytic, physiological, evolutionary, medical, psychological and sociological perspectives. Some of these ideas may have infiltrated the common-sense world, contributing towards relevant social representations, and influencing attitudes, opinions, images and stereotypes etc. regarding homosexuality. In this way, the different theories may affect the coming-out process.

Grouping the theories under headings of psychoanalytic, medical etc. does not provide exclusive categories, but the simpler division between physiological and environmental/social models of homosexuality is also problematic. Richardson (1981b, p. 6) pointed out that such a dichotomy is 'a false and meaningless one' as there must be interaction between biological and environmental influences.

Plummer (1981) suggested a distinction between essentialist and constructionist perspectives of homosexuality. Essentialists perceive homosexuality as developed in early life through biology or psychodynamics. Constructionists suggest an individual's identity is socially created and maintained, and thus an individual learns to see him- or herself as homosexual. There has been considerable debate concerning essentialist versus constructionist perspectives (Risman and Schwartz, 1988; Franklin and Stacey, 1988; Vance, 1989; Schippers, 1989; Weeks, 1989) and the usefulness of the distinction may be questioned. There are different forms of essentialism; different degrees of social constructionism; and essentialism and constructionism are not mutually exclusive: a perspective that incorporates both notions might be most useful. However, Kitzinger (1995) suggested that as social constructionism and essentialism raise different questions, and use the different approaches of rhetoric versus empiricism in seeking answers, the debate can have no resolution.

The following brief descriptions of different theories are not intended to provide comprehensive coverage of the areas, but are presented simply to illustrate the range of perspectives that may have influenced 'common-sense' notions of homosexuality.

Psychoanalytic

Freud (1905) described men whose sexual object was a man, and women whose sexual object was a woman, as 'inverts'. Those whose sexual objects were exclusively of the same sex, he described as 'absolute inverts'; those whose sexual objects may be of either sex, were 'amphigenic inverts'; and those whose sexual object was of the same sex under particular external conditions, he termed 'contingent inverts'. Freud (1905) suggested reasons why inversion could not be regarded as a degeneracy. He examined the question of innateness, and suggested that the choice between innate and acquired may not be exclusive. In a note added in 1915, Freud emphasized that homosexuals should not be separated from other people as a group of special character. However, Freud (1905, 1917) described associations between neuroses and inversion/homosexuality. He suggested that homosexual impulses were invariably discovered in neurotic people, and that paranoia arose through attempting to defend against such impulses. He also suggested that a narcissistic type of object choice tended to be associated with homosexuality.

Unresolved Oedipal conflicts have generally been suggested by the psychoanalytic perspective as the basis of homosexuality. The neo-Freudian perspective on homosexuality has focused on gender identity (Sternlicht, 1987).

Psychoanalytic interpretations of homosexuality described by Sternlicht (1987) included Adler's views of homosexuality as based on fear of the opposite sex and feelings of inferiority; Ernest Jones's focus on oral eroticism and sadism; and Melanie Klein's notion of oral frustrations in infancy. From the psychoanalytical perspective, homosexuality has often been seen as resulting from, or as a way of containing, anxieties (Socarides, 1981; Gershman, 1983; Krikler, 1988). It has been viewed as based on problems with individuation in early childhood (Socarides, 1981; Gershman, 1983). For Gershman 'homosexuality represents a deviation in the evolution of gender identity . . . I do not consider it a normal variation of human sexuality' (p. 137); and for Krikler, homosexuality is a 'perversion'. For Fine (1987) 'homosexuality is a curable deviation from the analytic ideal' (p. 87); and 'the homosexual is a person who has not grown up' (p. 93). Socarides (1981) made the distinction between 'true obligatory' homosexuals and those who were homosexual based on situational factors. Denman (1993) has suggested that the negative view of homosexuality in psychodynamic literature may be due to prejudice, and that an underlying reason for this may be the challenge that homosexuality presents to aspects of psychoanalytic theory. Its challenge, she suggested, focuses on the notion of a single path of development, as well as on the relationship psychoanalytic theory suggests between what is culturally 'normal', and biologically 'natural', regarding reproduction.

Although there have been attempts to interpret psychoanalytical ideas from feminist viewpoints (e.g. Horney, 1926; Mitchell, 1974), their impact on general perceptions of the psychoanalytic perspective is probably limited.

Psychoanalytic views generally have had a profound impact on common-sense notions of homosexuality. The notions put forward have reflected conflicting ideas of 'normality' and gender identity.

Physiological

Physiological studies on development of homosexuality have considered genetic factors, hormonal influences, brain structure and neuropsychological function (Bancroft, 1994). Genetic approaches have focused on monozygotic and dizygotic twin studies, and other statistical evidence of occurrence from family research, as well as investigating chromosomal sex linkage. Bancroft (1994) suggested that while biological factors may play a part in sexual orientation, psychosocial factors must be seen as crucial.

Money (1987, 1988) took a predominantly physiological perspective of homosexuality, but incorporated cultural and socialization viewpoints into his theories. Based on animal experiments indicating prenatal influence of sex hormones on male/female dimorphism of the brain, as well as data on hermaphroditism in humans, Money perceived erotic orientation as depending on both prenatal hormonization, and postnatal socialization. Furthermore, he suggested that postnatal determinants may be seen in biological terms, in the way that learning/memory may be understood as biological. Thus, Money perceived social and psychological determinants becoming biologically incorporated into the brain.

Bancroft (1994) has pointed out that 'scientific objectivity' has been hard to maintain in investigation of the origins of sexual orientation: moral and political distortions have occurred.

While homosexuality is as biologically natural as heterosexuality (Kirsch and Weinrich, 1991), biological explanations often underlie perceptions of homosexuality as unnatural. The possibility of a physiological basis for homosexuality has tended to be given media prominence (e.g. *Independent*, 16 July 1993; *Independent on Sunday*, 18 July 1993) allowing it to infiltrate common-sense understanding. While some media presentation has been reasonably sensitive, other reporting has incorporated the kind of distortions that arise through little awareness of methodological uncertainties, and a prejudiced perspective.

Evolutionary

Sociobiological explanations of homosexuality have been proposed. Among the hypotheses suggested by Ruse (1988) were 'balanced superior heterozygote fitness'; kin selection; and 'parental manipulation'.

One approach to research on development of homosexuality has been the study of animal behaviour (West, 1977; Tyler, 1984).

Nadler (1990) surveyed research on chimpanzees, rhesus monkeys and other non-human primates. He suggested much behaviour described as homosexual would be more appropriately classified as non-sexual/social. However, findings indicated occurrence of homosexual behaviour varied with species, sex, developmental stage, rearing/experience, environmental conditions, and endocrine status. Rosenblum (1990) pointed out that we cannot draw conclusions about human homosexuality from primate studies, but may generate hypotheses to be tested.

Implicit in the evolutionary and animal-behaviour-type approaches is the recurring theme of homosexuality as natural/unnatural.

Medical

The medical model of homosexuality has drawn on psychoanalytic and psychological ideas, as well as the physiological perspective. From the turn of the century there was strong influence from the ideas of the 'sexologists', particularly, Krafft-Ebing and Havelock Ellis (Faderman, 1981). During the first half of this century, lesbianism has primarily been regarded by the medical perspective as abnormal and deviant, and as an illness (Williams, 1987). Modifications in the American Psychiatric Association's *Diagnostic and Statistical Manual* (*DSM*) illustrate changes of the medical perspective in more recent years. Homosexuality was listed as a 'sexual deviation' until 1973 when it was removed from the *DSM* and 'ego-dystonic homosexuality' was included instead (Davison and Neale, 1982). Ego-dystonic homosexuality refers to someone who is distressed by experiencing homosexual arousal and wants to become heterosexual. Predisposing factors were suggested to be internalized negative societal attitudes towards homosexuality. As well as this, there may be features associated with heterosexuality that are viewed as desirable, but incompatible with homosexuality. Davison and Neale (1982, p. 364) suggested 'The fact that ego-dystonic *hetero*sexuality is not a diagnosis reflects a continuing implicit belief that homosexuality is abnormal'. The only reference to homosexuality in the diagnostic index of the revised third edition, *DSM-III-R* (American Psychiatric Association, 1987) was to ego-dystonic homosexuality. This was classified under 'sexual disorder not otherwise specified' with the example of 'persistent and marked distress about one's sexual orientation' (p. 296). *DSM IV* contains a similar reference (Davison and Neale, 1994).

The World Health Organization (WHO, 1992) now no longer

includes homosexuality as a category within its classification of mental and behavioural disorders (*ICD-10*). It notes 'Sexual orientation alone is not to be regarded as a disorder' (WHO, 1992, p. 221). It does include the disorder of 'egodystonic sexual orientation' (p. 222).

A position statement by the American Psychiatric Association is further illustration of the changing medical perspective on homosexuality:

> Whereas homosexuality per se implies no impairment in judgement, stability, reliability, or general social or vocational capabilities, the American Psychiatric Association (APA) calls on all international health organizations, psychiatric organizations, and individual psychiatrists in other countries to urge the repeal in their own countries of legislation that penalizes homosexual acts by consenting adults in private. Further, APA calls on these organizations and individuals to do all that is possible to decrease the stigma related to homosexuality wherever and whenever it may occur.
>
> (American Psychiatric Association, 1993, p. 686)

Although there has been positive change in the last twenty years, the predominant medical perspective this century has reflected homosexuality as abnormal. This conceptualization must be seen as having been highly influential in forming common-sense notions.

Psychological/sociological

Many of the more recent psychological and sociological studies have been concerned with homosexual identity formation rather than the origins or aetiology of homosexuality. Examples of these include stage theories of homosexuality and the symbolic interactionist approach. Such studies were discussed in Chapter 3. Some further relevant studies are mentioned here.

The notion of people's psychosexual reactions and/or activities lying on a continuum, ranging from entirely heterosexual at one end, to entirely homosexual at the other, as opposed to forming a dichotomy (Kinsey et al., 1953) has been very influential in subsequent thinking and research on homosexuality. DeCecco (1990) pointed out that the Kinsey reports reflected a conceptualization of sexuality as essentially physical. Cass (1990) suggested that Kinsey's model and scale of sexual preference is of limited use in understanding the experiences of lesbians today; and that stage of development in identity formation may provide more useful information. Emphasis now is on a multidimensional perspective of sexual orientation (e.g. Sanders et al., 1990; Coleman, 1990; Klein, 1990).

> Although nominal categories of heterosexual, homosexual, and bisexual exist, the application of such labels reflects a complex set of social, political, and developmental factors and does not always accurately reflect actual sexual behavior patterns or erotic desire.
>
> (Sanders et al., 1990, p. xxvi)

Examples of some recent psychological and sociological studies illustrate some of the varied current theories on development of homosexuality.

A constructionist perspective was provided by Weeks (1986). He suggested that what is known as 'sexuality' is 'a product of many influences and social interventions. It does not exist outside history but is a historical product' (Weeks, 1986, p. 31).

A model of development of sexual identity which takes into account interaction between a person's life experiences, the meanings ascribed to those experiences, and a person's self-constructs, was suggested by Richardson and Hart (1981). Development of a homosexual identity and its maintenance and meaning for each person was seen as unique.

Bell et al. (1981) provided a model of sexual preference based on path analysis. They found childhood gender nonconformity to be strongly associated with later homosexuality. Although data from their study does not provide physiological evidence, Bell et al. speculated that their findings were not inconsistent with a biological basis for homosexuality, in particular for those who were exclusively homosexual.

Green (1987) studied two groups of young boys growing up. Of the 'feminine' group of boys, a large proportion became homosexual, in contrast to only one boy from the conventionally masculine group becoming homosexual.

Findings of psychological and sociological studies have influenced general understanding of homosexuality to varying degrees, some having had little or no impact, and others, like the early Kinsey reports, having had a major effect on common-sense notions.

Feminist

Within the feminist perspective, there are some differing views, and there are obviously overlaps with some of the other perspectives, in particular, with those having a social emphasis.

Browning (1982) suggested the feminist perspective provides a social view of lesbianism. Thus, women's sexuality is seen as generally defined in male terms, and sexual inequality is seen as maintained by a patriarchal value system. Sexual preference from the feminist perspective is seen as a choice.

Providing a radical feminist viewpoint, Kitzinger (1987) suggested lesbianism must not be considered in individual terms, but must instead be seen from the political perspective. From the radical feminist point of view, both lesbianism and heterosexuality are perceived as political constructions, and neither is seen in terms of being 'natural'.

Limitations of theories

Research concerning the aetiology of homosexuality has basic limitations. There are methodological and theoretical inadequacies, and in particular, problems related to defining homosexuality, and to sampling (Richardson, 1981b; West, 1983). Further, such research raises serious moral, social and political questions. Overall findings in this area must be interpreted with extreme caution. However, the focus here is on the different ideas that have been suggested, since these may both underlie and reflect stereotypes and attitudes concerning lesbians, and thus affect the coming-out process. In particular, the underlying themes relating to notions of 'normality'/unnaturalness, and gender have been evident.

Self-disclosure

Notions of self/self-presentation

For a fuller understanding of the coming-out process, we must consider the notion of 'self'. Many different conceptualizations of self have been suggested (Burns, 1979). The perspective of Mead (1934) is particularly appropriate.

Mead (1934) presented a fundamentally social understanding of the self-concept. He perceived self as originating and developing through social experience and interaction with others. Within social interaction, an individual may become an object to herself and take the attitude of others towards herself. Meaning, Mead suggested, is given by the response of the other. He put forward the notion of 'the generalized other' which arises from the organization of the attitudes of others. Self, he suggested, may be seen in terms of 'I' and 'me', with 'I' corresponding to the response of the individual to the attitudes of others, and 'me' corresponding to the organized set of attitudes of others assumed by the individual.

From the perspective of Mead's notion of self, in perceiving oneself as lesbian, one would be an object to oneself and take the attitude of others towards oneself. Meaning would be derived from the response of others. While coming out to self and before meeting other lesbians, attitudes and responses of others would probably be those of the heterosexual community, and might tend to be negative. During the coming-out process, relative values of the 'I' and 'me' may vary. The 'I' would need to be emphasized over the 'me' while coming out to self within the heterosexual community, but would not require such emphasis once out within a lesbian community, since it would then be closer to the 'me' or organized attitudes of others.

Goffman's (1959) dramaturgical framework provides a further perspective from which coming out may be considered. Here, human social interaction is presented in terms of performances. Actors appear before their audience in the front region. In the back region, the actor's front may be dropped. Goffman's main concern was with expressions given off rather than expressions given. He suggested that performers tend to offer the audience an idealized impression. They may attempt to conceal certain information from the audience. These ideas on self-presentation are relevant to a number of aspects of coming out or not coming out, and passing as heterosexual. One example would be where a lesbian passed as heterosexual in front of the heterosexual audience of family or work colleagues, but dropped this front when backstage mixing with other lesbians.

Self-disclosure and other minority group experiences

Coming out may be examined in terms of self-disclosure generally, and also in comparison with other minority group experiences. The notion of self-disclosure is relevant mainly to an understanding of the coming out to others situation, whilst comparison with other minority group experiences may illuminate issues of self-acceptance and self-disclosure, with relevance both to coming out to self and to others. In particular, the notion of coping with threat to identity (Breakwell, 1986) forms a framework for interpretation of coming out.

Self-disclosure

How can research on self-disclosure add to our understanding of coming out? Self-disclosure has been defined and conceptualized in different ways. Cozby (1973) defined it in terms of information about self that one person communicates verbally to another person. Non-verbal communication is pertinent too. Women may disclose their lesbian identity verbally, or non-verbally, telling someone directly, or through their behaviour or appearance.

Studies of self-disclosure have looked at its relationship with mental health; effects of non-disclosure; self-disclosure and friendship formation; and disclosure reciprocity (Chaikin and Derlega, 1976). Derlega and Berg (1987) pointed out that decisions made about self-disclosure 'determine the kinds of relationships the person has with others; how others perceive him or her; and the degree of self-knowledge and awareness that the person possesses' (p. ix). Further, self-disclosure and relationships may be seen as mutually transformative: the nature of a relationship may be transformed by self-disclosure, as well as the meaning and effect of the self-disclosure being transformed by the nature of the relationship (Derlega et al., 1993).

The importance of self-disclosure to psychological health has been emphasized in many studies (e.g. Jourard, 1971; Berg and Derlega, 1987). Jourard suggested that individuals with healthy personalities have the ability to make themselves fully known to at least one other person. He linked non-disclosure with stress and illness. The woman who thinks that she is lesbian and feels she cannot disclose this to anyone is probably under extreme stress; and the risks to her psychological health are considerable.

Non-disclosure has further implications ranging from effects on personal growth to everyday interactions with others, friendships, and relationships. Jourard (1971) suggested people can only come to know themselves through disclosure to other people. In both the formation and maintenance of friendships, non-disclosure may be problematic, and reciprocity of disclosure plays an important role. Miell and Duck (1986) considered self-disclosure as a central strategy used in the development of friendship. Chaikin and Derlega suggested long-term self-disclosure may be affected by variables such as liking, proximity or commitment, and power or status. For the lesbian, non-disclosure may limit understanding and perceptions of self; and affect everyday interactions with others, friendships, and family relationships.

The role of the individual to whom disclosure is made requires consideration. For example, Miller, Berg and Archer (1983) found that some individuals ('high openers') tended to elicit greater self-disclosure from others than other individuals ('low openers').

One pertinent issue to consider is how people can avoid revealing information about themselves. Often a woman may not wish to disclose her lesbian identity to others. Refocusing conversational content and lowering information quality were the main tactics used to evade revealing information in a study by Berger and Kellermann (1989). If these tactics became less efficient, presentation of a negative self-image or conversational control were sometimes used. Another common situation may be where a lesbian has decided to tell a particular person, but does not wish the information to be passed on to others by this person. However, it has been found that a substantial proportion of disclosers and receivers of private information expect the information to be passed on, even where a prior restraint phrase like 'don't tell anyone' was used (Petronio and Bantz, 1991).

Thus, for a lesbian, disclosure reciprocity may be problematic in both the formation and maintenance of friendships. She may need to employ tactics of evading revealing information about herself in everyday conversations. Disclosure of her lesbianism may well relieve many of these problems, but it carries considerable risks too, ranging from rejection to avoidance or decreased liking. Making decisions regarding whether or not to disclose that she is lesbian to heterosexual friends or family will almost certainly demand much emotional energy and may involve a high level of stress.

Other variables may affect self-disclosure and have implications for lesbians coming out. The relationship between privacy, power and norms was discussed by Kelvin (1973). Disclosure and privacy may be balanced by individuals (Derlega et al., 1993).

Men and women may interpret self-disclosure differently (Derlega et al., 1993). Findings relating to gender and self-disclosure have been inconsistent (Hill and Stull, 1987). However, gender issues obviously play a role in disclosure of lesbian identity.

Brown and Gilligan (1992) suggested that for girls, adolescence is a time of disconnection or dissociation. They described a 'relational impasse' where girls recognized they risked losing relationships if they spoke of their strong feelings and thoughts, but by not speaking, the girls lost the authenticity of those relationships. For the lesbian adolescent such dissociations would intensify the isolation of coming out.

Different models of self-disclosure have been proposed. Miller and Read's (1987) goal-based model of self-disclosure has four components: goals, plans/strategies, resources and beliefs. This provides a possible framework for analysis of coming out to others as lesbian. However, although the model takes into account beliefs about the world, its emphasis on the individual, while illuminating some aspects of coming out, may obscure, or give insufficient emphasis to, some of the major determinants of the coming-out process.

In considering self-disclosure and coming out as lesbian, it is important that the level of analysis is not confined to the individual or interpersonal. Issues of self-disclosure in coming out must be viewed within the social context of intergroup relations, gender relations, power inequalities, and dominant social representations relevant to sexuality, gender and human nature.

Comparison of coming out with other individual/minority group experiences

There may be similarities between the experience of coming out for lesbians, or gay men, and the experiences of some other minority group members concerning self-acceptance and self-disclosure. Possible examples include the experiences of an alcoholic in coming to accept him- or herself as alcoholic; and the experiences of the ex-psychiatric patient or religious minority group member in disclosing this information about themselves to others. Children disclosing their experiences of being sexually abused to their mothers (Hooper, 1992) provide a further example. It is useful to consider both the similarities and differences of such experiences with those of lesbians in coming out.

The notion of stigma provides a particularly helpful framework for looking at coming out. Goffman (1963) considered the blind, deaf and physically handicapped, ex-mental patients, religious minority members, alcoholics and ex-prisoners, as well as homosexuals, in terms of the 'discredited' and the 'discreditable'. Where the individual's differentness is evident or already known about, she or he is 'discredited'. Where the individual's differentness is not known about, and cannot be seen, she or he is 'discreditable'. While the 'discredited' individual has tension to manage, the 'discreditable' individual is concerned with information management. The notions of 'discredited' and 'discreditable' can be seen to be directly applicable to the coming-out situation. Similarly, the analysis of marked relations (Jones et al., 1984), described earlier, can be applied to coming out.

A further perspective is provided by the model of identity, threat and coping suggested by Breakwell (1986). Examples of identity-threatening experiences cover a broad range. Included in Breakwell's examples were transsexualism, alcoholism, drug abuse and leprosy, and she examined, in particular, unemployment and sexually atypical employment.

The model of identity, threat and coping proposed by Breakwell

In Breakwell's (1986) model of coping with threatened identity, the identity structure is seen as consisting of a content dimension and a value dimension. The content elements each have a positive or negative value, and these values are open to revision. The identity processes are assimilation–accommodation and evaluation. Assimilation refers to absorbing new content into the identity structure. Accommodation is the adjusting of the existing identity structure to absorb the new content. The evaluation process concerns allocating meaning and value to new and old identity content. Identity principles guide the identity processes, specifying the desirable end states for identity structure. Breakwell suggested three identity principles: continuity, indicated by a continuation of some aspect of identity or behaviour across time and situation; distinctiveness, a sense of uniqueness, of being different from others, which may be positive or negative; and self-esteem, a sense of 'personal worth or social value' (p. 24). Identity is seen as developing within the social context. A threat to identity arises when the identity processes of assimilation–accommodation and evaluation cannot comply with the identity principles of continuity, self-esteem, and distinctiveness.

Intra-psychic, interpersonal and intergroup coping strategies were described by Breakwell. A coping strategy is any thought or action aimed at modifying or removing a threat to identity. Intra-psychic coping strategies include deflection and acceptance strategies which rely on the assimilation–accommodation process, and other strategies relying on the process of evaluation. Deflection strategies include denial; transient depersonalization; 'real selves and unreal selves'; fantasy; and reconstrual, and reattribution. Acceptance strategies include anticipatory restructuring; compartmentalism; compromise changes; fundamental change; and modification of salience of principles. Strategies relying on evaluation include re-evaluation of existing identity content and re-evaluation of prospective identity content. Interpersonal coping strategies include isolation; negativism; passing; and compliance. Breakwell's suggestions of intergroup coping strategies focus on multiple group membership; group support; and group action. Limits to coping that determine strategy choice, Breakwell suggested, include type of threat –

whether the threat originates internally or externally; social context; identity structure, including level of self-esteem; and cognitive resources. There may be phases in coping, with a succession of different strategies used in response to a threat.

Coming out and threatened identities

In the coming out to self situation, there may be conflict of continuity of experiencing lesbian feelings with the perceived negative distinctiveness of lesbianism. The threat to identity that arises may be dealt with on the intra-psychic level by deflection strategies of denial or fantasy, for example; or, maybe, acceptance strategies of compartmentalism or compromise change. Denial could range from Breakwell's first level where there would be denial that one is lesbian, through the lower levels where there would be denial that being lesbian is threatening to self, or denial that being lesbian requires any change to identity structures. Fantasy may involve wishful thinking with some more acceptable reality replacing the threat of lesbianism. Compartmentalism would probably be widely used in the initial stages of coming out to self. It would involve a woman assimilating the notion she is lesbian, but keeping this separate from the rest of her identity. An example of compromise change would be where a woman chose to define herself as bisexual rather than lesbian even though her feelings were actually exclusively homosexual. Conflict among the other identity principles may also arise, and other coping strategies may be used.

Threat to identity related to coming out to others would often be dealt with using the interpersonal strategies of 'passing' or isolation, as well as, possibly, intra-psychic strategies such as compartmentalism and, maybe, intergroup support. When 'passing', the lesbian allows herself to be perceived by others as a heterosexual woman. Using the strategy of isolation, the woman isolates herself from others in an attempt to minimize the effect of occupying the threatening position of being lesbian. These coping strategies are examples. The range of other strategies suggested within Breakwell's model are applicable to coming out.

Conclusion

The coming-out process may be interpreted from a social-psychological perspective, incorporating theories of social identity and social representations, within the context of an understanding of gender issues. Ideas on self-disclosure focus on more individual aspects. It is within this theoretical context of perspectives ranging from the intra-psychic level, through interpersonal and intergroup levels, to the societal/cultural level, and taking into account issues of gender, that the data from this study are to be interpreted.

5
The context of coming out

The investigation

This study was designed to investigate the coming-out process for lesbians, both in the sense of coming to identify self as lesbian; and in the sense of disclosure of this information to others. The focus was on the more isolated lesbian, functioning mainly within mainstream society, rather than on political lesbianism; that is, the study was concerned with women like those included in the imaginary lesbian, Clare. Figures are not available, but such women probably form a substantial proportion of the lesbian population, perhaps even the majority of those who define themselves as lesbian/gay women.

Coming out requires investigation not only from the perspective of individual and interpersonal relations, but also from intergroup and cultural/societal viewpoints.

We have seen that previous studies have suggested different lesbian identities, and that these could influence both coming out to self and to others. Lesbians have been described as 'homoemotional' rather than homosexual (Wolff, 1973). Lesbian identity formation has been interpreted in terms of stages, but general linear stage development is thought unlikely. Threat to identity (Breakwell, 1986) may occur in coming out. Further, salience of social category/group membership (Oakes, 1987) is likely to be pertinent.

Few previous studies have focused upon disclosure of homosexual orientation to significant others, yet whether or not to disclose one's orientation to family, heterosexual friends or work colleagues is a crucial issue for many lesbians. The comparatively numerous studies that have looked at heterosexuals' attitudes towards homosexuals have indicated a predominantly negative view. Further, these attitudes may be reflected in behaviour towards lesbians and gay men.

Theory and research on self-disclosure provide an individual/interpersonal level perspective that may illuminate some aspects of coming out. However, intergroup issues (e.g. Tajfel, 1981), and a societal/cultural perspective incorporating social representations (e.g. Moscovici, 1984) are also necessary for understanding coming out. In particular, social representations of human nature (Moscovici and Hewstone, 1983) and gender (Duveen and Lloyd, 1987) are fundamental.

Integral to any social-psychological framework for interpreting coming out for lesbians must be a comprehensive understanding of issues of gender; the underlying part played by heterosexual relations in notions of gender; and the power differences heterosexuality incorporates.

The main hypotheses

Coming out to self

Identification of self as lesbian is based upon primary emotional attachments with women. Additionally, awareness of lesbianism as an option, and a level of emotional acceptance of homosexuality are necessary for possible identification of self as lesbian. Coming out to self will generally be gradual, and while reconstruction of the past may or may not occur, for some women, feelings of differentness may reach back to childhood.

Coming out to others

Initially, a variety of issues are likely to contribute towards decisions on whether or not to come out to family or friends. These may include perception of general attitudes towards homosexuality; perceived risks of coming out; perceived possible gains; need for support. Perceptions of possible reactions of others may play a particularly important role. Approaches to coming out may vary in directness. Some women may simply assume others 'know' about them. However, communication of sensitive information may be planned. When a lesbian tells a heterosexual person about herself, personal understanding of what homosexuality means, perceptions of societal attitudes and stereotypes, and attributions may influence the situation. Reactions may modify over time. Circumstances will have been modified by coming out, and satisfaction with outcome will depend on perceptions of gains and losses. Underlying issues relating to self-disclosure may be loss, threat to self, and attempts to defend self.

Both coming out to self and coming out to others must be viewed within the social context of relevant social representations, intergroup relations, and issues of gender. This context incorporates historical period variations which will influence coming-out experiences.

Sampling and methodology

The coming-out process for lesbians was investigated from three main perspectives: firstly, the perceptions and experiences of lesbians in coming out; secondly, heterosexual men's and women's attitudes towards homosexuality, and their feelings about the hypothetical situation of friends or family members coming out to them; and thirdly, women's perceptions of communicating with family and friends on topics perceived as difficult to talk about.

Since coming out is a complex process, involving a multiplicity of issues and varying with cultural context, historical period, and individual variables, as well as social relations and social context, a methodological approach was selected that would permit the complexity of issues to emerge, imposing the minimum of structural restrictions, while at the same time permitting a systematic, scientific approach. Thus, the study was based on semi-structured, tape-recorded depth interviews. Lesbian and heterosexual interviews were supplemented with presentation of a short questionnaire of open-ended items, and sex-role inventories – the Bem Sex-Role Inventory (BSRI: Bem, 1974) and the short form of the Personal Attributes Questionnaire (PAQ: Spence et al., 1974) – for a focus on stereotyping.

Interviewing has been described as 'a task of daunting complexity' (Oppenheim, 1992, p. 65). Farr (1982) emphasized the social nature of the interview, and pointed out that it is necessary to take into account actions and experience of both interviewee and interviewer. Three sources of bias within the interview situation were suggested by Plummer (1983): the first source of bias arises from the interviewee; the second, from the researcher; and the third, from the interaction between interviewee and researcher. Oakley (1981a) suggested that the traditional approach in interviewing methodology may reflect a masculine social and sociological perspective. The necessity of precisely worded questions for accurate responses and maximum validity was emphasized by Sudman and Bradburn (1982). They identified four factors as related to response error: 'memory, motivation, communication, and knowledge' (Sudman and

Bradburn, 1982, p. 19). All these methodological issues must be considered in interpretation of the research findings.

Participants

Three groups of participants took part in this study.

The forty self-defined lesbian/gay women participants (mean age: 35.23 years; standard deviation: 10.88; range: 21–63 years) were mainly from one London group. Most, but not all, lived in London. All were resident in this country: approximately 10 per cent were from overseas. Occupations covered a wide range, including nursing, social work, journalism, secretarial work, teaching and accountancy. There were also women in the army and civil service; a doctor; and a traffic warden. A few of the lesbian sample were self-employed, and a few unemployed.

Representative sampling of lesbians was not possible. Some lesbians conceal their identity from most people, and do not participate in a lesbian community. This study was not designed to include those who had not come out within a lesbian community. Some level of confidence in coming out was probably needed to volunteer to take part in the investigation. Further, the study was not designed to investigate issues of race, class or disability, all of which would be likely to have some impact on coming out.

Of the thirty heterosexual participants (fifteen women and fifteen men; mean age: 33.97 years; standard deviation: 11.76; range: 18–60 years) who took part in this study, approximately half were students. Occupations of those in employment included secretarial work, teaching, the police force, accountancy and business. A criterion in selection of heterosexual participants was that, generally, they should be unaware that the researcher was lesbian.

The twenty women (mean age: 33.60 years; standard deviation: 12.88; range 20–54 years) who participated in the study on communication with family and friends were volunteers from within the university. Approximately two-thirds were students. The remainder were office, library or teaching staff.

The interviews

The lesbian study

Women at the London lesbian group were informed that the researcher was carrying out a study on women's experiences of 'coming out', both in the sense of 'coming out to self ', and 'coming out to others'; and that she was just as interested in interviewing women who had not come out to family or friends, as in interviewing women who had come out.

The interviews covered issues pertinent to both coming out to self and coming out to others. Examples of questions included the following:

- Can you remember when you first started feeling that you might be a lesbian/gay?
- Do you think there are any reasons why some women are lesbian/gay and some women are heterosexual?
- Do you see being a lesbian as a choice or not?
- How have you dealt with coming out, or not coming out, to your family?
- Have you come out to your friends?

Some of the other topic areas included were personal definitions, coming out to other lesbians, perceptions of the women's movement, relationship with men, coming out at work, influence of the media, and perceptions of heterosexuals' attitudes towards lesbians.

The heterosexual group study

Potential participants were informed that the researcher was carrying out a study on heterosexual people's views of gay men and lesbians.

Interviews were individual. The semi-structured interview schedule was designed to correspond where appropriate to the lesbian interview questions. Areas covered included attitudes towards homosexuality, and perceptions of feelings in the hypothetical situation of family, friends or work colleagues coming out to them. Examples of interview questions included the following:

- How do you think most heterosexual people feel about lesbians and gay men?
- Do you think there are any reasons why some people are homosexual and some people are heterosexual?
- How do you think you would feel if a friend told you that he or she were gay?
- How do you think you would feel if your sister told you that she were gay?

The communication group study

Potential participants were informed that the researcher was doing a study on communication with family and friends. The individual interviews looked at how the women had dealt with topics and incidents perceived as difficult to talk about with family and friends. The following are examples of interview questions:

- Were there topics you avoided talking about, or found difficult to talk about, with friends during your teens?
- As an adult are there topics you avoid talking about or find difficult to discuss with your family?
- Can you think of whatever you have found *most* difficult to talk to others about? You don't need to tell me what it was actually about. I'm just interested in your feelings about talking to others about it, and how you approached telling them . . .

Analysis

Analysis of lesbian and heterosexual interviews

All interviews were transcribed. For the content analysis (Krippendorff, 1980; Weber, 1985) of the interview material, it was decided that the most appropriate recording unit would be the theme. Krippendorff defined thematic units as

> identified by their correspondence to a particular structural definition of the content of narratives, explanations, or interpretations. They are distinguished from each other on conceptual grounds and are contrasted with the remaining portion of irrelevant material by their possessing the desired structural properties.
>
> (Krippendorff, 1980, pp. 62–3)

A coding frame was developed for analysis of both the lesbian and heterosexual interview material. The data were analysed using the statistical package SPSS-X. Frequencies and percentages were examined, and where appropriate, chi-squared tests were carried out.

Lesbian accounts were additionally analysed in the form of life-span lines, and tables for each participant, describing coming-out experiences to family and friends. Some case studies were also examined (see Chapters 6 and 8).

Communication group interview analysis

All communication group interviews were transcribed. Analysis was mainly on a descriptive level, focusing upon issues in communication with family and friends that might illuminate aspects of the coming-out process for lesbians.

In order to maintain confidentiality, 'names' used for participants from all three groups, throughout this book, are fictitious. Any 'name' corresponding to a real name of any participant is coincidental.

Stereotype investigation analysis

A coding frame was developed for analysis of the questionnaire responses as well as the interview material relating to a lesbian stereotype. BSRI and PAQ data were analysed using SPSS-X. Statistical techniques used included cluster analysis, factor analysis and multivariate analysis of variance.

The social context shapes individual experiences of coming out, and forms the basis for understanding the coming-out process. Therefore, it is from this perspective that we begin discussion of the findings.

The social context of coming out

Clare, the imaginary lesbian, experienced coming out within a context influenced by friends, family and school, newspapers and television, and their general reflections of homosexuality. Both coming out to self and coming out to others take place within a social context that includes personal understandings, attributions and stereotyping based on underlying social representations of human nature/gender/sexuality, and reflected in, for example, the media.

Personal definitions

Definitions relating to lesbianism constituted a fundamental difference in lesbian and heterosexual participants' perceptions. Love or emotion was emphasized by lesbian participants, and the sexual basis by the heterosexual sample.

Individuals' personal understandings of terms such as 'homosexual', 'heterosexual', 'gay', and 'lesbian' may be seen as arising from, and also contributing to, the social context in which a lesbian experiences coming out. Since society is predominantly heterosexual, heterosexuals' understandings, rather than those of lesbians, may reflect more closely the general understanding within our culture. Heterosexual participants tended to define the word 'lesbian' in sexual terms only. Lesbian participants were more likely to include something more than sex in their definitions: love or emotion; political or feminist; possibly celibate; a general relationship; the lesbian community or a predominant interest in women. Heterosexual participants were also significantly more likely than lesbian participants to define the terms 'gay' and 'homosexual' in sexual terms only. There were no differences between heterosexual men's and heterosexual women's responses. While for Clare, positive emotional feelings for women were predominant, for the world around her, lesbianism was viewed simply as sex.

Perceptions of reasons why people are homosexual or heterosexual

Explanations relating to why people may be homosexual form another aspect of the social context. They may underlie attitudes towards homosexuality, and in this way affect the coming out process.

> I'd love to know if it was genetic or it was caused by experience, and my attitude to it would be very different if I thought it was caused in different ways.
>
> (Vera, heterosexual group)

Just over a third of the total sample suggested a mixture of nature and nurture as the reasons why some people are heterosexual and some homosexual. (References to the 'total' sample in this section on the social context refer to the combined lesbian and heterosexual samples. The communication group is not included.) Only a few participants (9 per cent of the total sample) perceived the reasons solely in terms of nature. Half of the participants perceived the reasons in environmental terms only. Heterosexual participants perceived the reasons more in terms of a mixture of nature and nurture than lesbian participants, and less in terms solely of nurture than the lesbian participants.

Is homosexuality a choice? A third of the heterosexual sample perceived homosexuality as generally not a choice, while 20 per cent did perceive it as a choice. Just under a quarter of the heterosexual participants perceived it as a choice for some people and not for others. A few heterosexual participants suggested that there was no choice as to feelings, but a choice of behaviour. Uncertainty regarding the question of choice was expressed by some.

Distinctions between internal/external locus or dispositional/

situational attributions were not always clear. For example, while 'upbringing' was coded as nurture (external/situational), it often referred to very early experiences of infancy and seemed to reflect an essentialist rather than a constructionist viewpoint. Thus, although attributions were made, and must be recognized as having a role in the coming-out process, interpretation would seem problematic, reflecting some of the basic problems with the internal–external distinction (problems described by Hewstone, 1989a).

Stereotyping

Before meeting other lesbians, Clare was apprehensive and uncertain about what to expect. Responses to the questionnaire indicated that the stereotype of a lesbian was perceived as predominantly masculine, abnormal and aggressive by both lesbian and heterosexual participants. The stereotypical lesbian was also seen as unattractive or masculine-looking, and as negative in relationship towards men.

The heterosexual woman stereotype based on questionnaire data was perceived by the greatest number of participants as normal, attractive and feminine. The categories of 'maternal/family' and 'neutral in relationship to men', among the next most frequently mentioned categories, were mentioned more frequently by lesbian participants than by heterosexual participants. (The category 'maternal/family' indicates positive or neutral references to a woman's family role.)

The perception of a lesbian stereotype based on the interview material was derived mainly from responses to the question 'Do you remember what you thought lesbians might be like before you met others?' for the lesbian participants; and the question 'How do you think most people might describe a typical lesbian?' for the heterosexual participants. The stereotype was described in terms of masculinity, unattractiveness and aggressiveness.

> Butch – I hate that expression – that's the way that I've always thought of them as.
>
> (Teresa, lesbian group)

> A typical lesbian, she's a guy – she's more of a guy than most guys . . . personally, I would think of [a lesbian] as someone who is very masculine.
>
> (Robert, heterosexual group)

> The butch, the striding around in tweed skirts . . .
>
> (Felicity, heterosexual group)

> Physically strong and hard. Hard in physique, hard in personality.
> (Brian, heterosexual group)

> I just had this picture of all middle-aged women, all the butch types, and this terrified the life out of me!
> (Melanie, lesbian group)

The interview material on stereotypes, unlike that from the questionnaire, included a substantial proportion of comments, general observations, and personal thoughts and feelings. These accounted for nearly half of the lesbian participants' interview responses, and over a quarter of the heterosexual participants' responses. The lesbian participants' most frequent comment was in the category 'quite true'/'a lot of women are like that'. Their most frequently mentioned general observation was that their impressions arose from the media, popular culture or books. Personal thoughts and feelings mentioned by lesbian participants included that they had held a stereotype, been afraid of lesbians, or thought they might be attacked by them; that the image had put them off coming out; and, in contrast, that they had had no idea what lesbians were like.

> The stereotype I suppose, of the . . . rather masculine . . . with very short hair, a bit loud, maybe. But that's just the way that the media and popular misconceptions puts it across, really. I mean there are a few [lesbians like that] – rather a lot as far as I can see . . .
> (Dawn, lesbian group)

> I was terrified of them. I thought they were going to jump on me!
> (Marian, lesbian group)

> I thought they'd be dreadful. I mean I really was afraid of them.
> (Linda, lesbian group)

> I didn't think they were too different from anybody else.
> (Lucy, lesbian group)

> I had no idea what they were like at all . . .
> (Christine, lesbian group)

Heterosexual participants' most frequently occurring personal thoughts or feelings were that lesbians were not spoken about, and that they were harder to describe than gay men.

> I've never heard people describing a typical lesbian.
> (Keith, heterosexual group)

They're somebody that you wouldn't perhaps come across.

(Diane, heterosexual group)

The idea that there may be two types of lesbian, one masculine and one feminine, was evident from the interview material, but not from the sex-role inventory data, and less obviously from the questionnaire data.

> Well, frequently lesbians fall in my mind into two parts – one the female part and the other the male part. The male part is obvious by frequently the adoption of part of male dress: ties, severe haircuts and flat-heeled shoes, and striding steps, and plaid skirts.
>
> (David, heterosexual group)

> these very big, butch women who totally hate men. Short hair, deep voices and all that sort of thing. But – sometimes you get the odd one who's very feminine . . .
>
> (Stephanie, lesbian group)

> I knew there were two types. And then I heard about the butch and femme stuff . . .
>
> (Samantha, lesbian group)

Both the Personal Attributes Questionnaire (PAQ) and the Bem Sex-Role Inventory (BSRI) data indicated that the lesbian stereotype was perceived as masculine. Cluster analysis of the BSRI lesbian stereotype variables indicated a two-cluster solution that differentiated between masculine and feminine variables. Principal components analysis of the PAQ lesbian stereotype data with a criterion of three factors, and varimax rotation, produced a factor based on the eight female-valued items, together with six of the sex-specific items, while the male-valued items were divided between the other two factors. Cluster analysis of the BSRI personal view of lesbians data suggested a more complex structure, with the male heterosexual participants' data indicating the strongest distinctions between masculine and feminine variables. In contrast to the lesbian stereotype, the heterosexual woman stereotype derived from the PAQ data was seen as feminine. Multivariate analysis of variance of PAQ and BSRI data indicated some differences in perceptions between lesbian and heterosexual groups; between heterosexual male and female participants; and between younger and older participants. (Full details of all statistical analyses are provided in Markowe, 1992.)

Previous studies have indicated some of the limitations in conceptualization and structure of the BSRI and PAQ. Masculinity and femininity may be multidimensional. Fundamentally, gender requires a far more complex conceptual basis. However, within these limitations, findings in this study indicated a particularly clear distinction between 'masculine' and 'feminine' variables for the lesbian stereotype on the BSRI; and significant correlations between the BSRI and PAQ masculinity scales, as well as between the two femininity scales, for the lesbian stereotype. Thus the lesbian stereotype was very clearly perceived as 'masculine' in terms of the characteristics the BSRI and PAQ define as masculine or male valued.

In summary, the stereotype of a lesbian – masculine, abnormal, aggressive and unattractive – emerged using the three convergent methods of interview questions, questionnaire tasks and sex-role inventories. This contrasted with the stereotype of a heterosexual woman who was seen as normal, attractive and feminine. Sex role was generally the most important aspect of the lesbian stereotype, but notions of abnormality and unattractiveness were also basic components. Thus, social representations of human nature as well as gender are involved in people's perceptions of lesbians.

Notions of gender are central to perceptions of a lesbian stereotype and the data suggested clear distinctions between perceptions of masculinity and femininity. It is this rigid gender categorization, combined with notions of normality, that forms the basis for 'compulsory heterosexuality', and underlies heterosexism. Coming out as lesbian may be seen as challenging heterosexual assumptions and as threatening the power structure of male dominance.

If gender boundaries were flexible and open to negotiation (Condor, 1987), and if the power imbalance between women and men ceased to exist, emphasis on heterosexuality might diminish, permitting lesbianism to be perceived simply as part of the diversity of human relations. A gender aschematic society (Bem, 1981) is probably unlikely to emerge. The elimination of gender polarization is very unlikely: Bem (1993) pointed out how controversial this would be since it challenges both belief in male–female differences, and the women-centred perspective of many feminists; and would require a social and psychological revolution. However, greater flexibility in gender notions is a possibility, and may be seen, together with power equality between women and men, as essential for any decrease in emphasis on heterosexuality, and hence any reduction of heterosexism. As Condor (1987) pointed out, the gender boundaries approach allows for changes in social representations of 'male' and 'female'. It is change within these dominant social representations that is necessary.

Lesbian invisibility

Coming out to herself, the imaginary lesbian, Clare, had felt very alone.

Contact of heterosexual sample with lesbians

> I know gay men, I don't think I know any lesbians.
>
> (Karen, heterosexual group)

There had been little or no contact with lesbians for many of the heterosexual sample. Approximately half of them had no friends who were gay or lesbian. Almost three-quarters of the heterosexual participants had known a gay man, while less than half had known a lesbian. Only three heterosexual participants described having close gay male friends, and two participants close friends who were lesbian. Responses reflected 'lesbian invisibility'.

> I've like encountered them, but I've never known them – you know what I mean – like in pubs and stuff.
>
> (Simon, heterosexual group)

> I have acquaintances. They're not likely to be the sort of people I would make friends with.
>
> (David, heterosexual group)

> I know several gay men. I'm not sure if I know any lesbians. I think I might, but it's not the kind of question you'd go to put to someone.
>
> (Kevin, heterosexual group)

> I think I know some but I haven't asked them are they straight or not.
>
> (Denise, heterosexual group)

Considering how heterosexual participants had come to know that a person was gay/lesbian, some mentioned that the gay person had spoken about it in conversation or told them. However, many suggested that someone else had (probably) told them. Also, some suggested that it had been obvious, for example, from the way the person behaved; or that they had made the assumption that the person was gay.

Thus, direct self-disclosure by the gay person was not the most frequently mentioned way of coming out described by the heterosexual sample; and there was sometimes ambiguity or uncertainty relating to knowledge of a person's sexual orientation.

Within this context of invisibility, silence and uncertainty, it is not surprising that Clare felt isolated.

Media

Newspaper articles and television programmes had contributed to Clare's feelings of isolation. Responses regarding media were elicited by questions for the lesbian participants focusing on recall of books, films or television programmes during their early stages of coming out. For the heterosexual participants, the questions focused on whether they could recall reading any books or seeing any television programmes about lesbians or gay men. Thus, the lesbian responses were focused on a particular period of time, generally in the past, and in some cases many years ago; and the heterosexuals' responses may have included any awareness of media coverage of homosexuals at any time.

> you don't actually see so much media interest in lesbianism. There aren't the same situation comedy and role-playing on the television – and you don't really read very much about it either – it's not something as prominent as gay men.
>
> (Alan, heterosexual group)

Are lesbians a neglected and invisible group? A fifth of the total sample did not recall or mention any books on the subject. Over a quarter did not mention any relevant newspaper or magazine articles. A similar proportion did not recall or mention any related television programmes.

> I haven't really had the nerve to go into a shop and buy a book because I'd be too embarrassed . . . it's just as bad at the library because you have to take the books back! So, I've really avoided it.
>
> (Stephanie, lesbian group)

Although many participants mentioned books relating to homosexuality, these often focused on gay men rather than lesbians. The situation was similar for newspaper or magazine articles and television programmes.

> The first book I read which touched on homosexuality was *Maurice*. I think I read that when I was fifteen or sixteen. I was amazed – totally amazed by it.
>
> (Joan, lesbian group)

> One's aware of the usual shock-horror things in the press.
>
> (Brian, heterosexual group)

Just over half of the total sample mentioned some positive reaction to books, articles, television programmes, films or plays they had seen that included a lesbian or gay man as a main character. Some of the lesbian sample mentioned a strong positive impact on them by a specific programme, book or film.

> I can remember, sitting there by myself, feeling absolutely dumb-struck seeing this [television play], and knowing at that point that there were women out there somewhere who were lesbians like me, and I had to do something about reaching out, about contacting them.
>
> (Hilary, lesbian group)

Many of the total sample mentioned some kind of negative reaction towards a programme or book. These reactions ranged from reporting they had felt shocked, offended, repulsed, appalled, or disturbed, upset or uncomfortable, to not being interested or avoiding. There was no difference in the frequencies of lesbian and heterosexual group participants mentioning a negative reaction.

> [lesbian films] always left me with a sense of sadness that I felt so alone . . .
>
> (Sophie, lesbian group)

> I must say that if I realized a play was about homosexuality, I probably wouldn't want to go to it.
>
> (David, heterosexual group)

The media may be seen as both reflecting and contributing towards the relevant social representations. The main theme emerging from responses in this area was that of 'lesbian invisibility': little awareness of media material relating to lesbianism, and/or little coverage of lesbian issues by the media. At the same time, however, responses indicated that particular plays, books, films or television programmes had a strong positive or negative impact upon individuals. Media presentation of lesbians has been increasing in recent years. Clare's experiences and those of the study participants reflect the historical period.

Threat and normality

Clare was strongly influenced by how others seemed to perceive homosexuality. Perceptions of how 'most' people feel about gay people are a fundamental aspect of the social context within which lesbians experience the coming-out process and heterosexuals form their attitudes. In describing how they thought people perceived lesbians (or gay people generally), negative feelings were mentioned by many lesbian and heterosexual participants. These feelings included general fear or feeling threatened; suspiciousness; lack of understanding or acceptance; fear that homosexuality is catching; prejudice; and aggressive hostility. Feeling threatened was linked with the notion of normality, and perceived as occurring at both a societal level and a personal level:

> society feels threatened because it's not normal . . . it's a threat to the structure of society, and anything different has to be eliminated.
>
> (Stephanie, lesbian group)

> Anything that's different to the norm, the social norm, is regarded as an oddity, and therefore either ought to be shunned or watched very warily.
>
> (Teresa, lesbian group)

> I think the general view might be it's an abnormality. It's not the norm, it's abnormal, it's strange, it's threatening.
>
> (Brian, heterosexual group)

> Angry. I don't know why. Possibly because like racial differences, physical differences, there's a disgust to deformity, there's an anger to non-conformity . . . it's probably a fear of the unknown that produces the anger.
>
> (Felicity, heterosexual group)

> I think they're afraid . . . partly I think because of their own sexuality, and I think they, they haven't explored their own sexuality enough. Probably to do with ignorance, but I think they're afraid.
>
> (June, lesbian group)

> Not many people are very secure about their sexuality and . . . you can bring out their fears.
>
> (Emma, lesbian group)

Some participants suggested differences in women's and men's feelings; class differences; generation differences; or just general differences between people's feelings.

> Women are more threatened by it [lesbianism] than men.
>
> (Alice, lesbian group)

> I think it varies. I suppose – there are some people completely without prejudice here – there are some people who are just simply sympathetic – some . . . who just pity you – who say 'Oh, they're just sick'; and there are

other people who are completely hostile and think that it's an invasion of the devil . . . an abomination in the sight of the Lord.

(Gail, lesbian group)

Changing views?

Taking into account perceptions suggesting negative men's feelings, negative women's feelings, negative perceptions of lesbians in comparison to gay men, as well as general negative feelings mentioned, just under three-quarters of the total sample mentioned heterosexuals' negative feelings about homosexuality. About a third mentioned the positive feelings of some heterosexual people. A similar proportion mentioned neutral views. There was also mention of the invisibility of lesbians.

I don't think people know much about lesbians, I think they're kind of invisible. Or if they are [visible], they're kind of confused in the public eye with the images, sort of strident feminist, sort of wearing Doc Martens, this idea of butch.

(Amy, lesbian group)

I think it would be quite safe to bring in that great British adage of apathy . . .

(William, heterosexual group)

Most people couldn't care less.

(Margaret, heterosexual group)

You are always going to get extremes – but I do think a lot of heterosexual people may . . . have a more favourable attitude than meets the eye.

(Sophie, lesbian group)

Considering whether attitudes towards gay people had changed, many perceived attitudes had hardened or were becoming more negative, but some perceived little or no change. There were no significant differences between lesbian and heterosexual participants in these perceptions. However, while a third of the heterosexual sample perceived attitudes as improving and more tolerant now, significantly fewer lesbian participants perceived the situation in this way.

In considering changing attitudes, just under half the total sample mentioned AIDS.

I'm sure AIDS must have turned a lot of people against homosexuality.

(Stella, lesbian group)

Some saw perceptions of lesbians as affected by the issue of AIDS, while others did not.

> . . . in that lesbians are tarred with the same brush as homosexual men . . .
> (Joan, lesbian group)

> I see AIDS as being very much divorced from lesbians.
> (Hilary, lesbian group)

It was also questioned whether AIDS had actually affected attitudes:

> I think it's an excuse to justify an extreme view that probably already exists.
> (Brian, heterosexual group)

Few participants mentioned the Local Government Bill, passing through Parliament in 1988, with its clause concerned with preventing local authorities from 'promoting' homosexuality. Many of the heterosexual sample either had no knowledge of Clause 28/Section 28, or had heard of it, but knew nothing about it.

Further aspects of the social context

Additional points raised by heterosexual participants emphasized some issues, and reflected further aspects of the social context.

Lack of interest in the subject of homosexuality or the absence of any strong feelings about it were mentioned, as well as ambivalent personal attitudes.

> Many people just don't want to think about it. Maybe some people would have to face ambivalence in themselves . . .
> (Rosemary, heterosexual group)

> I don't think people will ever really stop [discriminating] because I think people find it too threatening, that they might be that themselves.
> (Viviene, heterosexual group)

The notion of homosexuality as a threat was re-emphasized, either as a general threat, or a threat specifically towards children. Also emphasized was the negative nature of attitudes towards gay people.

Different explanations of homosexuality underlying attitudes towards homosexuals were raised. These included notions of homosexuality as genetic or environmental; normal or abnormal; an illness; homosexuality as fashionable or trendy; homosexuality as fashionable versus something that cannot be helped; and homosexuality as existing through the ages.

Education may be seen as both contributing to, and reflecting, the social context. Only one in ten of the heterosexual sample recalled the subject of homosexuality being formally mentioned in lessons while they were at school, but about a third reported the subject had arisen indirectly. Over half reported having been unaware of gay/lesbian teachers or pupils while at school. Overall, heterosexual participants' responses reflected limited awareness of homosexuality in the school context. Although the majority suggested homosexuality should be taught about in school, some ambivalent feelings were evident.

The women's movement is part of the social context relevant to women's coming-out experiences. Many of the lesbian sample perceived the movement in positive terms, some suggesting it was supportive or helpful to lesbians. A few women suggested it had made their coming out easier or faster. Some perceived the women's movement in negative terms. There was evidence of ambivalence with some mentioning both positive and negative perceptions.

A further aspect of the social or cultural background is religion. For approximately half the lesbian sample, religion had been of some importance in connection with perception of self as lesbian. Some mentioned negative issues such as conflict or guilt, and the incompatibility of lesbianism and religion.

> I consciously left [the] Church because I couldn't handle feeling like this and going to church.
>
> (Pippa, lesbian group)

> I think for a lot of people it's made things more difficult and it certainly did for me.
>
> (Christine, lesbian group)

Positive experiences such as contact with the Catholic Lesbian Sisterhood, or the attitudes of other Quakers, were mentioned by a few women.

While Clare's coming-out experiences were affected in different ways by various aspects of the social context, the nature and impact of these influences must be seen as specific to historical period.

Summary

The social context in which coming out to self and others takes place includes a stereotype of lesbians as masculine, abnormal and aggressive; perceptions of most people's attitudes towards homosexuality as predominantly negative; and little or no actual contact with lesbians for many heterosexual people, compounded with minimal media coverage. The relevant social representations may be seen as reflecting gender issues, notions of abnormality and threat, and lesbian invisibility. A difference was found between lesbian and heterosexual groups in personal understandings of the terms 'lesbian'/'gay', with more heterosexual participants suggesting definitions in sexual terms only. Reasons for some people being homosexual were perceived mainly in terms of either a mixture of nature and nurture, or solely in environmental terms. Further aspects of the social or cultural background that may influence coming out were education, the women's movement and religion. For political lesbians and women coming out within a strong feminist context, the general societal context may have less impact. However, for many lesbians, like the imaginary lesbian, Clare, the social context described would form the main background to coming out.

6

Beginning with 'always' lesbian women . . .

Three case studies of women who, like the imaginary lesbian, Clare, had 'always' perceived themselves as lesbian, are presented in this chapter. These women are Jean, Hilary and Monica. Their cases were selected as representative of 'always' lesbian women in the sample from different age groups. Age/socio-historic period may influence coming-out experiences. Overall, the 'always' lesbian women formed just over a quarter of the sample. Their accounts indicated no heterosexual period. Other lesbians had had heterosexual experience. We shall look at cases illustrating these women's experiences mainly in Chapter 8. However, as an initial look at an example of a woman whose experiences were different from the 'always' lesbian women, we end this chapter with the case of Stephanie. All cases are presented within Breakwell's (1986) threatened-identity framework.

While the case studies are described on an individual level, the influence of the social context must be seen as permeating the individual women's experiences. Thus, dominant representations of gender and human nature are seen as underlying and influencing all aspects of coming out, including, for example, women's awareness of the negative distinctiveness of lesbianism, or feelings of isolation on coming out to self.

The case studies

Women who perceived themselves as 'always' lesbian

Jean: a woman under thirty years old who perceived herself as always having been lesbian

From a very, very young age. I don't know, possibly as young as eight or nine . . . at the time when my classmates say, or my friends, were noticing

> boys, I would be having those feelings towards girls . . . when I realized what the word lesbian meant, I knew that that's what I was.

Jean who was twenty-two years old, traced her initial lesbian feelings back to childhood, and had first become aware of the word 'homosexual' at about the age of nine or ten, and, a little later, of the word 'lesbian'.

> At first, and this might have even been pre-teens, but at first I thought that there was no way I could sort of live a life-style like men and women. I literally didn't realize there were other people like me. I literally went through that stage that a lot of people go through, I thought I was the only one, so I thought oh well, there's no future for me as far as that's concerned. I thought I'd have to live this lie for ever, and never be able to tell anybody, and just, you know, pretend that I liked boys and men. I thought I was unique!

Thus, with understanding of the term lesbian, there was some awareness of negative distinctiveness, and the need to use the interpersonal coping strategy of passing. Intra-psychic coping strategies employed were probably acceptance strategies rather than deflection strategies: possibly compartmentalism and compromise change. Conflict regarding a need for authenticity or integrity was also evident.

> Well, then a bit older, I realized there were people like that – like I did see documentaries on television and things like that . . . I suppose I did come to terms with it. The only problems it gave me was that I would have pressures of . . . keeping it secret . . . wishing you were not any different from the others; but apart from that I didn't really have any hang-ups – I never felt that it was wrong or anything like that – just different . . . that was probably in my early teens.

Jean looked for information and attempted to make some initial contact with other lesbians.

> When I was at school, I looked for information about it in the library, and when I was a bit older, well, fifteen or sixteen, I wanted to make contact I suppose with other people that were like me, and I was able to do that because I happened to find out about this contact magazine for lesbians . . . also, I'd felt really isolated at times, so . . . I rang Lesbian and Gay Switchboard a couple of times.

The image of homosexuals portrayed by the media, and the influence of the women's movement, formed part of the social context in which Jean was coming out to self.

> . . . anything about homosexuals really – in the paper or on television – I would make a point of trying to see.
>
> [The women's movement] literally gave them [lesbians] a voice, and gave them the opportunity to come out I suppose, and mix with each other, and the whole . . . offshoot really of it is lesbians being able to go on and form things like this contact magazine that I used as my first contact with the lesbian world, and helped to play its part in making homosexuality more acceptable.

Jean's perceptions of what lesbians might be like before she met any indicated both some awareness of a stereotype, and some awareness of lesbians as ordinary women.

> I thought that on the whole they would be less attractive than straight women, and more inclined, you know, to wear masculine clothes, and, you know, sort of appear quite masculine when you look at them . . . a lot of women are like that actually . . . pictures in newspapers and magazines, and things on television had given me that impression . . . but they would be, on the whole, no different from straight women, that's what I thought!

Jean perceived heterosexuals as having varied views about lesbians, many not having met any, some having the idea they all look like men, and some people being open-minded. Her apprehensiveness about meeting other lesbians for the first time also reflected awareness of some negative associations of lesbianism.

> I was quite scared to do that actually – I didn't know what it would be like meeting them, and how I would be able to cope with it.

Jean's perceptions of reasons why some women are gay and some heterosexual suggested both dispositional and situational attributions.

> Some are born to be gay or to be straight, and others are not forced into it, but others become that way through circumstances . . . I think for myself it's this combination of the two really . . .

Lesbianism was not seen as a choice.

> No, I don't think you can choose really. You are or you're not.

Jean suggested her feelings regarding men were friendly, but not sexual.

> Well, I like men generally . . . I just have no sexual feelings towards them whatsoever.

Continuity of lesbian feelings and emphasis on the need for authenticity or integrity within herself were predominant over her perceptions of negative distinctiveness. Possible challenge to her self-esteem was avoided with the interpersonal strategy of passing.

Jean's first experience of coming out to heterosexual people (an aunt and uncle) and her first contact with other lesbians all occurred within a short time interval. Telling her aunt and uncle was not approached in a direct manner.

> Well, I didn't actually tell them, they'd guessed – and from what my auntie in particular was saying, I'd sort of guessed that she'd guessed, and she sort of made it clear that she had, and made it very easy for me to say 'Yes, I am' sort of thing.

Asked how they had guessed, Jean reported her aunt had responded 'We've known you since you were very young . . . we could tell by seeing you and talking to you . . . ' This could be interpreted as further evidence of continuity.

Jean was unsure as to whether her mother knew about her.

> I think maybe that my mother could well have guessed, but I've never discussed it with her.

Other members of the family included a father, stepfather, sister and brother-in-law, and step-sister.

> I've never really felt the need to tell them . . . but just recently . . . I thought that maybe I would do.

However there was evidence of some mixed feelings about telling her family.

> I can't see that they would sort of cut me off really, but I don't know how they would react, and I just don't feel that I could find the words to tell them – but I do often think it would be easier if they did know really. So, er . . . maybe I'm waiting for them to sort of ask me about it before I'm brave enough to tell them!

Jean had not been in contact with her straight friends for a while, but suggested she may tell them about herself 'if the circumstances are right'. She was not generally out at work either.

> It does bother me that . . . I have to live on this pretence – and also, I feel I've never really formed any lasting friendships through work, and I think partly it's because . . . I don't feel I can with people that I'm not . . . open with . . .

Thus, Jean was relying heavily on the interpersonal coping strategy of passing with family, heterosexual friends and work colleagues. Considering the main benefits of coming out, Jean commented: 'I just don't like all this having to pretend that I'm straight . . . '

In summary, there was strong evidence of predominance of feelings directed towards the same sex from an early age for Jean. She seemed to be aware of the negative distinctiveness of lesbianism arising partly from the media. Initial intra-psychic coping tended to make use of acceptance rather than deflection strategies. Self-esteem was then largely maintained through interpersonal support from her aunt and uncle, and early contact with other lesbians; as well as some indirect intergroup support from the influence of the women's movement. Continuity of lesbian feelings had predominated throughout. The interpersonal coping strategy of passing was used extensively by Jean. There were indications, however, of her growing need for authenticity and integrity in her relations with family and friends.

Comparison of Jean's account with those of the other women in this group

Other participants under thirty years of age whose accounts were classified as falling into the 'always lesbian' group were Edith, Carol, Lucy, Sophie and Melanie. These women's accounts showed continuity of lesbian feelings and all indicated their first feelings as occurring around the time of their teenage years. Almost all had identified themselves as lesbian before having had a lesbian relationship. The majority of these accounts indicated experience of threat to identity and mentioned feelings of isolation or loneliness. Further, identity as lesbian was not perceived as a choice, and the women's movement was not seen as having affected coming out directly. Like Jean, all showed some awareness of the negative distinctiveness of lesbianism, but generally this aspect was not emphasized in the accounts of this group of participants. Nearly two-thirds of these accounts described the main benefits of coming out in terms of 'being oneself', not having to pretend, or freedom, thus reflecting a need for authenticity or integrity.

Hilary: a woman in her thirties who perceived herself as always having been lesbian

Hilary, aged thirty-one, traced her lesbian feelings back to the age of about ten. She recalled strong feelings towards a girl in her class that she identified then as indicating her to be lesbian. Before that time, she recalled experiencing fairly intense jealousies with changing alliances within a group of friends in her single-sex primary school. After having experienced the feelings that had arisen at the age of ten for a couple of years, Hilary attempted to find out more about homosexuality through books.

> I think that I almost knew that what I was feeling was a homosexual feeling before I'd even made a contact with that word. So maybe I had read it somewhere . . . I can't remember that the word ever sunk into my consciousness. It always just seemed to be there.

Conflict arose during her teens, not from the feeling of being lesbian itself, but from other people's attitudes towards homosexuality, and the effects of this upon a relationship Hilary was involved in. The possibility that this relationship might be discovered by others

> was a daily fear – never out of my mind actually . . . it was the most constant feeling in my life at that time – secrecy, fear of being found out, people's reaction to what we were doing, what was going to happen to the relationship if we were found out.

Eventually the relationship split up, largely as a result of the pressure from others. Dealing with the reactions of others

> I suffered all sorts of anger, upset, bitterness, sadness, jealousy – real emotional problems.

Continuity of lesbian feelings was given priority, in conflict with an awareness of the associated negative distinctiveness.

> So that was really what I went through most of my adolescence, my teens – a growing consciousness that I was, I suppose, outside the rest of society . . . I felt isolated as well, not just traumatized by what was going on.

While growing up, Hilary held a theory that you could only be lesbian or homosexual if you were an only child without brothers or sisters. Now, she viewed lesbianism as probably based on a mixture of nature and nurture, possibly with more to do with the latter. However, she pointed out

> I've always said what's the point in having theories about it, it doesn't matter, either you are or you're not . . .

She experienced her lesbian identity as 'a state of being' rather that deriving from choice.

> It's something I feel I was born with and grew up into . . . I never had the choice.

Overall, during this period of coming out to self, continuity of lesbian feelings was given priority throughout, producing challenges to both distinctiveness and self-esteem. As well as this, there was fundamental damage to Hilary's interpersonal connections and her need for affiliation. Coping strategies used were intra-psychic and interpersonal rather than intergroup. On the intra-psychic level, the strategies relying on the process of assimilation–accommodation tended to be those of acceptance rather than deflection. Interpersonally, Hilary was certainly using the coping strategy of 'passing', and she may, at times, have attempted to use either isolation or negativism.

Intergroup coping strategies were not made use of until some years later. Hilary eventually came out into the lesbian community in her mid twenties. Awareness of a negative stereotype of lesbians had delayed her attempting to meet other lesbians, and at university, she had chosen not to join the gay society. During this period, Hilary was coping with the possibility of further damage to self-esteem, partly through the use of the interpersonal coping strategy of isolation. Generally, her relationships with others were coped with by using the strategy of passing.

Social-context change formed the background to Hilary coming out into a lesbian community. First of all, there was a growing awareness of the existence of other lesbians. For example, at the age of twenty-four, Hilary recalled watching a television play that portrayed a lesbian relationship. She described 'sitting there absolutely spellbound' and realizing that there were women like herself whom she should try to make contact with. Around this period, at the end of the 1970s, there would also have been more lesbian/gay groups available.

By this time, group action, in the form of the women's movement, had provided a social context which Hilary was able to make use of to ease her eventual entry into a lesbian community. She perceived involvement with the women's movement as a means of moving towards meeting other lesbians.

> I'm not quite sure I could have just leapt out of being completely closeted, into coming out and being on the gay scene. I think I would have done if there had been no women's movement – I feel pretty sure that I would have done that eventually, but it was an easier way for me to be able to do that.

Hilary was thus provided with new criteria by the women's movement for judging her lesbian identity.

I could begin to identify with women instead of having to perceive a mixed situation as being the norm – I could actually see an all-women group as being another norm.

This enabled re-evaluation of identity content, aiding coping on the intra-psychic level. Looked at from the intergroup perspective, membership within the feminist movement helped to neutralize, to some extent, the effect of threat arising from membership of the gay movement (i.e. an intergroup coping strategy based on multiple group membership). Continuity of feelings was maintained throughout, and the conflict with self-esteem gradually decreased.

Coming out to straight women friends took place for this participant mainly once she had begun to experience group support – initially, that of the women's movement rather than that of a lesbian community. This diminished the challenge to self-esteem and distinctiveness, and helped meet Hilary's need for affiliation. Eventually, this need for affiliation was given priority.

It was following the traumatic break-up of a relationship that Hilary came out to her father. She described how she felt guilty about not having told her parents, yet embarrassed about the idea of telling them. The 'fairly good reaction' would have provided some immediate support to her self-esteem, as well as having longer-term implications for this identity principle.

Hilary perceived the main benefit of coming out as 'being yourself'. This need for authenticity and integrity regarding herself and her relations with others meant that coming out affected her self-esteem in a positive manner.

I would find it very hard to have any credibility with myself if I hadn't come out. I don't blame people for not having come out, of course I don't, but I find it very hard to be able to deal with myself I think, and that's why I did suffer over telling my parents, because of this credibility gap that I felt that I was guilty of myself. I think that's all it is, that's what it's about. You simply cannot live your life until people deal with you and accept you for what you are, and to have the strength if you like, not to care or not to worry if they can't relate to you on that level. But until you've tested those waters, you don't really know, and the knowledge is the beginning of self approval, I think. Until you have that knowledge then you are not going to know whereabouts you fit in the greater scheme of things, and I think that's fundamentally important to your own well being.

Comparison of cases with other women in the group

There was one other woman with an 'always' lesbian background in her thirties: Joan, aged thirty years old. Her account indicated that she had experienced considerable threat to identity during her teens and twenties. She had initially coped with the threat predominantly by using the intra-psychic acceptance strategy of compartmentalism rather than deflection strategies such as denial. The interpersonal strategy of passing was used with parents and at work. From heterosexual friends and a sibling there had been some interpersonal support. This participant's account indicated that she was still experiencing conflict regarding lesbianism in relation to her work and religious beliefs. Some group support from meeting other lesbians was evident. A benefit of coming out mentioned was that others would stop making assumptions. This may be seen as indicating some need for authenticity.

Monica: a woman over forty years old who perceived herself as always having been lesbian

First thoughts that she might be gay occurred for Monica at the age of seventeen or eighteen. This participant, aged forty-seven years old at the time of interview, also recalled having felt attracted to women while younger, with crushes on senior girls at school.

> I was probably about seventeen or eighteen, although I guess it goes further back than that, because when I was at school, yes, I did feel attracted to women, but then at a younger age, I didn't know why . . . Probably, if I'm honest, I perhaps thought it was only a phase . . .

From her description of her feelings at this time, there is little evidence of conflict related to lesbianism itself.

> I didn't have mixed feelings at all. It didn't worry me. I wasn't upset by it. I mean, I can't honestly say whether I thought it was normal or abnormal or anything. It just seemed to be right, I suppose, and I didn't think I was wrong in any way.

At eighteen years old, having left school and joined the services, Monica had her first affair. There was no conflict within herself about being lesbian, but there was an awareness of others viewing homosexuality negatively, and feelings of guilt arising from this. This could be interpreted in terms of continuity of feelings conflicting with self-esteem.

> I haven't ever had mixed feelings. Not in the way I felt. I suppose the only other feeling I would have against – sort of in relation to it – would be the worry, possibly, of my parents finding out. I suppose not because I felt it

> was wrong, but I thought they would think it was wrong – and so you get this – I suppose guilt, really, because subconsciously you maybe think that you're letting them down, because we all accept that society evolves because heterosexuality is considered the norm.

Monica had had no important relationships with men. She reported generally getting on quite well with men, but never having been interested in them sexually.

Monica's present feelings about being gay reflected a similar lack of conflict within herself regarding lesbianism, but an awareness of other's negative attitudes.

> Oh, very positive. I mean I'm not worried about the way I am. Well, I suppose I would be worried . . . if I thought somebody was going to be nasty enough to phone work and create havoc for me, then, yes, I would be worried – but it wouldn't change the way I am.

During Monica's early stages of coming out, there was little contact with books about lesbianism, and she could recall no films or television programmes on the subject. This probably reflected the comparative lack of books and low media coverage of gay issues, in the early 1960s.

> I think the only book I ever read was *The Well of Loneliness* . . .

Before meeting other lesbians, Monica suggested she had had no thoughts about what they might be like. Her first meetings were with her girlfriend and the friends they made together during the early 1960s. She suggested she had 'never been much of a scene person'. There would have been few groups to attend during the period Monica was first coming out. The influence of feminism at this time was comparatively weak. Monica felt the women's movement had played no part in her coming out as gay, or in her life as a gay person generally. Overall, Monica had made little use of group coping strategies, although this is probably at least partly due to limited availability.

Monica considered it possible that homosexuality may be within everyone, and circumstances may influence 'which road one takes'. She did not, however, perceive that lesbianism was a choice for her.

> A choice? No, I am the way I am. End of story, really.

Her attributions relating to sexual orientation were both dispositional and situational.

Thus, the early stages of coming out for Monica involved

continuity of lesbian feelings predominating, but in conflict with some awareness of the negative distinctiveness of lesbianism. On the intra-psychic level, possibly the main coping strategy used was compartmentalism – the notion of lesbianism having been assimilated into her identity structure, but kept largely separate from other identity content. On the interpersonal level, the main coping strategy used at this stage was passing. Intergroup coping strategies were probably limited in availability, and little use was made of them.

Coming out to family members for Monica occurred mainly as a result of her need for support. She told her aunt and uncle when she was upset at being separated for a period of time from her girlfriend. The major need for support occurred later, when in the mid 1970s, the girlfriend with whom she had been in a long-term relationship suddenly died.

> It was a tremendous shock, totally unexpected – and my mother just couldn't understand why I was in such a state.

Monica chose to tell some old friends of her parents and have them tell her parents for her. Her sister was also told about her being gay at this time. The sister had 'known' before, but it had not been discussed previously. Thus, for Monica, at this time in her life, the interpersonal strategy of passing was no longer adequate for coping with her situation, and had to be dropped. If the death of her girlfriend had not occurred, Monica suggested she would not have spoken to her family about herself, as they had accepted her relationship, and she did not think she had gained by telling them.

The issue of coming out to heterosexual friends was dealt with by Monica in a similar manner to her initial situation with family. She assumed that they knew because they were aware that she lived with a woman, and seemed to accept this, but she had never actually spoken to them about it.

> Well – I say yes [I have come out to heterosexual friends] – no, I don't think I've ever sort of stood up and said 'you know I'm gay', not as blatant as that, but I think people are tuned in to it . . .

At work, Monica was not out.

> I mean I wouldn't lose my job, but I'm not a hundred per cent certain that I would be accepted as readily as I am, if they categorically knew. I mean, I may be totally wrong, but all the same I'm not prepared to take that risk.

She suggested that she perceived coming out as an individual issue.

> I think it's an individualistic thing. I mean some people do it quietly, and if

> that's what they want to do, fair enough. Other people make a big scene about doing it, and equally, if that's the way they want to do it, again fair enough. But I personally would do it the quieter way.

Thus, Monica coped with the issue of whether or not to tell others about herself by generally assuming that they 'knew'.

In summary, continuity of lesbian feelings was predominant in Monica's experiences. An awareness of the negative distinctiveness of lesbianism was probably indicated in her reluctance to tell others about herself. For some time, the intra-psychic coping strategy of compartmentalism and the interpersonal coping strategy of passing were successful in avoiding threat. However, with crises – in particular with the death of her partner – passing was no longer adequate for her needs, and this interpersonal strategy had to be dropped regarding her family. With most heterosexual friends, Monica tended to assume they 'knew' and perceived it as unnecessary to tell them directly. Monica became aware of herself as lesbian during the early 1960s, a time when there was comparatively little media coverage of gay issues, and little availability of group support. Her limited use of intergroup coping strategies may be seen as to some extent a reflection of the historical period during which her initial coming out occurred.

Comparison of cases with other women in the group

The two further cases in this group were Alex and Audrey, both in their early forties. In both accounts, there was some evidence of continuity of lesbian feelings with the recall of crushes on other girls at school. Identification of self as lesbian occurred during her early twenties for Alex, and in her late twenties for Audrey. Alex reported having dressed in men's clothing which she suggested may have indicated her sexual orientation to others. She may have been using the interpersonal coping strategy of compliance. Audrey had chosen not to tell her family about herself, and therefore used the coping strategy of passing with them. She reported having told some heterosexual friends about herself. Both these participants suggested the women's movement had played an indirect part in their lives, and both seemed to have derived some group support from a lesbian community. Alex's account emphasized her dislike of deception, while Audrey's account mentioned 'being true to yourself ' as a main benefit of coming out. Thus, both accounts indicated a need for authenticity.

These case studies have provided us with a first picture of coming out, interpretable within the social context. However, women's experiences of coming out vary. In particular, many lesbians, unlike Clare, and the women just described, have perceived themselves as heterosexual for a period of time. Now, as an initial look at these lesbians' experiences, we consider Stephanie, a woman in the early stages of coming out, selected as a case that fits well within the threatened-identity framework.

A woman who had not always perceived herself as lesbian

Stephanie

Stephanie had attended her first lesbian meeting only a week before the interview. She was thirty-one years old. There was evidence of some continuity of lesbian feelings, conflicting with self-esteem, arising from perceptions of negative distinctiveness; and the use of some form of denial as a coping strategy. Thus, she recalled:

> On and off for a few years I've thought [I might be gay] . . . it passed through my mind and I've pushed it back, and not really given it any thought, not even for five minutes . . . I keep diaries and sort of I read back through some of my diaries . . . mentions thinking 'Oh dear', you know, 'Maybe' for a few years, but I've never actually sort of given it any serious thought until about – oh, some time last year I think . . . even now I don't think I've really acknowledged it, I'm just trying to come to terms with it, I think.

The negative distinctiveness of lesbianism for Stephanie was reflected in a number of ways including a stereotypical image of lesbians held before coming out to others and negative feelings about the words lesbian and gay.

> . . . very big, butch women who totally hate men.

> I don't like either of them [the words lesbian and gay] really . . . I can't think of anything to use instead, but I don't like any of them.

Her perception of how most heterosexuals feel about lesbians was also negative.

> I think men feel threatened because they wonder what they have got, why a woman has to go to another woman. And I think some women feel threatened in case they're going to be leapt on. And I think society feels threatened because it's not normal.

A further reflection of Stephanie's rather negative perceptions of homosexuality is provided by her response to the question concerning possible similarities of coming out with other minority group experiences.

> All I can really think of is like telling someone you've got some contagious disease, I suppose, because you don't want anyone to know in case you do get rejected or . . . You know, it's like saying to someone 'I've got AIDS' or 'I've got cancer' because people have the same sort of reaction, they move back because they don't want to catch it.

There was evidence of conflict in assimilating a lesbian identity, related to perceptions of continuity regarding expectations for life generally, that Stephanie had held for many years.

> I often thought I'd get married . . . I wanted to have six children or seven children, but then again, I also knew that I wouldn't get married . . . half of me still wants to get married, but the other half knows I won't . . .

> The two don't go together, being a Catholic and being gay. And it's very difficult, so I'm going through quite a traumatic time at the moment, trying to decide. It goes against everything I was taught and it's very difficult to change an attitude that's been put there since you were very tiny.

Coping on the interpersonal level, the conflict between the perceived negative distinctiveness and Stephanie's need for affiliation was reflected in her use of strategies of isolation and passing, and her decision not to come out to friends or family.

> I haven't really been associating with my friends recently because I've been trying to sort myself out. I've become quite a hermit . . .

> There are a couple of friends I think I would like to [come out to] but I won't, because of that risk again of rejecting me, changing their attitudes towards me.

There was evidence of the strain of using this method as a means of coping.

> It is very difficult keeping it all to yourself, and wanting to tell them, but not telling them. It's very, very difficult.

Stephanie suggested she would deal with not coming out to her heterosexual friends using a form of compartmentalizing her life, and the interpersonal coping strategy of passing.

> I just start a new set of friends, and have one set, and the other set, and keep them separate.

For family too, Stephanie was choosing not to come out. The aim was to maintain affiliation.

> I don't think I want to [tell family], I don't think so. It would change everything, and I don't want everything to change, because we get on well.

Maintaining the continuity in her relationship with heterosexual friends and family was most important for Stephanie. She was very concerned not to upset her parents.

> I'm the eldest in my family. I'm the one that's supposed to be the good example to all my brothers and sisters, and so I could never tell my parents. My mother would just die on the spot, and my father wouldn't be very far behind I don't think . . . I think too much of my parents to put them through that.

This participant was only just beginning to make use of intergroup strategies. She had contacted a counselling service (PACE).

> It's like a transitional period from one life to another . . .

She expressed uncertainty about her identity.

> I don't really know if I've accepted it [being gay] yet. I'm still a bit ambiguous I think. I can't make up my mind how I feel about it. I don't fully accept that I am, but I think, well, I'm not exactly a heterosexual, I suppose. I'm not too sure what I am at the moment. I'm still trying to decide, and I can't make up my mind about it. I think maybe I am, but I don't want to accept it.

There was some evidence of modifications in Stephanie's perceptions of homosexuality arising from involvement with other lesbians. Her stereotypical notions of lesbians were disappearing.

> . . . it's not like that at all, just ordinary women. I was very surprised really. Quite pleased to have that image shattered anyway.

Stephanie had not perceived lesbianism as a choice.

> If it is a choice, then I don't know why I made it, because it makes life very, very difficult and, you know, there's a part of my life that I can't share with my friends or my family, and it cuts you off from a lot of things – marriage and everything else – and you're not accepted as part of normal society. So, I don't think – if it is a choice – I think people are mad to make it, really, I mean absolutely crazy . . .

At the lesbian discussion group, it had been suggested that 'people were not born that way, but decided to be that way', and Stephanie was attempting to incorporate this understanding of lesbianism into her own views.

Stephanie's response regarding the main benefits of coming out stressed the difficulties of passing, and like many of the lesbian participants, emphasized the notion of 'being yourself'. This may be understood in terms of a need for authenticity or integrity.

> I think if you do [come out] you're not so alone and you have people to talk to, and you can relax more because you haven't got to hide anything. And you can go where you want, say what you want and – if you do keep it to yourself then you have to act differently, you have to be very furtive and you can't enjoy yourself. You're on the lookout all the time in case anyone's watching or there's anyone you know, that sort of thing. And I think it makes you probably have a nervous breakdown because you're so worried about things, on edge all the time. I think it's the fact that you can just act the way you want to act, and be yourself, I think that's the most important.

In summary, Stephanie had experienced, and was still experiencing, considerable threat in attempting to assimilate the notion of herself as lesbian into her identity. For some years, she had coped with this largely through the use of the intra-psychic deflection strategy of denial. Now, she was beginning to use the acceptance strategy of compartmentalism. On the interpersonal level, Stephanie had for a while coped through isolation, and was now emphasizing the use of the strategy of passing. Continuity of lesbian feelings had conflicted with the perceived negative distinctiveness of lesbianism, and thus, seriously challenged self-esteem. Her present strategy on the interpersonal level of passing was aimed at maintaining her positive relationship with family and friends. In this situation, lesbianism was a serious threat to the social value aspect of self-esteem, and Stephanie's need for affiliation was paramount. Intergroup coping strategies were just beginning to be explored.

It is clear from Stephanie's account that she has not always perceived herself as lesbian, and she has had heterosexual experience. We must now broaden our perspective on coming out.

7

Coming out to self and others

Coming out to self

Coming out to self must be viewed as taking place within the social context of predominantly negative attitudes towards homosexuality, stereotypical perceptions, and lesbian invisibility. The hypothesis that coming out to self may be considered in terms of an emotional basis of feelings directed towards women, together with awareness of lesbianism as an option, and a level of emotional acceptance of homosexuality was generally confirmed.

The emotional basis

As for the imaginary lesbian, Clare, awareness of self as possibly lesbian was found to be based firmly on strong emotional feelings towards girls or women. Falling in love/crushes, etc. were mentioned by almost all of the lesbian sample. Recalling how they had felt before perceiving themselves as lesbian, most mentioned having felt strongly about women/girls. Comparatively few women mentioned physical contact. (In this section on 'coming out to self', use of the term 'women', in reference to sample or participants, applies to lesbian participants rather than female participants from either of the other groups. All quotes within the section are from the lesbian group participants.) Some women mentioned having felt 'different'.

> I'd already had crushes on school teachers and . . . I'd read that this was perfectly normal for teenage girls . . . But this one, having a crush on someone I knew who was young – that one hadn't been mentioned. A crush on older women, OK, yeah; a crush on a woman your own age, that one isn't talked about. And when this continued, and it carried on continuing

> right through my teenage years and into my twenties, then I began to think there is something considerably different about me.
>
> (Alex)

The general emphasis on emotional feelings is consistent with both Wolff's (1973) conceptualization of lesbians as 'homoemotional' rather than 'homosexual'; and Faderman's (1981) historical perspective of lesbianism based on romantic friendship. This must be understood within the context of love and emotion as social constructs, reflecting culture and socio-historic period. In particular, there is reflection of our society's representations of gender, and the beliefs about women and emotionality that these incorporate.

A gradual process

Like Clare, some women perceived the origins of their lesbian feelings reaching back to early childhood.

> I just know I had these feelings always . . .
>
> (Jean)

> Yeah, it's a cliché, you know, 'I always knew I was different' sort of thing, but I didn't know why – you don't really know when you are five . . . The way you look at things and the way you respond to things even then. I always knew I wasn't going to get married. I couldn't have said why . . . I just knew that wasn't going to be me.
>
> (Lucy)

This was in complete contrast to the perceptions of a small number of the sample who regarded being lesbian as a conscious choice they had taken during adulthood, and perceived themselves as previously heterosexual.

> It was never really a question of feeling I might be a lesbian, but kind of seeing lesbianism as an option.
>
> (Alice)

This provides some support for earlier studies that have suggested a distinction between two types of lesbian (e.g. Bell et al., 1981; Golden, 1987).

Reported or estimated age at time of first lesbian feelings ranged from three years old to one case of over fifty years old. For about two-thirds of the women, first feelings were estimated as occurring between the ages of ten and nineteen years old.

Personal definitions

Pertinent to identification of self as lesbian/gay were the women's personal understandings of the terms. Forty per cent of the sample suggested that they preferred the term 'gay'; just over a quarter of the women preferred the word 'lesbian'; and thirty per cent of the women suggested they had no preference between the terms 'gay' and 'lesbian'. Several women suggested they would prefer some other term.

> When I first came out, I didn't like the word 'lesbian' . . . in fact I couldn't even write it down . . . I couldn't watch myself writing [it].
>
> (Lucy)

Reasons given for word preference were that 'lesbian' has negative associations or was disliked; that 'gay' was associated with male homosexuality and 'lesbian' associated specifically with women; and that 'lesbian' has political or feminist associations. These latter reasons were given in support of both preferences for 'lesbian' and 'gay'. Generally, negative associations of lesbianism may be seen as part of the dominant social representations of human nature, gender or sexuality. From the perspective of social identity theory, the negative associations may be viewed as affecting salience of social categorization through accessibility and perceived fit of category (Oakes, 1987).

Love or emotion were included within lesbian participants' definitions of the term 'lesbian' by substantial proportions of women in both questionnaire and interview responses. Few gave a sexual definition only.

> Women whose emotions, time, energies on the personal and/or political level centre round other ♀ and who choose in various ways to act on this in their daily lives.
>
> (Shirley)

> [A] woman who loves and/or is sexually attracted to other women. She may well be celibate too.
>
> (Emma)

> Love and friendship and possibly sex between women.
>
> (June)

> Women loving women, a political state as well as emotional.
>
> (Linda)

A woman who identifies emotionally and sometimes sexually to other women.

(Gail)

Following Sappho in caring about women, giving them validity, nurturing them, looking to them for intimacy and nurture, supporting them, furthering their perception of the world, etc., etc.

(Valerie)

These definitions reinforce the emphasis on an emotional basis for lesbianism.

Awareness of lesbianism as an option

Before identification as lesbian could occur, women had to be aware of lesbianism as an option. Some were uncertain as to when they had first heard words relating to homosexuality. For some, the words had always seemed to be there, or they recalled hearing them as young children.

Still in the junior school, sort of about ten or eleven – in the playground, that sort of thing.

(Dawn)

For others, first awareness of such words was at secondary school age, and for a few women, it was not until adulthood.

Many of the lesbian participants first heard the words at school or amongst other children, and a few mentioned first reading about it. For some the circumstances were rather different:

I think it was probably when I got whisked off to the doctor's by my mother at fifteen.

(Irene)

Some women mentioned being aware of the negative connotations of the terms, knowing it was something not to be discussed or being frightened. For a few, first understanding came from gossip or from the media. Two-thirds of the women had either held some kind of stereotype of lesbians, or mentioned feeling frightened of lesbians before meeting others, as described in Chapter 5.

While school was the context for initially meeting words relating to homosexuality for some women, over half the lesbian sample had been unaware of gay/lesbian teachers or pupils. Further, three-quarters of the women did not recall homosexuality having been mentioned in lessons. There was general support for homosexuality being taught about in school: nearly 90 per cent of the lesbian sample indicated they would like this, some suggesting they felt very strongly.

Only three women (less than 8 per cent of the sample) had come to identify themselves as lesbian through their involvement with feminism.

> I'm not sure whether I would have been a lesbian but for women's liberation.
>
> (Mary)

Just under half the sample did perceive the women's movement as having played a role in their coming out. However, while some suggested it had had an indirect influence, a substantial proportion of the sample (nearly 40 per cent) perceived it as not having played any part in their coming out.

> I always think of my number one identity as being . . . a lesbian, and my number two as being a woman, as opposed to the other way round.
>
> (Hilary)

In summary, women began to understand the terms relating to homosexuality at different stages of their lives, often having experienced lesbian feelings previously without having labelled them. Awareness of the negative connotations attached to lesbianism was evident. Women's personal definitions emphasized the emotional basis of lesbianism, involving more than just sex. School experiences and the women's movement contributed for some towards awareness of lesbianism as an option. Generally, awareness of lesbianism must be viewed as based on available social representations concerning human nature, gender or sexuality; and the attitudes, stereotypes and attributions relating to homosexuality that these representations reflect.

Perceptions of reasons why some women are lesbian

While perceptions may change over time, about a quarter of the lesbian participants currently perceived the reasons why some women are lesbian (and some women are heterosexual) in terms of both nature and nurture.

> Well, I think it must be a mixture of nature and nurture, and I don't know how much of each.
>
> (Joan)

Over 60 per cent of the lesbian participants perceived the reasons solely in terms of nurture: circumstances, environment or upbringing.

> I tend to think that it's an environmental, emotional situation that happens through circumstances. I think we're all born able to be either or both.
>
> (Evelyn)

Only a few women perceived the reasons in terms of nature only (i.e. born with a tendency or predisposition; possibly genetic or hormonal).

> I think they were born that way. I don't really believe that society or their upbringing sort of pushes them in one direction. I don't know that you can make a heterosexual person gay. I'm not saying they wouldn't try it, but I think at the end of the day it's just the way you're born.
>
> (Stella)

Some women expressed uncertainty regarding reasons.

Is being a lesbian a choice or not? Some of the lesbian sample did not perceive being lesbian as a choice for themselves.

> No, it's not a choice, no, not at all.
>
> (Hazel)

> I don't really think it is [a choice]. I mean, I think it's part of your nature, you can't change the way you're born.
>
> (Amy)

Some of the sample perceived being lesbian as a choice for certain women but not for others. A few suggested there was no choice regarding feelings, but a choice as to behaviour.

> Well, if you're dishonest with yourself, then you've got a choice. You can live a lie as a heterosexual, or you can be honest with yourself, and live your life as you want to live.
>
> (Stella)

> I didn't choose . . . I think it's in you and the choice is whether or not you acknowledge it, and do something about it. I just don't see how you can choose.
>
> (Lucy)

Other women perceived lesbianism as a general choice.

> Yes, very clearly, it is a choice.
>
> (Isabel)

In summary, over half the lesbian sample perceived at least some limitations to the notion of lesbianism as a choice. Perception of no choice, or restricted choice, was not necessarily linked to perception of reasons underlying homosexuality in terms of nature. Nurture, upbringing, etc. could be viewed as predisposing a woman to lesbianism.

Relationship towards men

> I suppose the only thing that [the relationships with men] did teach me was that I liked women.
>
> (Stella)

Women's relationship towards men affected their experiences of coming out to self. Many, like the imaginary lesbian Clare, had not been in any important relationship with a male (40 per cent of the sample). Two women were currently married; seven women (18 per cent of the sample) had been married and were now separated or divorced; and just under a third of the sample had been in some other important relationship with a male. Thus over half of this sample (55 per cent) had been in at least one important relationship with a male.

For nearly half of the lesbian sample, unlike Clare, there was a period during adulthood when they had considered themselves heterosexual. Of these women, half mentioned either that their relationships with men had been difficult or unsatisfactory, or that there was the problem of inequality. Some women had attempted heterosexual relationships, but perceived themselves as possibly lesbian. Two participants suggested they went out with men or married to prove that they were normal, not gay.

In relating to men generally, many of the lesbian sample suggested that they had good friendships with men, got on well with them, or felt friendly towards them, but of these, a majority pointed out that they had no romantic or sexual interests in men. Nearly half of the sample reported slightly negative feelings towards men. Some participants responded both that they felt friendly or got on well with men, and that they felt slightly negative towards men. Some gave neutral responses. Several participants mentioned they related more easily to feminine or gay men.

These generally friendly, although sometimes slightly negative, feelings towards men must be contrasted with the strong emotional feelings described towards other women. Rather than the stereotypical 'hatred of men', it is the strength of women's positive emotional feelings for other women that provides the basis for identification as lesbian.

Becoming aware of self as lesbian

The minimum age of first identifying self as lesbian (as distinct from estimated age of first lesbian feelings) was ten years old. About half the participants identified themselves as gay/lesbian between the ages of fifteen and twenty-four years old. A quarter of the women were aged thirty years or over on first identifying self as lesbian.

> I mean looking back on it, in retrospect, I can see that I had feelings towards other women, and attraction towards other women, much sooner than that, but I don't think that I was really prepared to sort of acknowledge that in myself at the time, but, you know, now I can see it.
> (Audrey)

Estimated length of time between first feelings and first identifying self as gay/lesbian ranged from less than a year to over twenty years.

The process of becoming aware of oneself as possibly lesbian began for many with negative or conflicting feelings. Over half the lesbian sample mentioned negative feelings related to self, and 40 per cent mentioned having repressed or denied feelings. No difference was found between younger and older participants in mentioning these feelings.

Conflicting feelings, as for Clare, arose from perceptions of how others such as parents might react, as well as from an awareness of the negative connotations attached to lesbianism within society. Perceptions of others viewing lesbianism as abnormal, and of isolation within a predominantly heterosexual society were evident.

> It was terrifying at first because . . . I'd never heard anything other than the fact that it was abnormal and abhorrent which was why I tried to repress it, you know, for years.
> (Hazel)

> I felt absolutely awful and scared – mostly because of . . . my parents finding out – what the world would say.
> (Emma)

> My attitude towards the fact that I was gay – I was never in any doubt about it, I was never confused about it through that time, and that actual

> condition never worried me at all . . . the only thing that did affect me was how other people seemed to perceive homosexuality . . .
>
> (Hilary)

> Very worried. Frightened. I hoped it was a phase . . . I didn't think it was going to be – or after a bit I felt it wasn't going to be – and I think I felt isolated.
>
> (Joan)

> I was very excited. I thought it was wonderful to think of, to have this wonderful relationship, and I really wanted to share it with everybody, but I knew I couldn't.
>
> (June)

Some of the participants were still in the initial stages of coming out to self at time of interview.

> At the moment, I feel as though I'm beginning to accept the fact that I am [gay] . . . I suppose coming to terms with it, actually coming into an accepting state of mind. I'm feeling more relaxed than I have been.
>
> (Dawn)

Emotional acceptance of a lesbian identity was a gradual process for most of the women which may be understood from the perspective of Breakwell's model of threatened identity; and also within the context of salience of social categorization (Oakes, 1987).

Considering current feelings about being lesbian, both positive and negative feelings were mentioned by the majority of the sample. Having accepted self as lesbian, many women described their feelings in very positive terms:

> Well, I can say now I'm happy with myself.
>
> (Stella)

> I wouldn't change – completely positive.
>
> (Sophie)

Some further issues

The range of experiences of coming out to self described by the women in this study do not indicate support for a linear stage model of lesbian identity formation. They reflect instead a more complex interaction between emotional experiences, awareness of options, and emotional acceptance of homosexuality. It is women's strong positive emotional feelings for other women that form the basis for identification as lesbian. Awareness of options is related to available social representations, and the beliefs, attitudes, images and attributions these reflect. Emotional acceptance of homosexuality may be understood in terms of threat to identity, and needs to be viewed in relation to the underlying social representations of human nature, gender and sexuality. Women come to identify themselves as lesbian at different ages, in different circumstances, having had a variety of life experiences. Rather than focusing on average ages of first identifying self as lesbian, first lesbian experience etc., it may be more useful to consider the social and cultural context that would facilitate women identifying as lesbian, minimizing threat to identity.

Some differences between lesbian identities have been indicated in this study. Since the study was based on retrospective accounts, reinterpretation or reconstruction of the past may – or may not – have occurred to varying degrees. Although aspects of Kitzinger's five lesbian identities (Kitzinger and Stainton Rogers, 1985; Kitzinger, 1987) were reflected within these women's accounts, generally such categorization of the women's accounts appears inappropriate. Any category boundaries would need to be seen as flexible: intersecting, permeable, and not static.

This study has mainly focused upon women, like Clare, who have become aware of self as lesbian initially without direct involvement in women's movement activities. Their experiences of coming out to self almost certainly differ from those of political lesbians. The influence of predominant societal notions of gender and human nature is likely to have had a profound impact on these more isolated lesbians.

Coming out to others

Coming out to others, whether to other lesbians, or to heterosexual people such as family or friends, takes place within the social context described in Chapter 5, reflecting dominant social representations of human nature, gender and sexuality. Thus, whether a woman is contacting other lesbians for the first time, or telling a parent or friend about herself, she is acting within a context that is likely to include some awareness of a lesbian stereotype; notions of normality/abnormality; perceptions of generally negative attitudes towards homosexuality; and possibly some ideas relating to explanations of homosexuality as innate or environmental. Further, she is acting within a context in which other lesbians have probably been largely invisible. Like the imaginary lesbian, Clare, women approach coming out to others with these influences forming the background.

Coming out to other lesbians

The influence of the social context on the woman coming out to other lesbians for the first time was reflected in the experiences described.

> I had the standard image. I thought they were all built like bulldozers, all wore boiler suits and ripped jeans or whatever, spiky hair, as ugly as anyone could possibly be . . . very much because I had that image in my mind of what a lesbian was like, and it probably put me off for quite a few years doing anything about it, coming out.
>
> (Hilary, lesbian group)

Before coming out to others, nearly half of the lesbian sample thought lesbians might be masculine or look like men. Some suggested they had believed in or held a stereotype. Some mentioned being frightened. This ranged from feeling terrified to being nervous. Some were frightened of being attacked, or had thought lesbians would be predatory or aggressive. However, some of the lesbian sample suggested that they had been unaware of a stereotype; had had no thoughts about lesbians; or had not wanted to think about them.

The period of time between first identifying self as lesbian and coming out into a lesbian community was negligible for some, but for others had lasted many years. What further reasons were there for this?

> I made a point of not joining the Gay Soc. at . . . university . . . I couldn't cope with it then.
>
> (Emma, lesbian group)

The general invisibility of lesbians often meant that a woman needed to take active steps in order to meet other lesbians. Stereotypical ideas of what lesbians may be like, and perceptions of generally negative attitudes within society towards homosexuality made this hard to approach:

> I looked in *Time Out* and saw all these clubs, and I thought, well, there's no way I can go to all these places on my own because I'd walk in, I'd just die, I think.
>
> (Teresa, lesbian group)

> I was walking outside for a bit because I thought 'I can't do this!', I wasn't going to go in.
>
> (Melanie, lesbian group)

> I tried going to the . . . Lesbian and Gay Society. I went up there, walked past three or four times, and scuttled down the stairs. I couldn't bring myself to walk in.
>
> (Kim, lesbian group)

Many women reported having felt scared or concerned at the idea of going to lesbian places on their own; going to the lesbian section in bookshops, or buying a lesbian book; or contacting a gay helpline. Over a third eventually contacted Lesbian Line or Gay Switchboard. Feelings of isolation or that there was no one to confide in were mentioned. About a third of the women had talked to a therapist or counsellor. A few women had looked for support from straight friends. Four had joined a feminist group.

The first lesbian meeting attended was vividly recalled:

> I just sat in a corner and couldn't believe my eyes – I was terrified!
>
> (Marian, lesbian group)

> Of course, it was completely different from what I'd imagined – they were perfectly ordinary women who you would never believe were lesbians, and it came as a complete shock – a bolt out of the blue for me to think that these women were actually lesbians – complete shock.
>
> (Gail, lesbian group)

> – a real feeling of 'it's OK' . . . they're not all nutcases.
>
> (Brenda, lesbian group)

> It was amazing actually – I thought I would be absolutely terrified – well, I was quite frightened, but it wasn't as bad . . . so, that was the biggest step I felt I'd ever made.
>
> (Joan, lesbian group)

The relief reported at finding that lesbians were just 'ordinary women' provides further evidence of the women having been aware of stereotypical notions of lesbians. Present perceptions of lesbians for many reflected there being 'all sorts' – no typical lesbians; lesbians were just people, like other women.

For some women, however, first experiences of meeting others supported images of lesbians as masculine or political.

> Lesbians there are very political . . . they were very, very male lesbians . . . you know, they were very butch. So, I did have that preconceived idea which seemed to be borne out by what I saw.
>
> (Hazel, lesbian group)

Over a third of the lesbian sample described their present perceptions of some lesbians as masculine or political. Perceptions of lesbians now were both positive and negative.

In the process of coming out to other lesbians, the effects of the underlying social representations of human nature/gender, reflecting stereotyping of lesbians, and generally negative attitudes towards homosexuality, were clear. From the social identity theory perspective, before coming out, lesbians were likely to be viewed as a negatively valued group. On meeting other lesbian women, however, there was usually positive reinforcement of lesbian identity.

Coming out to heterosexual friends or family

The initial circumstances

Clare had come out to some family members but not others, and to some heterosexual friends, but not others. Making a decision on whether to come out to a family member or heterosexual friend is based on a complexity of issues. The social context, reflected in relevant social representations, as already described, involves notions of stereotyping; normality; perceptions of generally negative attitudes towards homosexuality; and the general invisibility of lesbians within society. Within this context, the lesbian makes her decision on whether to come out. Reasons given for not wanting to tell a family member or friend give some indication of the issues a woman may consider.

Over half the lesbian sample mentioned the need to protect the other person in some way as a reason for not coming out to them.

> I can't bear the thought of them [parents] feeling dreadful about it.
>
> (Joan, lesbian group)

> My parents, I could never have told – it would have killed them.
>
> (Hazel, lesbian group)

> I wouldn't tell him [grandfather] for the world – it would destroy him.
>
> (Sophie, lesbian group)

> At their age they [her teenage children] are coming to terms with their own identity and sexuality.
>
> (Christine, lesbian group)

> I've got no business telling him [her father] at ninety-two, unless I want to finish him off!
>
> (Sylvia, lesbian group)

Just under half the lesbian sample mentioned the negative views of the other person as a reason for not coming out. These ranged from the lesbian perceiving the others as viewing homosexuality as 'evil and wrong' or 'dirty and sordid', to perceiving the others as probably not understanding, or being very conventional heterosexuals, and the possibility of being cut off by them.

> They're [her cousins] terribly right-wing fascists and real East-Enders . . .
> (Brenda, lesbian group)

> They'd [other students] probably gossip behind my back.
> (Kim, lesbian group)

> She'd [friend] be afraid of being tarred with the same brush by association.
> (Christine, lesbian group)

Reasons to do with self were mentioned by some participants. These included feeling guilty or afraid, or that it was only one aspect of themselves.

> They would see me as . . . the queer . . . and all the other things that they otherwise admire and value would be counted for nothing and invalidated.
> (Christine, lesbian group)

That there was no necessity to tell the other person either because the participant was not close to them, or because the participant perceived no need to tell them, was mentioned by almost half the lesbian sample.

> My private life is my own business [not my flatmates'].
> (Stephanie, lesbian group)

> Heterosexual people don't go around saying 'Hey, I'm heterosexual!'
> (Kim, lesbian group)

> I don't see any point in it. We're not close [her parents and sister].
> (Marian, lesbian group)

Other reasons given for not coming out to parents, family or friends included that the other may have guessed; that the woman did not know what was stopping her/would tell when the circumstances were right; or that the woman could not find the words/could not get around to telling.

> He probably does have an idea, but he wouldn't want the 'i's dotted or the 't's crossed.
> (Sylvia, lesbian group)

Underlying many of these reasons for not wishing to come out are perceptions relating to societal notions of 'normality'. Whether or not to come out to family and friends was a dilemma for many.

The initial circumstances in which women took the decision to tell family or friends about themselves were mainly of three types. Firstly, there was the context in which the woman was in a state, confused, needed support, or had lesbian relationship problems.

> I was in a desperate state at the time, and I rang both of them [friends] up on the same evening.
>
> (Joan, lesbian group)

Secondly, there was the context where the woman felt guilty, or felt that she was leading a double life, and having to lie. She wanted to be able to speak freely and did not want people assuming her to be heterosexual.

> I'm the type of person that – I couldn't lead a double life, I couldn't – I mean, I knew my parents wouldn't agree to it, wouldn't like it, whatever, but there's no way I could go round trying to pretend that I was something that I wasn't.
>
> (Teresa, lesbian group)

The third major context involved the woman feeling that the other person would not mind. She may have expected approval, felt close to the other person, or have always told them everything. 'If they're real friends, it wouldn't bother them.'

Additionally, some participants mentioned something having happened so that it was appropriate for them to come out. This included cases of bereavement and blackmail. Political lesbians may have different reasons for coming out to family and friends.

Overall, the initial circumstances that prompted disclosure can be seen as involving some crisis that forces the situation; circumstances such that the woman is ready to challenge notions of normality in order not to live a double life; or a context where the woman perceives her close relationship with the other person as overriding any negative societal notions of lesbianism.

What kind of other situations may be compared with the initial circumstances of coming out? The interviews on communication with family and friends provided some examples.

One participant had not yet told her parents of her involvement with religion and future career plans based on this.

> Really they should know because it's such an important part of me now, that they can't know me, because they don't know this part of me, and it's

> only right they should know . . . they'll think it's a phase – they'll hope it's a phase . . . I'm quite sad and I wish I could [talk about it] because I want to tell them. I want them to know all the different parts of me . . . I'm thinking of a particular chance [to tell them] I had a few weeks ago . . . they'd made a comment which was very against what I wanted to tell them, and I almost joked and laughed with them – making it the opposite of what I actually wanted to do.
>
> (Charlotte, communication group)

Parallels with the coming-out situation for lesbians include the issue being related very much to the participant's identity; her perceptions of the possible reaction of her parents; and her management of the situation through isolating self, or attempting to 'pass'. Perhaps the main difference of this example from coming out as lesbian lies in the nature of the issue involved – religion being part of the traditional establishment; and lesbianism associated with alternative culture.

An example of another situation with some similarities to coming out was a participant's account of telling her parents about a non-Jewish boyfriend.

> I mean like there was one major thing which I refused to talk about with my parents – it was the fact I was going out with someone who wasn't Jewish – and I felt this overpowering need to tell them. I wanted them to know so they could start to accept, because I was completely in love with him – then, that was horrible, that was bad, that was really not a nice experience. They didn't accept. They never would have done.
>
> (Judith, communication group)

Here, the similarities with coming out included the dilemma of the participant wishing to share her positive feelings about a relationship with someone, but perceiving the likelihood of a negative reaction. A main difference to the coming-out situation was that the participant would not have been telling her parents anything about her identity in telling them about the relationship.

Contrasting with the situation of coming out was the example of Jessica (Communication Group) who as a child had been wrongly accused by a teacher and felt unable to talk to anyone about it. This incident had a profound effect on the participant, leading to her truanting from school for three days. It differs from the coming-out situation in that the participant viewed the accusation as mistaken – it was not something that was perceived as part of her identity that was being challenged.

In summary, for lesbian participants, on the one hand, against coming out there were perceptions of negative attitudes towards homosexuality; a desire to protect others from being upset; and the feeling that it was unnecessary to tell certain people. On the other hand, in favour of coming out, there was need for support, particularly regarding lesbian relationship problems; there were feelings of guilt at not being able to speak freely, and being assumed to be heterosexual; and there was the feeling that the other person would not mind. Generally, where a decision not to come out was made, awareness of negative attitudes, and perceptions of some heterosexual people as vulnerable, or threatened by the potential knowledge, predominated. Where a decision to come out was made, the lesbians' own needs were given precedence; or perceptions of negative attitudes, and of homosexuality as a threat to heterosexuals, were replaced by the perception that the heterosexual person would be able to handle it/would not mind – in other words, a positive reaction was expected from the heterosexual person. On an individual or interpersonal level, parallels from the communication study involved issues related to identity and relationship, perceived as likely to provoke a negative reaction from others. From a more social perspective, perceptions of societal notions of 'normality' may be seen as underlying lesbians' decision-making.

The approach to coming out

Almost three-quarters of the lesbian participants had told a parent, family member or friend about themselves in a direct manner.

> She [her mother] was driving towards the traffic lights and she went through the red.
>
> (Lucy, lesbian group)

Some described situations in which someone had been told about them by somebody else. Some just assumed that another person knew, or thought the person had guessed. Sometimes the subject had arisen naturally. In some cases, a person had asked the woman whether she was lesbian ('a friend forced it out of me'). Sometimes, there had been gossip that the woman was lesbian. Few women were recorded as 'testing the water' before telling someone about themselves.

Indirect ways of coming out included not hiding a relationship – 'I just act as I am'. Sometimes the words 'lesbian' or 'gay' were avoided, and the other person told that the woman was having a relationship with another woman, or 'attracted to women', or just not interested in men. Such approaches reflect concern with negative perceptions of homosexuality in our society. Where the approach taken in coming out has been indirect, and particularly in cases where assumptions have simply been made that others 'know', the situation must be seen as ambiguous. The others may or may not actually 'know'/understand that the woman is lesbian. This uncertainty would affect the relationships concerned. In terms of Goffman's (1963) notion of discredited/discreditable individuals, or Jones et al.'s (1984) marked relationships, whether the woman perceived herself as 'discredited' or 'marked' or, on the other hand, 'discreditable' or 'markable'; and whether she was perceived by the other as 'discredited' or 'marked', or not, would be uncertain.

Coming out tended to be on an individual basis. However, a few women described coming out to both parents at the same time, or to a family group.

How might one approach discussion of a 'difficult' topic with family or friends? Communication group interviewees described some planned approaches.

> I suppose I'd try to approach it in a very roundabout fashion, and see what kind of response I got. If they . . . weren't embarrassed, or wanted to change the subject, then I'd probably go on and tell them a bit more, and a bit more, and so on.
>
> (Sandra, communication group)

> I asked key questions to other people first so that I would have a clue as to how this other person would react. It's a very, very cold and calculating procedure. I completely distanced myself from it . . . Planned out every single thing I was going to say in advance . . . made sure nobody else was in the room, or coming into the room. I don't remember if I locked the door . . .
>
> (Trudy, communication group)

> Well, I would probably, if I decided that I wanted to talk to a particular person, I would make sure that there was an occasion where it would be easy to do so . . . or more likely go for . . . a couple of days' walking – that's always a good way to talk about anything.
>
> (Jessica, communication group)

> Well, I'd make sure she's in a good mood to start with – I might drop a few subtle hints before . . . I make sure either she's on her own, or if I want my dad there . . . I'd wait for my dad to be there . . . it's basically getting them in the right mood, and when they're not rushing around – when they've got time to sit and talk. It's pointless trying to start a conversation if they're trying to cook or clean or something!
>
> (Beverley, communication group)

Some approaches may be less strategically worked out; or the opportunity to talk may arise naturally.

> The thing which I still can't do unless I'm totally drunk, is to talk about my feelings to a guy . . . usually when I have something to say, I usually do really get drunk, and then I can say it.
>
> (Eve, communication group)

> It kind of fed in to that discussion . . . I didn't just say I have something to talk to you about.
>
> (Sharon, communication group)

> It just sort of happened. It was very much the moment and the person, and the conversation we were having I guess . . .
>
> (Judith, communication group)

In summary, lesbian participants tended to approach coming out to others in a direct manner. Indirect approaches could lead to ambiguity and reflected concern with societal attitudes. Some of the communication interviews indicated the possibility and advantages of planning one's approach, and perhaps testing possible reactions.

'Out'/'not out' to family and friends

While just over three-quarters of the lesbian sample were out to one or more members of their family, most of the participants mentioned one or more family members they had not come out to. Nearly two-thirds of the women had come out to their mothers, but over a third had not. A lower proportion had come out to their fathers.

> I never really dared to mention it and he [her father] never asked.
>
> (Edith, lesbian group)

> Well, I went home once with the express intention of telling them [her parents] – but I . . . I chickened out.
>
> (Joan, lesbian group)

> It was such a relief when it came out [to her mother, sister and brother-in-law], and since then I've been able to go home with my friend, and talk about things I do without hiding anything. It's great – because I now feel that I'm back in the family, and I feel that they can share my life, and I can share family life.
>
> (Stella, lesbian group)

Of those who had sister(s), two-thirds had come out to one or more of them. Of those who had brother(s), one-third had come out to one or more.

> I told them both actually, my sister and my brother-in-law, and they were very receptive. We had quite a good conversation.
>
> (Joan, lesbian group)

Just under a quarter of the lesbian sample had been, or still were, married. Some, but not all, had come out to their husbands. Those with older or adult children tended to have come out to them, but those with younger children had not.

> My husband, no problem, because I think he knew before I did . . . I just told him as soon as I knew, and told him what I was going to do, because he knew that I wouldn't leave him, because we have such a close relationship . . .
>
> The children are difficult. I still don't know what to do about the children.
>
> (Hazel, lesbian group)

Since family relationships may reflect more traditional notions of gender, it might be expected that coming out to heterosexual friends would be easier than coming out to family members. Although many of the sample had come out to some heterosexual friends, almost one in four had come out to few or none.

> At first I didn't [come out to heterosexual friends] because I felt that I was something wrong you see . . . then I sorted out the fact that there were certain people I couldn't come out to because I had to protect my family; then I worked out there were certain people I couldn't come out to because of my job; and then when I thought of the rest, I thought why can't I tell my friends – if I call them friends – if they're my friends – so I started telling them . . .
>
> (Hazel, lesbian group)

Like the imaginary lesbian, Clare, there were specific people that some lesbian participants chose not to come out to. In response to questions concerning whether there were people participants would/would not like to come out to, some women mentioned they would like to come out to friends, and several mentioned they would like to come out to parents. Approximately a third of the sample stated that they would not like to come out to people at work.

Coming out or not at work

> I'd like it if I was totally out, I think, but I'm not going to do it now.
>
> (Linda, lesbian group)

> They wouldn't like to know about it. They would not like to know!
>
> (Christine, lesbian group)

Few lesbian participants were out to most or all of the people at work. Almost a third were not out to anyone at work. Some were out to just one person or a very few people. A few women simply assumed their colleagues knew.

Reasons mentioned for not coming out at work included potential difficulties in relations with others: that other women might be concerned; that it might shock or embarrass people; that others may see you as a threat. Some suggested difficulties with the men at work.

> I think the men would just start making stupid jokes. I think I might lose respect.
>
> (Amy, lesbian group)

The possibility of difficulties in relations with others at work, particularly with men, was reflected in some of the heterosexual participants' responses to the question of how they would feel about someone at work being gay.

> If she was the masculine-type lesbian then she would become some sort of joke in the office anyway.
>
> (David, heterosexual group)

> I don't try to hide the fact that I don't find it agreeable . . . I suppose you can't help despising them slightly for it.
>
> (Edward, heterosexual group)

> Well, I'd accept them, but I'd probably find it difficult to be friendly with them, because I wouldn't know how to behave or what to say.
>
> (Andrew, heterosexual group)

Some women suggested that coming out might harm their career prospects, or they might lose their job. Again, there was reflection of these issues in some heterosexual participants' responses.

> I certainly wouldn't engage anybody for appointment that I thought either gay or lesbian.
>
> (David, heterosexual group)

Further reasons suggested by the lesbian sample for not coming out at work included that others did not tell them about themselves. This too was reflected in responses from the heterosexual and communication groups.

I don't see it having anything to do with work.

(Viviene, heterosexual group)

Some of the women from the communication interview group suggested they avoided talking about anything to do with their personal life at work. However, this restriction of discussion area did not exclude mentioning of husband or boyfriend.

> Well, I mean, I avoid talking about anything personal, except you know sometimes if you're working together with people . . . you talk about certain things: 'Oh, I'm going out with so and so', and you talk about your relationship a little bit . . . but you don't talk about anything overtly personal.
>
> (Eve, communication group)

Other concerns mentioned by lesbian participants were the possibility of gossip, rejection or hostility; being known as a lesbian rather than oneself; and being scared/unsure of how others would react. Lending some support to the notion of gossip at work, 40 per cent of the heterosexual sample mentioned the topic of homosexuality arising with work colleagues. The most commonly mentioned types of conversation regarding homosexuality, generally (i.e. not necessarily occurring specifically with work colleagues), were discussion; jokes, comments or derogatory slights; and comments on or speculations about someone being gay.

Although over half of the heterosexual sample suggested that it would make no difference to them if someone at work was gay, over a quarter suggested it would make some difference. Several expressed their personal concern about gay men or lesbians working with children and being teachers. Over half perceived this issue as a general concern. Some also suggested 'most people' would consider it unsuitable for gay men or lesbians to work as doctors or politicians, or in other responsible jobs.

In favour of being out at work, lesbian participants mentioned 'being oneself ': 'I don't like pretending to be something I'm not'; 'I wish I didn't have to hide it'; 'it is a strain to lie'; 'I can talk freely'.

> At work now, it's awkward with the other girls talking about boyfriends and husbands all the time, because I can't talk about what I do.
>
> (Carol, lesbian group)

Other reasons included closer friendship with colleagues, and increased confidence.

This analysis has focused on the issue of coming out at work from an individual perspective. Work situations must be understood as incorporating the social context of gender relations, and notions of human nature, of the society within which they exist. It is this context that creates the individual-level experiences of lesbians at work.

First coming-out experience to a heterosexual person

Over half the lesbian sample had selected a heterosexual female friend – in some cases the girl/woman they were attracted to – as the first heterosexual person they had come out to. Some came out first to parents or other family members.

Coming out to other lesbians before coming out to heterosexual people may provide some background support for women, but less than a quarter of the lesbian group had come out to other lesbians before first coming out to a heterosexual person. Just over a third of the participants had been in a relationship before their first experience of coming out to a heterosexual person. Length of time between first identifying self as lesbian and first coming out to a heterosexual person varied from less than a year to many years. Substantial lengths of time, in delaying first coming out to heterosexual friends or family, must be seen as reflecting the influence of the generally negative social context relating to lesbianism.

Perceptions of reactions to coming out

Reactions to coming out described by the lesbian participants were based on their perceptions of friends' or family members' responses to the lesbian telling them about herself. Reactions described for the heterosexual sample were based on their perceptions of how they would react in the hypothetical situation of a friend or family member coming out to them. Responses were often a mixture of positive, neutral or negative reactions.

The majority of the lesbian sample described some kind of positive reaction to their coming out from friends or family. This included perceptions of the other as understanding, interested, sympathetic, supportive, or receptive. Most women described some positive response from friends; just under a third described a positive reaction from one or more family members, other than parents; and about a quarter described some positive response from one or both parents.

> It's just been thoroughly accepted that aunt is a lesbian and it hasn't made any difference.
>
> (Yvonne, lesbian group)

Corresponding to the lesbian participants' perceptions of positive reactions of family and friends, just over half the heterosexual participants described some positive reaction to the hypothetical situation of a child, sibling or friend coming out to them. These responses included that it would not bother them at all; they would be happy if the gay person was happy; they would try to understand, accept or be supportive; they would help with any problems. A third of the heterosexual participants described some kind of positive response to the possibility of a friend coming out to them; a similar number perceived some positive response to a sibling coming out to them; and just under a quarter of the heterosexual participants described some positive response in the hypothetical situation of a child coming out to them. The following quote illustrates a response categorized as both neutral and positive.

> What you ought to do, I think, with any teenage child who says he or she is gay is to make it clear that, you know, there are alternatives, and that all sorts of things during a period of great sexual upheaval can happen. But I don't think you should say 'Oh, this is dreadful . . . never darken my doors again' – you have to help them to try and understand their own sexuality.
>
> (Rosemary, heterosexual group)

A positive change in reaction over time by one or more family members or friends was described by over a third of the lesbian sample. Included in this were reactions such as 'is coming to terms with', or an improved relationship. Only one heterosexual participant was recorded as describing any positive change in reaction over time.

Overall, significantly more lesbian participants than heterosexual participants mentioned either an initial positive response or a positive change over time.

Some kind of negative reaction from one or more friends or family members was also described by the majority of the lesbian sample. Correspondingly, some negative response in the hypothetical situation of a child, sibling or friend coming out to them was described by most of the heterosexual sample. General negative responses included: shocked, upset, disapproved, does not believe it, cannot understand, does not accept, sorrow or unhelpful. Extreme negative responses included: went mad, appalled, horrified, felt revolted, anger or extremely disappointed. These extreme reactions were described by almost a quarter of lesbian participants, but few heterosexual participants. The lesbian participants described such reactions mainly from parents and friends rather than siblings or other family. The heterosexual extreme reactions were towards children and siblings, rather than friends.

> I think I'd be very, very angry [to discover my children were gay/lesbian] and annoyed, and go all out to find blame and that sort of thing.
>
> (Edward, heterosexual group)

Several lesbian participants described rejection by a family member or friend. Only one heterosexual participant suggested he would reject. Altogether, just over a quarter of the total sample described one or more reactions categorized as either extreme negative, or rejection.

> And as I say, I have lost a couple of friends, people . . . who've just not approved, who've just sort of been judgemental . . . I haven't missed them because I – after the original hurt – I thought, well . . . they weren't friends. There've been some who've stayed friends who say 'Well, I really can't understand it' . . . but there are still some friends that I know that if I came out to, I would lose them, and I like them too much to want to risk losing them . . . and there are some again that I've come out to, and they've gone gulp, OK, and stayed friends, but it's not the same – there's a distancing, an awkwardness . . .
>
> (Hazel, lesbian group)

Social stigma or societal pressure were mentioned by 40 per cent of the heterosexual participants, but by significantly fewer lesbian participants.

> It's not just the individual, it's the immediate family as well that actually get affected.
>
> (Rosalind, heterosexual group)

One of the major reasons given for wishing to come out was to be able to speak freely with others. However, just over half the total sample described reactions of either a distancing, or of the subject not being easy to talk about, or not having been discussed since coming out. The heterosexual sample tended to respond more in terms of the distancing category, and the lesbian sample in terms of the subject not having been discussed since.

Almost a third of the total sample described reactions categorized as 'hopes it was a phase' or 'would prefer them to be straight/unhappy they couldn't have children'. Responses blaming self were mainly concerned with the parent–child relationship.

Some kind of neutral response was mentioned by all the heterosexual participants, and the majority of the lesbian participants. Surprise was mentioned by some, while not being surprised/having suspected, was also mentioned.

> I just can't imagine that within the family you wouldn't have some gradual knowledge of it . . . you wouldn't suddenly discover that your brother or your sister were gay . . .
>
> (Rosemary, heterosexual group)

Uncertainty as to how they would react or not being able to tell until the situation arises was mentioned by half of the heterosexual sample.

> A lot would depend on the context in which they're telling me, like why are they telling me, why has it come to light.
>
> (Brian, heterosexual group)

Sex differences were a further issue. Over a quarter of the heterosexual sample mentioned one or more incidences of feeling less bothered or more understanding if a male rather than a female came out to them.

> It's terrible, I think I'm much more tolerant of men than I am of women being gay. I've thought about that sometimes and I think it's because since I like men, I can be sympathetic with anybody liking men . . .
>
> (Viviene, heterosexual group)

More female participants than male participants mentioned feeling less bothered about a male coming out to them.

For the communication group women, perceptions of possible reactions of others to issues they had found difficult to discuss were usually negative. Perceived possible reactions included that the other would not understand; would disapprove; would be upset or embarrassed; or that the other was not interested, or did not want to discuss it. Where the topic was eventually talked about, actual reactions of the other person were often perceived in positive terms.

> I would think that almost everyone would not understand what I was feeling [about marriage, fidelity and trust].
>
> (Sharon, communication group)

> Very, very understanding. She couldn't offer much help, but she did listen and I think she did understand.
>
> (Sharon)

With mixed feelings about the possible reaction of others, the woman may not have attempted to discuss the issue.

> I'm sure they would be fine . . . I don't see why they shouldn't be. I'm just not brave enough – I haven't quite got the confidence and courage yet.
>
> (Charlotte, communication group, on having eczema)

Overall, perceptions of possible reactions to issues that communication group participants had found difficult to talk about with family or friends, and the participants' related feelings, were quite similar in range to the perceptions of possible reactions, and associated feelings, of the lesbian participants in coming out.

Generally, reactions to coming out must be seen as rooted in societal notions of gender and 'normality'. The perceptions of both lesbian and heterosexual participants reflected these influences.

The outcome: satisfaction/dissatisfaction with coming out

> So that's why I feel content with myself because the people that are important to me have accepted it.
>
> (Irene, lesbian group)

Being yourself or being open was mentioned as a positive aspect of being lesbian. Negative feelings included wanting to be whole self, wanting to talk freely, hating to deny the essence of self, being weary of lies and fighting. Many mentioned negative feelings about being lesbian connected with others' attitudes.

Describing the main benefit of coming out, three-quarters of the lesbian sample mentioned being yourself: being true to yourself, having credibility with yourself, being a whole person; not having to pretend that you are straight or keep part of yourself secret; feeling freer.

> Being yourself – it has to be.
>
> (Hilary, lesbian group)

Other benefits of coming out concerned the women's general relationship to others: being able to stop lying, pretending or covering up; being more relaxed; being able to share feelings with friends or family, not having to hide, being accepted by others as oneself; people stopping making assumptions of heterosexuality and becoming aware we exist; people perhaps becoming more positive towards gays.

> You can't live your life keeping a whole part of yourself a big secret. I think it's immoral to expect anyone to do that.
>
> (Evelyn, lesbian group)

> The nice thing, I find, about being able to be open with straight people is I can make jokes about myself!
>
> (Christine, lesbian group)

> You simply cannot live your life until people deal with you and accept you for what you are.
>
> (Hilary, lesbian group)

The emphasis emerging from the communication group accounts regarding feelings about having talked to someone about a difficult topic concerned relief or feeling better in some way. This was mentioned by almost all of the communication group participants.

> I generally feel an incredible sense of relief.
>
> (Sharon, communication group)

> I understand things – usually a lot clearer – a lot calmer; a lot stronger; more confident.
>
> (Elaine, communication group)

'Relief' was mentioned by some lesbian group participants, but their focus tended to be on authenticity and integrity as a person.

Although the lesbian group women interpreted their feelings about being lesbian and coming out in individual terms, it is important that these perceptions are understood from a social/societal perspective as well. The women's perceptions reflect a general cultural understanding of sexuality as part of one's essence or essential being. The influence of social representations with restrictive conceptualizations of gender and human nature is evident.

Some further issues

From a social-psychological theoretical perspective, coming out to others must be seen within the context of social representations of gender and human nature, and their content of stereotypes, beliefs, attitudes and attributions relating to lesbianism. In social interaction where the lesbian has not come out, she is perceived primarily as a woman, and gender-related behaviour as described by Deaux and Major (1987) may occur. Coming out as lesbian adds further complexity to interactions. From the viewpoint of social identity theory, when a lesbian tells a heterosexual person about herself, her social identity as lesbian, rather than her personal identity, becomes salient. This may threaten distinctiveness relating to heterosexuality and/or gender roles for the heterosexual person. Further, the heterosexual person may make attributions about the lesbian based on social category membership. Ambiguous situations in which assumptions may have been made by either lesbian or heterosexual person, and may or may not have been perceived accurately by the other, may occur.

Issues that many studies of 'attitudes towards homosexuals' have failed to consider have included sex of participant and/or sex of target person; variation with situation or social/ideological context; and that knowledge of a person's homosexuality may vary. Interpretation of findings of some previous studies relating to attitudes towards homosexuals is thus somewhat problematic. This study has indicated that it is essential to take into account such issues. There were some differences in male and female heterosexual participants' attitudes and perceptions. Perceived reactions in the hypothetical situation of a family member or friend coming out sometimes varied with sex of person coming out, relationship to that person, and/or the perceived situation. There were varying levels or ways of 'knowing' someone was homosexual. These ranged from speculation, guessing or making assumptions, to having been told in a direct manner; and also from having been told but not believing it, or perceiving it as a phase, to having been told and accepting it.

The focus here, starting with the imaginary lesbian, Clare, has been largely upon the non-political lesbian. One may speculate that while reasons for coming out, and perceptions of outcome, may well vary for political lesbians, other aspects – for example, telling one's family and their reactions – may not be very different. However, it must also be recognized that the more isolated a lesbian is from other lesbian women, the greater her dependence on relations with heterosexual friends and family is likely to be.

On an individual level, functions of attitudes (Herek, 1984b) may serve as a starting point for considering possibilities of changing attitudes. However, for more fundamental attitude modification, change would need to occur within dominant social representations of human nature and gender.

Interplay of influences in the coming-out process

Interaction between aspects of coming out

Coming out to self and coming out to others have been described separately for clarity, but they do interact with each other. This interaction needs to be understood within the general social context of stereotyping and attitudes towards homosexuals, and the encompassing social representations.

Coming out to self is an intrinsically social process. It is shaped by perceptions of the attitudes of others; of stereotyping within society; and of social representations of human nature, gender and sexuality. Whether or not the woman has been in an actual relationship before identifying herself as lesbian, coming out to self is based on her perceptions of her feelings directed towards other women. Her emotional acceptance of these feelings will be strongly related to her perceptions of the social context; and her awareness of lesbianism as an option will be firmly based within this context too.

Perceptions of self as lesbian are likely to be reinforced on coming out to others, particularly on coming out to other lesbians. Some women come out to other lesbians at a stage when they feel they might be lesbian, rather than having fully identified themselves as lesbian. On coming out to heterosexual friends or family, perceptions of self as lesbian are again likely to be reinforced, whatever their reactions.

A life-span perspective

Coming out takes place over a woman's life-span within the context of the cultural background specific to the historical period, and interacting with particular events within a woman's life. Life-span lines for each lesbian participant focused on coming out to self and others in the context of the personal events, relationships, and emotions occurring within a woman's life over the historical period specific to her life.

From an examination of all the life-span lines, it was evident that while for some participants (e.g. Amy, Alice, Emma, Mary and Yvonne), first feelings, identification as lesbian, coming out to other lesbians and to some heterosexual significant others, had occurred within a very short space of time, for most participants these had taken place over a long time-scale. Often, first feelings were traced back to teens or childhood, with lesbian identification occurring many years later. For approximately half the sample, identification of self as lesbian occurred before coming out into a lesbian community – in some cases, many years before.

Events happening in a woman's life at a particular time may provide opportunities for different aspects of coming out to occur. Examples of such life events included a marriage ending; starting work in an occupation, such as the services, where there are many lesbians; meeting an 'out' lesbian for the first time; moving to a different country; becoming involved with feminism; or going to university as a mature student. Other personal events may hinder aspects of coming out. An example of this would be marriage.

As a background to these personal events, there is the cultural context of the time period. Almost half the participants first identified self as lesbian/gay during the last half of the 1970s and the first half of the 1980s. During this period there was a largely positive influence from the women's movement; equal opportunities initiatives; and, in London, positive initiatives from the Greater London Council on gay and lesbian issues. It was before the main awareness of AIDS as a problem in this country; and before the introduction of Clause 28. This period probably formed a more positive context for coming out to take place than either the preceding years, or the more recent years.

Age itself may also be relevant. Approximately a quarter of the communication group participants mentioned talking to others had become easier as they became older.

> Certainly as I've got older, I've got better at communicating.
>
> (Sandra, communication group)

Comparison with other minority group or life experiences

Asked to make comparisons of the experiences of gay people with those of other minority groups, most of the lesbian and heterosexual sample mentioned ethnic or religious groups. Comparisons were also made with other sexually defined groups, the mentally ill or disabled and women. Some suggested there were no other groups whose experiences were the same.

Some lesbian participants, asked to consider if there were any individual experiences similar to coming out, mentioned change in political ideas, philosophical beliefs or religion. Some mentioned knowing something that you think may adversely affect how others think or feel about you, or telling something that you have hidden because you have not thought people would accept it. Possible events mentioned by small numbers of participants included telling someone you are pregnant; telling parents you want to marry a black boyfriend; being politically active in an extreme group; and telling parents/others of career plans or that you do not want to go to college.

Comparisons between different minority groups or life experiences tended to be made considering discrimination or prejudice; or by considering having to hide or invisibility.

Lesbians themselves, as well as being members of a double minority, as women and lesbians, may also belong to other minority groups. The sample included a very small number of ethnic minority lesbians, insufficient in size for separate analysis of their coming-out experiences. No physically disabled women participated in the study. However, all women belonging to such groups must be recognized as experiencing further oppression based on their different group memberships. Racism occurs within lesbian communities, as within the wider British society. Disabled women may encounter serious practical problems, relating to access, mobility and independence, as well as discrimination.

General communication with family and friends

Disclosure of self as lesbian to significant others is often perceived as difficult or problematic. It is helpful to consider what kind of topics generally may be difficult to discuss with others.

The most frequently mentioned topic in the communication interviews that teenagers found difficult to discuss with others was sex. This was mentioned by almost all the participants, either in the general case of communication between teenagers and their parents, or relating to their own teenage years and communication with parents, siblings or friends. Other topics mentioned as difficult for teenagers to discuss included feelings about parents or siblings, and family problems; friends; school work; and drugs or alcohol.

Topics found difficult to discuss with others as adults included relationships and/or sex, mentioned by approximately two-thirds of the participants. Career, money, death and religion were further topics mentioned by some.

Issues or topics that the communication group participants reported having found difficult to discuss with others may be seen as akin to aspects of the coming-out process for lesbians in terms of relating to identity, personal relationships, or a different way of life; to threat, loss or stigma; or concerning the reactions of others. Examples in which there was potential threat to identity included inner conflicts; vocational aims related to religious beliefs and conflicting with family expectations; fear as a child that one was adopted; and concern with academic failings, or fear of failing at work. In some of the issues where identity was threatened, stigma may have been involved too. Examples were a weight problem; and having a son in prison, which the participant considered might lead others to view her as a failure as a mother. Sometimes issues of identity were linked to a different way of life from others. This was the case where career aspirations conflicted with others' expectations; and where there was difficulty settling into living in a different country.

Communication about relationships also has obvious parallels with the process of coming out, and was mentioned as a source of difficulty by a number of women. Examples included telling parents about a non-Jewish boyfriend; telling others that one was leaving one's husband; marriage to a man not accepted by parents; and cases of choosing not to talk to others about affairs.

Some participants mentioned choosing not to talk about topics they perceived might upset others, or that they perceived others did not want to discuss. Examples included not discussing sex with one's children; and not discussing religion with work colleagues.

Loss or threat may be seen as relevant to difficulties in communication with others relating to death. This was found difficult to talk about in different ways, which included planning for the future, such as parents making wills; experiencing bereavement; and talking to bereaved people.

The difficulty of talking to others about money would seem to have little or no connection with the issues involved in coming out. Possibly for some, however, it may be associated with identity.

Thus, comparison of topics reported difficult to discuss with others would suggest that those most akin to aspects of the coming-out process may involve threat to identity and/or relationships. Threat to identity may sometimes be associated with stigma or a different way of life. Protecting others and loss were further aspects relating to difficulties in communication: the former has been seen as a direct issue in the decision of whether or not to come out to others; the latter is associated in a more indirect manner. Loss may relate to the coming-out process in terms of rejection and the potential loss of friends, for example; or to the loss of the expected heterosexual future of marriage and family.

In an 'ideal' world

'In an ideal world, how would lesbians be perceived?' Responses to this question emphasized how lesbians would be seen as 'normal'; 'like everyone else'; or 'equal'.

> Just as good – or bad; just as normal – or extraordinary; just as worthy – or unworthy; just as important – or insignificant; just as special, just as individual, as anyone else.
>
> (Shirley, lesbian group)

> In exactly the same way as everyone else – i.e. they should be judged or valued on their acts and words, and not on their sexuality.
>
> (Rosemary, heterosexual group)

Some of the lesbian sample, but very few heterosexual participants, mentioned positive qualities of lesbians.

> Perhaps, to some extent they could be seen as standard-bearers for women believing that their qualities, traditionally regarded as weaknesses, such as emotional, gentle, co-operative, unaggressive, should be seen *as* qualities by society.
>
> (Hilary, lesbian group)

> As caring, compassionate, reliable, tolerant, friends.
>
> (Sylvia, lesbian group)

Several heterosexual participants, but no lesbian participants, responded negatively.

> Misguided, possibly in need of help. To be discouraged.
>
> (David, heterosexual group)

> There would be no homosexual people. All people would be heterosexual.
>
> (Lynn, heterosexual group, giving the religious view)

Some lesbian and heterosexual participants mentioned equal rights for lesbians in an ideal world.

Some further issues

The coming-out process must be understood within a context that takes into account interplay of phenomena at intra-psychic, interpersonal, intergroup and societal/cultural levels of analysis. No single social-psychological theory seems sufficient by itself to explain the coming-out process. A substantial part of the process may be understood from the perspective of social identity theory, but its view tends to be ahistorical. Social representations are crucial to the understanding of the coming-out process, but do not provide an adequate basis for analysis at the level of the individual. A social understanding of self (e.g. Mead, 1934) needs to be incorporated. Attribution theory is relevant to limited aspects of coming out. In addition to the positive contributions of these theories, Breakwell's model of coping with threatened identity provides a useful basis for analysis. Ideas on self-disclosure and stigma are also helpful.

It is thought essential that coming out be examined from both the lesbian and heterosexual perspectives. This study has suggested some basic differences in the understanding of homosexuality between lesbians and heterosexuals which require further consideration.

The study has focused upon lesbians, like the imaginary lesbian, Clare, with a less political, or non-political, background. Experiences of coming out for political lesbians might be expected to display both differences and similarities. Suggestions about any differences have been speculative. A future study would be required to investigate this.

General methodological issues relating to sampling, interviews and interpretation of qualitative data should be taken into account in considering the findings.

Fundamentally, it is suggested here that coming out is only an issue within a heterosexist society; and underlying heterosexism are inflexible notions of gender, and ideas of 'normality'. Thus, any interpretation of the coming-out process for lesbians must be based within the context of an understanding of gender relations in our society, as well as of our more general notions of human nature.

8

Lesbians with some heterosexual background

Many lesbians, unlike the imaginary lesbian, Clare, have had heterosexual relationships in the past. Some of these women perceived themselves as heterosexual at the time. Others had thought of themselves as possibly lesbian while living as heterosexual. In this chapter we look at case studies of some of these women. We also consider a case study of a woman with a political background. Finally, we contrast the accounts of women with these different backgrounds with one another, and with those of women who have 'always' perceived themselves as lesbian.

In this chapter, to limit the number of cases presented, only two age categories are used: aged under thirty years old, and aged thirty years or more. This basically separates women who reached adulthood before the main impact of the gay movement and women's movement around the 1970s, from younger women who may have experienced a more positive environment while growing up. (The political group is not broken down into age categories.)

The case studies

Lesbians with heterosexual backgrounds

Amy: a lesbian under thirty years old with a heterosexual background

Twenty-three-year-old Amy had perceived herself as heterosexual until only a few months ago. She had had two serious relationships with men but neither had been satisfactory. She had been living abroad.

> Then, I thought, well, go out with a woman – and I thought no, no, you

> can't just think that, because your relationships with men don't work out, turn to women, that's ridiculous.

Soon afterwards, while still living overseas, she was staying in the flat of a woman,

> I realized I was very attracted to her.

It was from this time that Amy began to perceive herself as lesbian. Looking back to earlier years, Amy described her perceptions of her feelings then:

> [My sister] started going out with boys, I was about eleven, and I was really upset. I don't know why, but I used to lie awake at night and cry. I sort of felt she was moving away . . .
>
> When I was about thirteen, I remember everyone suddenly got interested in doing their hair and everything, reading *My Guy* magazine, and talking about boys. I didn't really go along with that – but then eventually I did, and sort of grew up, and went on diets, and all these kind of things.
>
> When I was about sixteen . . . I never had a boyfriend. I used to think, sort of abstractly . . . not 'What if I am a lesbian' but 'What if I *were* a lesbian. What would I do, wouldn't it be awful. Oh God, never let me be a lesbian!' I'd sort of forgotten about that, until recently.

During this period she was certainly aware to some extent of the negative distinctiveness of lesbianism; and correspondingly, she was aware of the general positive evaluation of heterosexuality.

> It was a real status symbol to have a boyfriend.

When a radical lesbian feminist stood as a candidate in an election while Amy was at university, and went round canvassing, Amy recalled a friend warning her about letting the woman into her room.

> I think it's so embarrassing that I could have thought such a thing! You know, because I was eighteen years old, supposedly an adult, thinking things like that. As if you let a lesbian into your room, you would be contaminated – she sat on your bed, you might catch it!

Thus, during Amy's teenage years, lesbianism may be seen as constituting a threat to her identity – a threat that was dealt with using the intra-psychic deflection strategy of denial. In this way self-esteem, need for affiliation and positive distinctiveness were maintained. To what extent any threat may have been present is difficult to determine. The possibility of reinterpretation of the past by the participant needs to be taken into account. However, it would seem that lesbian feelings emerged at a point in Amy's life where attempts to conform with heterosexuality were not succeeding. On the intra-psychic level there was probably re-evaluation of existing and prospective identity content. Lesbianism, it would seem, no longer constituted the threat that it had previously to this participant's identity.

Amy tended to perceive lesbianism in dispositional terms.

> I think it's part of your nature, you can't change the way you're born. And I think that it is something that you've got or you haven't – even though some people don't really realize it till they're fifty or – you know. I don't think you can choose. It's like deciding what colour you want to be born, or something.

Amy recalled reading or seeing little about homosexuality, in books or the media, during her early stages of coming out. She did, though, perceive the women's movement as influencing her life as a lesbian.

> All the sort of events that I go to now, I don't think they would have existed . . . I think the women's movement sort of focused attention on women, and gave lesbians a voice as well.

Considering how 'most' heterosexuals feel about lesbians, Amy suggested lesbians either tended to be invisible, or seen as 'strident' feminists and butch. The social context of Amy's coming out may be seen as reflecting both the general invisibility of lesbianism, and the more open aspects influenced by the women's movement.

Coming out to self, to other lesbians, and to some family and heterosexual friends, all occurred for Amy within a very short period. As she was not living in the United Kingdom at the time, telling some people was by post rather than a face-to-face conversation.

> I wrote postcards to all my friends in [X], but they were very cryptically worded, sort of saying 'Hey, something wonderful's happened' . . . they were postcards which definitely invited a response, which I got. I got all these letters back saying 'Would you mind telling me what's going on!

> I wrote and told [my brother] in great detail . . . I remember after I wrote the letter I was sort of shaking all over.

Coming out to her brother was complicated by his relationship to the woman that Amy was involved with. His reaction, she later heard, had been extreme.

> When he got my letter, he reacted massively, and went storming around the house, sobbing and things, and ripped up my letter!

Relations with her brother remained 'very strained'. She suggested his reaction may be partly based on his religious beliefs.

Amy had not come out to her mother or sisters.

> My mum would be the obvious next person to tell, but I don't know. I'm having all these arguments with myself . . . If I don't see her that often, why should it matter anyway, we don't know very much about each other anyway. But then I've always prided myself on what, you know, my mother and my family talk about freely to each other.

Additionally, apart from one work colleague, Amy was reluctant to come out at work (teaching adults):

> I think they would change their attitude towards me.

Thus, there probably has been some threat to identity arising from the situation regarding disclosure to family and coming out at work.

Back in her home town, Amy came out to friends.

> [My friend] had sort of half twigged from the postcard and the things I'd said on the phone . . . she just accepted it! But I was relieved that she did, and after that I didn't have to tell anyone because it went round on the grapevine. People were coming up to me at parties and saying 'How does it feel to be a lesbian?', people that I haven't seen for, you know, a year or so. So I just told [the one friend] and that was the [home town] people told, it went around.

This was an experience reported by very few other participants. More usually, if friends were told, they did not tend to pass it on to others. Amy's friends all seemed accepting, and thus have provided her with interpersonal support for her new identity. This support was supplemented by the group support of the lesbian community. The support from these two sources had minimized potential threat to identity for Amy, but she still had to cope with possible threat arising from family, work and societal attitudes.

> I get very annoyed about this assumption about, you know, universal heterosexuality, and generally things against women annoy me much more as well now . . . I sometimes think, I feel so angry a lot of the time, wouldn't it be easier just to forget it, but I couldn't now.

Overall, however, Amy seemed positive about her lesbian identity, emphasizing authenticity and integrity.

> It's just generally made me feel more positive, more me. I've learnt a lot about myself over the last few months, and now I feel I've got a lot stronger identity.

In summary, Amy had only relatively recently assumed a lesbian identity, having previously perceived herself as heterosexual. There were some indications of earlier feelings possibly related to lesbianism, but there may have been some reinterpretation of the past. If there were lesbian feelings during her teens, these would have threatened her identity and been coped with using the intra-psychic strategy of denial. Unsatisfactory heterosexual relationships, together with awareness of lesbian feelings, prompted Amy to re-evaluate her identity. Within a social context of interpersonal support from friends, and intergroup support from a lesbian community and feminism, the potential threat of a lesbian identity had been minimized. Thus, in spite of her awareness of the negative distinctiveness of a lesbian identity, her self-esteem was maintained at a high level. Potential sources of threat regarding her lesbian identity, such as the family or people at work, were dealt with by using the interpersonal coping strategy of 'passing'.

Comparison of the case with other participants in the group

The only other woman with a heterosexual background and aged under thirty was Alice who had defined herself as lesbian through her involvement with feminism, and is therefore discussed within the 'political' group.

Christine: a lesbian woman over thirty years old with a heterosexual background

Divorced from her husband, and in her early forties, Christine had three children ranging in age from eight to sixteen. Identification of self as lesbian did not occur until her mid thirties. There was some evidence, however, of possibly lesbian feelings reaching back to her teens and early twenties.

> I also had very intense emotional crushes on older women, that were completely asexual, but went on for a lot, lot longer than is normally supposed, right through my teens and early twenties.

Christine described how she had had no interest in boys except on a friendship level. Although Christine was aware of the words 'queer', 'poofter' or 'homosexual' being used by others while in the sixth form at school, they were used to refer to men only.

> In the nurses' home was the first time that I was aware that this odd situation could occur between women . . . I don't ever remember hearing the word 'lesbian' or knowing what it meant until by my thirties . . .

It was while living in the nurses' home that Christine briefly confronted the idea for the first time that she might be homosexual. There was a scandal centred on a nurse she had been friendly with who was required to leave the hospital.

> I went to the nurses' home where she was living, absolutely terrified that anyone would see me, in case I would be tarred with the same brush, and she was very, very upset. I can still see the scene now – I was sitting on her bed and she was sitting in her armchair – and I remember her looking across at me and saying 'You know, there really isn't very much difference between you and me . . .' . . . for a moment, it was yes, that explains it, but I couldn't cope with it and immediately I shut down on it, and I think from that point was determined to prove to everybody else, and me myself particularly, that there was nothing wrong with me, and I was perfectly normal, and it was the following weekend that I started to become involved with one of the young fellows . . . and we eventually married.

Thus, the possibility that she might be homosexual led to immediate conflict between continuity of feelings and self-esteem, arising from perceptions of negative distinctiveness. The intra-psychic coping strategies used were denial – at the first stage i.e. denial of the fact that one occupies a threatening position; and re-evaluation of existing identity content by focusing attention on heterosexuality and giving it increased value. Continuity of lesbian feelings was sacrificed to maintain self-esteem.

These coping strategies broke down when Christine was around thirty years old. By this time, her marriage had become very unhappy and she was becoming very depressed. An older heterosexual woman friend was very supportive, and Christine became emotionally involved with her.

> I began to be aware that I was having – as I termed it – 'unhealthy' thoughts about her.

Threat to identity was intense at this point. Self-esteem was extremely low; continuity of sexual orientation was disrupted; and there were very negative perceptions concerning the distinctiveness of lesbianism: 'totally abhorrent, repulsive'.

> Now, I first began . . . to have some idea of my identity when I was thirty, it's only twelve years ago. Now, when I found out, I damn nearly killed myself, I was so horrified.

Suffering from depression, Christine was having psychotherapy.

> I waited for about a year before I broached the subject with my psychotherapist, and then I said 'I think it's possible that I might be having bisexual feelings'.

The therapist suggested Christine contact a feminist group which included both gay and straight women. This may have helped Christine to begin to use the intra-psychic coping strategy of re-evaluation of prospective identity content, providing her with different criteria to judge the issue. Group support has played an important part in helping this participant to accept a lesbian identity.

> I became aware of feminism and lesbianism more or less in tandem.

The process of accepting herself as lesbian was slow.

> Gradually, I came through to a sort of intellectual acceptance of it . . . then I had to accept it at an emotional . . . level. That took quite a while too . . . it took me, I guess, about ten years to come from the point of view of wanting to kill myself because of it, to a point where I value it as one aspect . . . of myself.

At first, Christine avoided reading about lesbianism. She told a friend: 'Look, I want to find out who I am first'. When she later did start reading, she was able to identify with women described, and found it 'quite validating and enriching'.

Religion formed a very strong background to Christine's experiences. She perceived it as having made things more difficult for her.

Partly because she has custody of her children, Christine felt unable to disclose her lesbian orientation to certain people. In particular, she had avoided letting her husband or other family members know. Thus, she has had to rely quite heavily on the interpersonal coping strategy of passing. With some heterosexual friends, she also made use of this strategy.

Since her marriage broke down and her husband left home on a court order, Christine has had the opportunity to mix more with other lesbians. Thus, she has had further group support, aiding self-esteem by lowering the negative distinctiveness of lesbianism, and diminishing the conflict between maintaining continuity of lesbian feelings and distinctiveness.

> I have never felt more at ease with myself. I have never felt more validated as a woman since coming to terms with myself as a gay person.

Christine perceived coming out to self as of fundamental importance.

> I would reiterate that I think the important thing about coming out is coming out to yourself, coming to terms with yourself, and coming to accept yourself; and what you do to others, what you say to others, will very largely depend on how well you've come to terms with yourself.

She remained apprehensive of heterosexual people's possible reactions to her disclosing her sexuality to them.

> If they knew I was gay, I know that's the only label they would see. They would see me as [Christine] the queer . . .

Using the interpersonal coping strategy of passing, however, was not easy.

> . . . [other people] have no idea of what it means to have to deny yourself, when it's taken so long to fight against yourself, to accept yourself as you are – and then, not to be able to do anything about it is very hard.

Thus, from a threatened-identities model perspective, Christine may be perceived as having progressed from a position of extreme threat to which her main response was denial; through the breakdown of this intra-psychic coping strategy; and the subsequent use of interpersonal and intergroup strategies. Christine's marriage may possibly be seen partly as a response to the first awareness of the threat to identity of lesbianism, and as occurring during the period that the strategy of denial was being used successfully. However, this interpretation could be questioned as it rests upon Christine's reinterpretation of her past experiences. It is, nevertheless, one possible interpretation of her heterosexual past. Potential threat has continued to be present in Christine's life as she has had to use the interpersonal strategy of passing quite heavily due to her home circumstances and having custody of young children. Group support was of importance for Christine, helping her to maintain a good level of self-esteem with continuity of lesbian feelings, in spite of some continuing perceptions of the negative distinctiveness of lesbianism.

Comparison of the case with other participants in the group

Of the other women with heterosexual backgrounds, two (Mary and Shirley) had come to define themselves as lesbian through their involvement with feminism, and they are discussed in the group of women with a political understanding of lesbianism. Other lesbian participants in the heterosexual background group aged in their thirties were Stephanie, Samantha and Emma. Stephanie, in the early stages of coming out, was looked at in Chapter 6. Her case illustrated considerable threat to identity. Six years previously, at the age of twenty-nine, Emma had experienced initial acute challenge to continuity of self as heterosexual, with vital implications for self-esteem and affiliation. Awareness of negative distinctiveness of lesbianism had been present for many years for Emma, and like Stephanie and Samantha, she perceived herself as having repressed lesbian feelings over a long period.

The nine other women in this group were aged forty or over. Like Christine, six of these nine women had been, or were still, married. In the majority of these women's accounts there was some tracing back of lesbian feelings as existing prior to, or during, the period in which they had led heterosexual lives. The majority of accounts also indicated awareness of lesbianism as having negative connotations. Approximately half of these women's accounts described their previous sexual relationships with men in positive terms, and indicated that lesbianism was a choice they had taken. Two other women's accounts suggested they had had unsatisfactory heterosexual relationships and had no choice regarding a lesbian identity. For three of the nine women, as for Christine, there was some evidence of threat connected with identifying self as lesbian, dealt with mainly using intra-psychic deflection coping strategies such as denial. For other women in this group, threat tended to arise more from external sources such as conflicts with marriage or religion, or coming out to others, rather than from accepting self as lesbian. A need for authenticity or integrity was indicated by most women in this group.

Lesbians who had had heterosexual relations, while perceiving themselves as possibly lesbian

Penny: a woman under thirty years of age who had heterosexual relationships but perceived herself as possibly lesbian at the time

Penny, a twenty-four-year-old nurse, recalled both trying to conform while at school, and her intense friendships with other girls.

> I remember trying very hard to do what my friends were doing, sort of

> following around boys . . . and thinking 'I don't find these people attractive', but still trying very hard, and going to parties with people, and, you know, sort of joining in the general feeling without really feeling it . . .
>
> I remember being really infatuated with her, I just wanted to be with her all the time . . . after about a year, I suppose, I wanted to have more physical affection than this, and then her mother suddenly got very shirty about the whole thing, and virtually said I wasn't to see her daughter or anything else, because she felt that I was a lesbian – and I said 'I'm not, no'.

Penny continued to have boyfriends at university, while also having close friendships.

> The boyfriends that I had at school and university were very much me trying to prove something, trying to just lock myself into a role model. And I think for that reason – because I didn't particularly want to have a boyfriend – they were completely unsuccessful . . .

There was evidence of awareness of possible homosexuality.

> . . . you know universities usually have a lesbian and gay society . . . I used to walk past, and look sneakily at the board, and not actually look at it, and that was the closest I got at university.

At this stage, therefore, there was emphasis on attempting to conform by trying to lead a heterosexual lifestyle. There was also some evidence to suggest that lesbianism was perceived as having negative connotations and as threatening.

> I prefer 'gay' to 'lesbian'. Lesbian conjures up an image of a very . . . butch, sort of angry feminist . . .
>
> I remember thinking that they couldn't all be like the stereotypes . . . somebody who was fairly butch, and sort of short hair, and, you know, very strong feminist . . .

There was further evidence that there was conflict for Penny in the process of becoming aware of herself as lesbian.

> I think when I first thought about it, I actually 'mourned', in inverted commas, the idea that I wasn't going to get married and have all the relatives saying 'Jolly good' and 'Isn't this wonderful?'. I think I – for a short while – was a bit sad about that . . .
>
> The idea of coming out to yourself, and literally acknowledging to yourself that that's what's going wrong, rather than trying to give yourself other reasons for doing things, and actually realizing for yourself that that's

what's going on. There's a huge stumbling-block and sort of took years of fairly self-destructive analysis to acknowledge and to accept.

It must have taken me five or six years to come out to myself . . .

Thus, lesbianism did initially constitute a threat to identity for Penny. The threat was at first dealt with by use of the intra-psychic coping strategy of denial, and possibly by perceiving the lesbian feelings as not part of her 'real' self.

The social context seemed to provide little support for Penny's emerging lesbian identity. Until she came to live in London, she came across little reading material on lesbianism.

There was a huge lull while I was at university when I really didn't do much about it at all, and then suddenly coming to London and finding all this information, I then started to read in a big way, but during the early times *The Well of Loneliness* was about the only thing I ever saw.

She also felt the women's movement had played little part in her coming out as lesbian.

I think it almost had a negative effect, that I didn't want to feel that I was part of that idea . . .

Ultimately, Penny came to perceive herself as gay in the context of falling in love with a friend.

So gradually, with that particular friend, it evolved, because we were both trying to work out whether we were or whether we weren't gay, and then we just sort of fell into being in love, and just suddenly looked at each other and realized that we were quite happy about it, and it wasn't such a big deal, and it just seemed exactly the right thing to do.

First coming out into a lesbian community was eased by doing it with her girlfriend. By this stage negative distinctiveness of lesbianism had been minimized, and continuity of lesbian feelings could be allowed to predominate, not only without damage to self-esteem, but possibly even serving to enhance it.

Penny perceived heterosexuals' feelings about gay women as involving fear, but she suggested a positive approach may encourage them to respond positively.

I think – they're frightened of something that I feel they perhaps don't understand, or they don't want to have anything to do with it, and therefore it represents quite an unknown . . . but if you can present a positive approach they can then take it positively. If you present a negative

> approach, then it will be taken negatively – people can feel quite aggressive and quite threatened . . . Given the opportunity, people will respond well.

Penny's perceptions of reasons why some women are gay and some women are heterosexual have changed over time. At first she had thought it might have something to do with upbringing, but later dismissed this notion. She suggested that she did not perceive it as innate.

> It's just something that is, without actually coming from anywhere.

Her views on whether or not being gay was a choice seemed to suggest some kind of dispositional attributions.

> . . . the pain and anguish of coming to accept and enjoy it, I don't think anyone would ever choose to go through that . . . As far as I'm concerned, I don't see that it's a choice for me, it's something that I feel is right, and I've chosen to accept it.

Acknowledgement of self as gay led Penny to want to come out to others.

> So, I think I'd actually been gay for about – or at least acknowledged and enjoyed it – for about two months I suppose, and then I was so full enjoying it all that I wanted to tell everybody . . .

Penny's experiences of coming out to friends and family have generally been positive. Before coming out, Penny found herself having to tell her mother 'half-truths'.

> And I just thought 'This is ridiculous, this is my mother and I don't want to lie to her, and I'd quite like to let her enjoy what I'm enjoying'.

Coming out to her mother was very successful.

> And she just sort of took it all in her stride, and gave me exactly the sort of affection and response that, you know, one dreams about . . . and the overriding thing was that my mother was just concerned that I was happy, and that I was going to be happy, and that's the way it happened.

Penny's father was told by her mother. Her father has found it difficult to believe and does not talk about it much. Penny was unsure whether or not her brother realizes, but did not seem concerned about this. She decided not to tell her grandparents – 'partly because I didn't want to upset that [high] opinion of me, and also I just didn't feel that it was something that I needed to say to them'. All Penny's close friends know and have responded positively. At work she had come out to some people, but was generally quite cautious about disclosing the information about herself in the work situation.

> I don't think I'd make a definite statement, because I think it would influence how I got on.

Reactions to Penny's coming out were generally very supportive. Self-esteem was raised by not having to make heavy use of the coping strategies of passing or isolation. On the interpersonal level, she had derived considerable aid in minimizing any threat to identity. She had also begun to make more use of intergroup strategies.

> Having met more women, and I suppose grown up a bit anyway, and realized that there is a lot more to feminism than an angry feminist, I think [the women's movement is] beginning to play an increasing part in what I do.

Thus, for Penny being gay was largely no longer perceived as negatively distinctive; her self-esteem was high; and there was little challenge now to continuity of lesbian feelings for her. Overall, threat to identity for Penny is now minimal in comparison to the period during which she was coming out to self, as she indicated in her perceptions of the main benefits of coming out.

> . . . a large amount of self-esteem. Once you've come out to yourself, I think if you still carry on denying it to other people, it's still sort of denying it to yourself. And then you can enjoy the fact that other people are happy because you're happy . . . as I say, it's brought me quite a lot of good friends.

Comparison of the case with other women in the group

The other participants in the group of women under thirty years old who had had heterosexual relationships, but had perceived themselves as possibly lesbian at the time were Kim, Teresa, Beryl, Dawn and Stella. Three of these women were in the early stages of coming out to themselves and/or coming out into the lesbian community. Like Penny, all reported some dissatisfaction in their previous relationships with men. For all these women, too, there was some evidence of continuity of lesbian feelings with reports of such feelings traced back to teenage years, or in one case, the age of ten years old. There was some evidence of possible threat to identity from most of these women's accounts. For the majority of lesbians in this group, there was little evidence of use of the intra-psychic coping strategy of denial at Breakwell's first level – denial of occupying a threatening position – but denial at one of the higher levels may have been used. Most of these women's accounts indicated a need for authenticity or integrity.

Gail: a woman over thirty years old who had heterosexual relationships but perceived herself as possibly lesbian at the time

> From what I can remember . . . I've always found girls, women, females, much more appealing to be with than boys or men really. I have to say girls because that's when I go back to the first thing I can remember, which is about three I suppose.

Gail, who was thirty-three years old, traced her lesbian feelings back to childhood. She first became aware of terms relating to homosexuality around the age of eleven, and realized that the issue might relate to her. She described her feelings about it during her teens.

> You know it's there and you know you feel it . . . and there's absolutely nothing you can do about it. But at the same time you are on the other hand denying it – certainly not doing anything – well, I didn't do anything about it . . . there was such a stigma attached to it, and I'm sure that if anything was suspected, I would have been immediately ostracized . . . it was terribly difficult to be different.

Gail described her view of the situation during the period in which she was having heterosexual relationships.

> I think I sort of held back [from having a relationship with a woman] simply because of the constrictive ideas of society on sexuality and lesbianism. But I went on even though I was seeing men, being attracted to women. I'm sort of what they call a born lesbian I think . . .

There seems to have been continuity of lesbian feelings throughout. This conflicted with an awareness of the negative distinctiveness of lesbianism. Self-esteem was maintained by employing the intra-psychic coping strategy of denial, at the level of recognizing the threat, but denying the need to modify her identity structure.

Gail's heterosexual lifestyle and denial of lesbianism were challenged when, at the age of twenty-four, she unexpectedly became involved in a relationship with a married woman.

> It came out of the blue when I wasn't really looking for it . . . It was only after that happened that I began to have to admit to myself that there was something more that I was feeling. Even though I still wasn't prepared to actually say to myself 'You are a lesbian, face it and do something about it' . . . eventually when I did . . . finally disappointed with men . . . nothing would ever be the same with men after this, then I started to do something positive about it . . .

Thus, with the challenge to her coping strategy of denial, Gail came to re-evaluate existing and prospective identity content, eventually devaluing her heterosexual identity, and reconsidering lesbianism in the light of her recent experience.

> I couldn't reconcile wanting to be my own person and having to be submissive to a man.

> I think initially, when I first admitted it [being lesbian] to myself, I went through all the arguments that are put against – moral sort of . . . and I found an answer to all those things and justified it. It made me feel much happier that all the arguments against it were actually groundless and rooted in prejudice.

Gail's awareness of the negative distinctiveness of lesbianism was evident at this time.

> When I knew I had to end this relationship, I thought well, I've got to do something about it, I have to meet other women, and I thought I can't possibly – all those dreadful women. I mean, I had the stereotyped idea of tweeds and . . . the usual Radclyffe Hall type of idea.

This view of what lesbians might be like made it harder for her to contact others.

> I couldn't have rung Lesbian Line at that stage because I thought that I would speak to the types of women I had in mind. Rather off-putting, to put it mildly.

There was some awareness of both positive and negative images of lesbians in the media. Gail's perceptions of most heterosexual people's views of lesbians ranged from the sympathetic to those who regard it as an abomination. She also pointed out the possibility of physical assault if one wore badges relating to being lesbian.

Both situational and dispositional attributions were reflected by Gail's perceptions of reasons why some women are lesbian and some women are heterosexual, and whether lesbianism is a choice.

> I think, it's sometimes that people want certain things from life, if you like, and if having children and having security, and having status, and having social acceptability are the most important things to you, I think that you would get married, whether you are a lesbian or not.

> I still don't think that I've made a choice, I think it's something that I've come to because it's me.

First contact with other lesbians was made through *Sappho* magazine. Gail reported 'complete shock' in meeting 'perfectly ordinary women'. This provided further evidence that she had held a stereotypical view of lesbians.

Coming out to family and heterosexual friends, Gail used the approach of telling them about her relationship rather than stating that she was a lesbian. The first person told was a friend.

> Even when I had a relationship with a woman, she was still, as far as I was concerned, a one-off thing . . . I didn't actually come out and say 'I'm a lesbian' – it was far too traumatic a thing to say.

Gail had become very depressed after her relationship.

> I became so depressed about it that it began to show in various different ways, until my mother actually demanded to know what was wrong, and it just simply came out that I'd been involved with another woman . . .

Concern was expressed at the reaction of her mother.

> . . . that was about, I suppose, about seven years ago, and she hasn't mentioned it since. She doesn't want to know, which I find very disappointing, because if she's my mother, and I need her, she should try and understand, but if she doesn't want to know, I see no point in upsetting her . . . and the same reaction from my sister . . . I mentioned it to her at that time, and she's never mentioned it since, so I haven't mentioned it since . . . and . . . my father doesn't know.

> Occasionally, something might crop up on the television . . . and [my mother] might say something like . . . 'I can't stand that woman' – primarily because she's a lesbian. But that's about the only reference to it at all.

Both family and heterosexual friends seem to have perceived the relationship as a 'one-off' occurrence, and have not accepted Gail as lesbian. Thus, support from heterosexual significant others was limited. Also, Gail had chosen not to come out at work in the Civil Service.

There had been some group support for Gail since coming out into a lesbian community. The women's movement, however, was initially perceived as a negative influence.

> I had a very bad introduction to feminism which put me off for a number of years. I was introduced to feminism . . . by two revolutionary radical feminists who, as far as they were concerned, my hair was too long, I had a flashy car, and you shouldn't shave your legs . . . and if you weren't right on, you were right off . . . [now] I've come round to feminism in my own way, under my own steam, in a different way, and I would say, in the last year or so, that feminism has helped me put views in much more perspective again.

Thus, feminism now provided Gail with some group support.

Benefits of coming out expressed by Gail focused on aspects of authenticity and integrity.

> The good thing that has come out of it, of course, is that I've actually begun to find out who I really am . . . The very core of one's being is there, whereas before when I was just sort of a shell – a shallow sort of existence – trying to be what you really are not.
>
> . . . giving back to yourself, finding out 'this is me' . . .

In summary, there seemed to be strong evidence of continuity of lesbian feelings for Gail. During her teens and twenties there was awareness of the negative distinctiveness of lesbianism. This was initially dealt with by denial and the assumption of a heterosexual lifestyle. After an unexpected lesbian relationship in her mid twenties, there was re-evaluation of a lesbian identity and, ultimately, acceptance of self as a lesbian. On the interpersonal level, Gail told heterosexual friends and family about the one relationship, but not that she was lesbian. This could be seen as a partial form of passing. Support on the interpersonal level for Gail tended to be from other lesbians rather than from family or heterosexual friends. Group support was playing an increasingly important role. Self-esteem was being maintained with continuity of lesbian feelings, and awareness of satisfying needs of authenticity and integrity, outweighing remaining perceptions of the negative distinctiveness of lesbianism.

Comparison of the case with other women in the group

The two other women in this group were both older. For Irene, in her forties, the process of accepting herself as gay was gradual and involved dealing with the initial negative reactions of her mother. Although she had boyfriends over a period of time during her teens and into her early twenties, the relationships were not of a serious nature. Intra-psychic coping strategies ranged from the deflection strategy of denial of herself as lesbian, when attempting to conform and have boyfriends, to acceptance strategies of anticipatory restructuring, and eventually re-evaluation of identity content, and fundamental change. During the time when Irene had boyfriends, the negative distinctiveness of lesbianism was predominant. Afterwards, as she came to identify herself as lesbian, and came out into a lesbian community, continuity of lesbian feelings was given priority. Group support at this stage aided maintenance of self-esteem. On the interpersonal level, acceptance by significant others minimized potential threat.

Sylvia, at sixty-three years old, was the oldest lesbian participant. Her account indicated that she had had heterosexual relationships which she had 'thoroughly enjoyed' but did not find 'emotionally fulfilling'. Feelings possibly connected with being gay were traced back in Sylvia's account to a woman she had been attracted to when she started work at the age of fourteen. There seemed to be little evidence of threat in the account related to coming to perceive herself as lesbian: 'I've never really been burdened with any sense of guilt'. However, Sylvia had not told most of her heterosexual friends about herself, and reported that she did not think most of them had realized. Further, she described how before meeting other lesbians she had thought they would be like men, and she would be frightened of them. Thus, there was some awareness of negative associations of lesbianism, and evidence of some conflict.

Shirley: a woman who perceived her lesbian identity in political terms

Shirley did not define herself as a 'political lesbian', and would probably not be perceived as such by others. However, her understanding of lesbianism emphasized a political perspective; and she had initially defined herself as lesbian within the context of involvement with feminism and women's groups. Thus, Shirley provides an example from the small group of women within this lesbian sample who had a fundamentally political understanding of their lesbian identity.

Shirley defined 'lesbian' in terms of putting women first:

> [It] has to do with priorities and who you prioritize; whether you are prepared to give a lot of emotional and/or sexual energy to men or not, or whether you want to reserve that for women.

Further, Shirley's perceptions of reasons why some women were lesbian and some heterosexual reflected situational rather than dispositional attributions:

> . . . opportunity, choice, knowledge, those sorts of reasons.

First awareness of lesbian feelings occurred for this participant while at university:

> I can actually remember an evening sitting in my room and having these thoughts about this woman, and thinking 'gosh, that means I'm a lesbian'.

Shirley suggested that she could not trust her memory regarding whether or not she had had 'schoolgirl crushes' before this time; and further, she questioned whether such experiences would be connected with lesbian sexuality. She was 'dubious' about people claiming to be lesbian from an early age.

Following her first awareness of lesbian feelings, she 'buried that notion completely for a while' and 'went off and got married'.

> Obviously I'd absorbed subconsciously from all sorts of places that it was 'bad' . . . so it was just a totally negative thing that you just shut the door on.

In terms of the threatened-identity model, this could be interpreted as conflict between Shirley's self-esteem and her perceptions of the negative distinctiveness of lesbianism, preventing assimilation of a lesbian identity, and leading to the use of the intra-psychic coping strategy of denial.

It is not clear whether Shirley's marriage was or was not partially a reaction against her lesbian feelings.

> Well, I did – as I say – I did get married, and in fact it was weird. It wasn't having thought . . . 'this means I'm a lesbian, oh no I'm not going to be'. [I] didn't actually very consciously say 'I'm going to get married, I'm going to find someone'. I was actually in love with a bloke and got married, and it was sort of 'normal' in that sense.

The marriage came to an end, but exactly when this occurred was not clear from the interview.

It was through involvement with feminism and women's groups that Shirley eventually came to perceive herself as lesbian.

> . . . I was living in [X] at the time and started to get involved with the Women's Centre and various women's groups – not specifically lesbian groups, and not mixed gay groups either. What I felt was that what I was doing was making a decision about being involved with women and spending my time with women, and my energies.

Regarding the part played by the women's movement in her coming out as lesbian, Shirley emphasized that she perceived coming out and defining one's sexuality as a continuing process. Of the women's movement she suggested:

> It's a context. Without that context, and in a different context, I would, no doubt, either not be a lesbian, or feel differently about it in various ways.

From the perspective of the threatened-identities model, the change in social context, arising from Shirley's involvement with the women's movement, may be seen as having provided group support, diminished her perceptions of the negative distinctiveness of lesbianism, and, hence, reduced the conflict between distinctiveness and self-esteem. It was no longer necessary for Shirley to use a coping strategy of denial. On the intra-psychic level, she was now able to re-evaluate prospective identity content. There was association of the prospective identity content of lesbianism with the more positively valued feminism.

Within a feminist environment, much of the threat posed by lesbianism may be removed. However, within the larger context of heterosexual society generally, potential threat remained. Shirley described her experience of working in 'a very heterosexist, racist, bigoted institution'.

> I was getting really fed-up with being in the closet at work because I felt very much that it was distorting how I was feeling about myself and about my lesbianism . . . if you're having to spend quite a lot of your life in some way, however implicitly, denying something that matters to you, it's going to affect how you think about yourself.

In her present work, Shirley was able to be open about herself.

> I think what's good is having spent time, particularly at work, not being open, it's very important to me to be able to, and not to have to split things up or shut things off; and I feel that I've, by doing that, I've got rid of a lot

of – not guilt – a lot of negative feelings about my way of life in general, and that includes my sexuality.

Shirley had told her mother about herself.

I think she must have been a bit thrown because there were lots of very contradictory reactions very quickly, one after the other.

She has never told her father as her mother did not want her to, but she suggested he must be aware of it. Her brother lives overseas, and she has little to do with him. With heterosexual friends, she reported that she tended to assume people knew she was lesbian, and avoided telling them directly as this put 'a false emphasis on things'.

It doesn't actually mean anything to anybody without some context, and I'm not sure that people have that context of what I do and where I live, and who I'm involved with, and how I'm involved with them.

Generally, Shirley seemed to find it easier to cope with being out than with concealing her lesbianism.

Being in the closet is damaging to your identity and self-respect.

Lying of any sort, deception of any sort, makes things more complicated because you've got to remember what you said, and who you said it to, and you've got to keep up the act . . . I just find it tiresome. I've got more energy to do other things.

Thus Shirley preferred where possible not to have to use the coping strategy of passing. She emphasized a need for authenticity and integrity. In terms of Goffman's (1963) notion of stigma, Shirley may be seen as preferring to occupy the position of the 'discredited' in which she has the social situation to manage, rather than occupying the position of the 'discreditable', where she has control of information to deal with.

To summarize, there was some evidence to suggest that first awareness of lesbian feelings may have initiated a threat to identity for Shirley, with self-esteem challenged by negative distinctiveness, and thus leading to the use of the coping strategy of denial. A few years later, however, within the context of her involvement with feminism, Shirley was able to re-evaluate the prospective identity content relating to perceiving self as lesbian. Now, she perceived being lesbian 'very much as choice'. Thus, accepting awareness of herself as lesbian was within a social context providing group support. Shirley did not perceive continuity in her lesbian feelings.

However, as has been seen, there was some evidence of possible repression or denial. On the interpersonal level, Shirley preferred not to use the coping strategy of passing. A need for authenticity and integrity was emphasized.

Comparison of the case with other women in the group

The other cases of women falling into the group of those who had come to identify themselves as lesbian through their involvement with feminism were Alice and Mary. Within these accounts, attributions regarding lesbian identity were situational, and lesbianism was perceived as a choice. The accounts indicated that all had previously had sexual relationships with men and had perceived themselves as heterosexual at the time. There was little or no evidence of previous lesbian feelings from these women's accounts. Thus, continuity of lesbian feelings did not seem to have been an issue for these women. One of these women's accounts indicated some conflict of feelings during the time she had taken the decision to stop having heterosexual relationships, and before she began to have lesbian relationships. The other woman's account reflected very positive feelings during this period, but indicated later conflict in dealing with the 'shock' of having coming out as lesbian. This latter participant also mentioned conflict regarding continuing sexual feelings for men. The accounts for all three of the lesbians in this group indicated threat, or awareness of potential threat, arising from coming out to heterosexual significant others.

A comparison of the groups

All the lesbian accounts indicated some evidence of threat to identity occurring at various stages of the coming-out process, and being coped with through the use of different intra-psychic, interpersonal or intergroup strategies. There was variation in intensity or type of threat, and in choice of coping strategy.

Accounts from the 'always' lesbian groups (see Chapter 6), in comparison to the accounts from those lesbians who had had heterosexual relationships, indicated considerable threat during the women's teenage years and early twenties. For these women, lesbianism tended not to be seen as a choice, and the women's movement was generally perceived as either having played no part or as having contributed indirectly rather than directly. In most cases, the accounts of the 'always' lesbian women indicated perceptions of continuity of lesbian feelings from a relatively early age. There was also usually evidence of some awareness of the negative distinctiveness of lesbianism within these accounts. This was often associated with perceptions of others' attitudes rather than with feelings that lesbianism itself was wrong. Intra-psychic coping strategies occurring during the coming out to self period for these women tended to be acceptance rather than deflection strategies; but where Breakwell's strategy of denial may have been used by these women, it would have been at one of the higher levels rather than the first 'layer' of denying that one occupies a threatening position. None of the 'always' lesbian women's accounts had been classified as indicating evidence of repression, suppression or denial (of Breakwell's layer one type) of feelings on coming out to self. In contrast, just over half of the accounts from the two groups of women with heterosexual backgrounds had indicated this.

Use of the interpersonal coping strategy of passing was indicated in a number of accounts of the 'always' lesbian group. The majority of these accounts also indicated a need for authenticity or integrity. For the women in this group, self-esteem was maintained, and continuity of lesbian feelings allowed to predominate, while perceptions of the negative distinctiveness of a lesbian identity often tended to be minimized. Others' attitudes and reactions towards lesbianism, rather than the lesbian identity itself, tended to be perceived in negative terms. Initial identification of self as lesbian had occurred at an older age for some of those aged forty or over; and these women had also probably experienced less group support than the younger women.

The accounts of the majority of women who perceived themselves as having been heterosexual in the past indicated some continuity of lesbian feelings. This tracing back of homosexual feelings may have been a re-interpretation of the past; such feelings may or may not have occurred at the times suggested. Approximately a third of these women perceived their relationships with men in positive terms; the remaining two-thirds suggested their relationships with males had been unsatisfactory. There were indications of some quite strong perceptions of the negative distinctiveness of lesbianism, and as has been described, about half of these accounts of women with a heterosexual background were categorized as reflecting initial repression, suppression or denial of a lesbian identity. Some of these women's accounts indicated experience of considerable threat on becoming aware of self as lesbian. Others, however, seemed to indicate little threat from internal sources, but greater threat arising from external issues such as conflict with marriage. Intergroup coping strategies were used by many of these women. The majority of women in the heterosexual background group, like those women from the other two groups, suggested that being oneself/not having to pretend/freedom was a main benefit of coming out.

For the group of women who had a heterosexual background, but had perceived themselves as possibly lesbian during that time, accounts reflected at least some continuity of lesbian feelings. For the majority of women with this background, there were perceptions of their heterosexual relationships having been unsatisfactory. This contrasted with the proportion of women within the group of women who had perceived themselves as completely heterosexual, who viewed their relationships with men positively. There was some evidence of threat to identity occurring on coming out to self from many of these women, and just over half had been recorded as having initially repressed or denied lesbian feelings. All but one of the women's accounts in this group indicated that 'being yourself', not having to pretend, having freedom were the main benefits of coming out. Thus, a need for authenticity or integrity was evident across the groupings.

With the addition of an identity principle relating to need for integrity/authenticity, and possibly a further principle relating to need for affiliation, Breakwell's model of coping with threatened identity provides a basis for analysis of coming out. Need for affiliation may be seen as underlying both decisions to tell significant others about self, and decisions not to come out to others. In the first case, the aim is to improve the relationship, and in the second, to maintain a relationship, rather than risk damaging and perhaps losing it.

As Breakwell has pointed out, a limit to choice of coping strategy is the ideological social context. This is of particular importance in considering coming out. The values and beliefs associated with the ideological background may be seen reflected in the dominant social representations of human nature and gender. Individual experiences are structured by this context, and may only be understood in relation to it.

Thus, a broad overview, based on this case-study analysis, has suggested differences between the groups. The extent of influence of the context of dominant notions of gender and human nature was reflected in part in the level of awareness of the negative distinctiveness of lesbianism. Although almost all lesbian participants showed some such awareness, it was the women with a background of heterosexual experience, whether or not they had perceived themselves as possibly lesbian at the time, who tended to show most evidence of such perceptions. A further aspect of the influence of predominant representations on some of these women was a positive evaluation of heterosexuality. It was women with an 'always' lesbian background, however, in contrast to women from the other groups, whose accounts reflected greater isolation in experiencing coming out. These feelings of isolation may also be seen as relating to perceptions of dominant notions of gender and human nature. Thus, the 'always' lesbian women were as influenced by societal representations as the women with heterosexual, or lesbian and heterosexual backgrounds, but this was shown in experiences of isolation rather than in perceptions of lesbianism itself as negative. Initially in coming out, women with an 'always' lesbian, or lesbian and heterosexual background, tended to have had less direct experience of the women's movement, or to report more negative perceptions of feminism, than lesbians in the heterosexual background or political groups. Perceptions of the negative distinctiveness of lesbianism, experiences of isolation, and extent and nature of involvement with feminism, must all be seen as influenced by the context of social representations of gender and human nature – a context that changes over time. The different groups of lesbians may be viewed as having dealt with, or reacted towards, the dominant notions of gender and human nature in different ways.

9

Therapy for lesbians: some issues

While Clare, the imaginary lesbian, was growing up, and identifying herself as lesbian, she was aware that homosexuality was regarded by many as a mental illness. This obviously had an impact on her coming-out experiences. Changes have taken place now in medical perceptions. Homosexuality is no longer classified as a mental illness. However, many lesbians, for a variety of reasons, seek therapy. A considerable number of the lesbians in this study reported having experienced counselling or therapy. This chapter does not attempt to provide a comprehensive coverage of psychotherapy for lesbians. More simply, it aims to consider some issues concerning therapy with lesbians that are related to the process of coming out.

We start by looking at why lesbians may wish for therapy. Following this, two issues relevant to therapy generally are raised: emphasis on the individual, and the relationship of gender to mental health. The nature and limitations of therapy for lesbians are then focused upon. Finally some further issues of therapy relevant to coming out are considered. These include identity development and the notion of internalized homophobia; issues for adolescents and older lesbians; family concerns; and some feminist perspectives on therapy.

Why therapy?

For what kind of reasons do lesbians seek therapy? Reconsidering the picture of coming out that emerged from this study, we may speculate that threat to identity, isolation and lack of social support and heterosexism within society are just a few of the contributing factors. However, it seems likely too that these very reasons may also deter women from seeking help. What have previous studies found? Lesbian participants in a study by Morgan and Eliason (1992) mentioned family of origin issues, relationships, coming out and depression most frequently as reasons for entering therapy. Their perceptions of why there are so many lesbians in therapy included oppression creating stressors, acceptance of therapy within the lesbian community, fewer social supports and that coming out is hard. The National Lesbian Health Care Survey (Bradford et al., 1994) gives us further insight into reasons for lesbians seeking therapy. With a sample of just under two thousand, from across the United States, this survey focused on demographic and lifestyle information as well as mental health issues including depression, anxiety, suicide and eating disorders. Almost three-quarters of the sample had received counselling, and of these, half reported sadness/depression as the reason.

General issues of therapy

Counselling/therapy for lesbians must be considered in the context of issues that relate to therapy generally. Two issues are of particular relevance: emphasis on the individual; and differing perspectives of mental health related to gender.

Psychotherapy has tended to focus on the individual and inner feelings, neglecting the shaping of experiences on the personal level by social and cultural structures (Salmon, 1991). Pilgrim (1991) has argued that psychotherapy is socially blinkered, relating this to psychological reductionism (e.g. reducing actions within a social context to individual motives), and power issues of professionalism. Smail (1991) has suggested the need for an 'environmentalist psychology of help' taking into account interpersonal relations; and has emphasized the role of power. We have seen the impact of the social context on lesbians' experiences of coming out. Where psychotherapy is focused on the individual, neglecting this context, its usefulness to lesbians coming out must be seen as limited.

There are also general issues of perceptions of mental health/illness and gender. Over twenty years ago Broverman et al. (1970) found that while clinicians' perceptions of a healthy man did not differ from their perceptions of a healthy, mature adult, their perceptions of a healthy woman were different. Gove (1980), using a definition of mental illness that makes a distinction between personality disorders and mental illness, and excludes, for example, alcoholism and drug addiction, suggested that women have a higher rate of mental illness than men. However, Johnson (1980) challenged Gove's definition of mental illness and pointed out that it excluded categories in which men are predominant. Ussher (1991) has described femininity and madness as closely aligned within patriarchal discourse. Examining whether women's madness is misogyny or mental illness, she came to the conclusion there was no simple answer: 'It is both. It is neither' (Ussher, 1991, p. 306). Notions of 'normality' and gender clearly underlie conceptualization of mental illness.

Therapy with lesbians: its nature and limitations

What are some of the current ideas on counselling/therapy for lesbian/gay people that relate to issues of coming out? In the past, homosexuality tended to be regarded by many as an illness (as we have seen, the American Psychiatric Association's *DSM* listed homosexuality as a 'sexual deviation' until 1973). Even today, there are those who regard homosexual behaviour as a deviation from the normal developmental process and something to be treated (e.g. Fine, 1987). However, most current counselling/therapy approaches tend to emphasize instead positive adjustment to one's sexual orientation, and helping the individual to overcome 'internalized homophobia' and cope with stigma. Some radical lesbian feminists have challenged the notion of internalized homophobia and questioned the appropriateness of therapy for lesbians (Kitzinger, 1987; Perkins, 1991; Kitzinger and Perkins, 1993).

General research on mental health issues for lesbians has been limited. Rothblum (1990) pointed out that while there had been a great increase in research on depression among women, there had been very little research on depression among lesbians. Rothblum (1994) suggested a need for research on gay and lesbian mental health, but illustrated how methodological issues relating to definition of sexual orientation and selection of research participants may affect findings.

The scarcity of research relating to mental health issues of lesbian/gay ethnic minority group members must be noted in particular (Greene, 1994a).

Further, there has tended to be neglect of gay and lesbian issues in counsellor/therapist training programmes (Dworkin and Gutierrez, 1989; Garnets et al., 1991; Hancock, 1995). There has been material available, however, on counselling of gay men and lesbians, for some years now (e.g. Woodman and Lenna, 1980; Moses and Hawkins, 1982). Some ways in which counsellor training may be provided have been suggested (Iasenza, 1989; Buhrke, 1989). Emphasizing the need for training, it has been suggested that homophobia among non-gay counsellors may be a problem (McDermott et al. 1989).

Garnets et al. (1991) looked at bias in psychotherapy of lesbians and gay men. This was a large-scale survey, on a sample of psychologists, contacted through the American Psychological Association. Garnets et al. (1991) identified both themes that illustrated 'biased, inadequate, or inappropriate practice' and themes that reflected 'exemplary practice' (p. 966). Areas focused on included assessment, intervention, identity, relationships, family, and therapist expertise and education. Among the biases were perceptions of homosexuality as pathology; attributions of clients' problems to their sexual orientation where this was inappropriate; not recognizing clients may have internalized negative attitudes towards homosexuality; and making the assumption of heterosexuality. Good practice included recognition that homosexuality is not pathological in itself; awareness of societal prejudice/discrimination; and not assuming sexual orientation is pertinent in all the clients' problems. Garnets et al. recommended the development of guidelines for psychotherapists, and appropriate training.

Generally, therapeutic approaches suggested have varied with theoretical perspective adopted; perceptions of the nature of homosexuality; perception of the 'problems' to be dealt with; and therapeutic goals.

Theoretical perspectives

A variety of theoretical perspectives have been used in counselling or therapy for lesbians and gay men. Coleman (1987) suggested that the most effective and widely used treatment methods have included cognitive approaches and attitude modification; psychoanalytic approaches; group therapy; role play; and client-centred therapy.

Perspectives on the nature of homosexuality

Perspectives on the nature of homosexuality carry implications for therapy, and may be viewed as ranging between essentialist and social constructionist views; and as based on diverse theoretical perspectives such as biological determinism, for example, or psychoanalytic notions.

Thus, for instance, Mihalik (1988) argued that gender-related and erotic functioning may be based on a pre-structured neurobiological core; and viewed sexual diversity as deriving from the evolutionary processes underlying general biopsychological variability among human beings. Contrastingly, Richardson (1987a) viewed sexual identity as socially constructed and possibly changing over time. Viewing homosexuality from a different perspective, Golden (1987) made the distinction between 'primary lesbians', who do not perceive their lesbianism as a conscious choice; and 'elective lesbians' who perceived their lesbian identity as consciously chosen.

Psychoanalytic perspectives on homosexuality have had a particularly strong influence with their focus on gender identity, unresolved conflicts and ideas of natural/'normal' development.

Generally, underlying perspectives on the nature of homosexuality, we see the influence of perceptions of 'normality' and gender. Whether homosexuality is seen as biologically based; determined by early experiences; of a deviant nature; as a response to anxieties or an immaturity; as 'curable' or modifiable; or as fixed and permanent, will obviously help determine the therapeutic approach selected, perception of 'problem(s)', and goals of therapy.

Some issues in counselling/therapy of lesbians

External factors that may lead to lesbians and gay men experiencing psychological problems have been summarized as follows:

> (a) the lack of an accepting and nurturing environment for homosexual expression, (b) myths and misinformation regarding homosexuality, (c) lack of information regarding methods for developing a positive self-identity and improvement of interpersonal functioning, (d) lack of survival techniques for living in a predominately heterosexual and heterosexually-biased society, and (e) lack of healthy role models.
>
> (Coleman, 1987, p. 1)

Issues pertinent to coming out that recent psychological and sociological studies have examined include identity development, and family conflict. The problems of adolescents require particular attention.

Identity development and 'internalized homophobia'

Underlying many studies on therapy with lesbians has been the notion of 'homophobia', and in particular, 'internalized homophobia' (e.g. Sophie, 1987; Margolies et al., 1987; Hanley-Hackenbruck, 1988; Forstein, 1988; Browning, 1987; Hall, 1985). Shidlo (1994, p. 178) defined internalized homophobia as 'a set of negative attitudes and affects toward homosexuality in other persons and toward homosexual features in oneself'. In order to develop a positive lesbian identity, studies have suggested a reduction in internalized homophobia as a basic therapeutic goal.

Reduction of internalized homophobia through therapy based on psychoanalytic conceptualizations was suggested by Margolies et al. (1987) and Hanley-Hackenbruck (1988). Margolies et al. described some of the ways internalized homophobia may be expressed and the underlying defence mechanisms. They suggested that, internalized homophobia may consist of fear or discomfort based on sexuality (erotophobia), and/or that based on one's differentness (xenophobia). The latter may take the form of fear of rejection by family. Id and superego anxieties would require focusing upon.

Hanley-Hackenbruck suggested that modifications are needed to the superego during three stages of the coming-out process, in order to reach a positive, integrated identity. She referred to these stages as 'must not', 'must' and 'choice'. During the 'must not' stage there may be confusion, depression or anxiety, and superego modification begins with dispelling myths about homosexuality. During the 'must' stage, further modification of the superego takes place, and the individual copes with the tasks of adolescence that may have been neglected at the appropriate chronological stage. Work on internalized homophobia needs to go on during the 'choice' stage, with losses and rejections continuing to occur as the person remains 'out'. Hanley-Hackenbruck emphasized throughout that the problem lies not in an individual's homosexuality, but in the homophobia of society and the individual's internalization of this.

In another psychoanalytic interpretation, Gonsiorek and Rudolph (1991) took the perspective of Kohut's self-psychology. They suggested that most lesbian and gay young people experience narcissistic injury – 'a profound blow to one's self-esteem' – on becoming aware of their homosexuality (p. 170).

Further studies of therapeutic approaches that have focused on reduction of internalized homophobia have incorporated different theoretical frameworks. Sophie (1987), taking a cognitive perspective, suggested examples of possible coping strategies in order to encourage self-acceptance and reduce internalized homophobia. These included cognitive restructuring, self-disclosure and meeting other lesbians. Browning (1987) considered therapy issues within an adult developmental context, viewing a woman's identity as emerging through her resolution of her perceptions of the discrepancy between her own identity, and the cultural definition of adult identity.

From adolescence to old age

Adolescence or young adulthood is an important time during identity development. The stigma of homosexuality contributes towards psychological problems for adolescents (Coleman and Remafedi, 1989). Adjusting to a socially stigmatized role was seen by Hetrick and Martin (1987) as the major task of the gay adolescent. The seriousness of problems during adolescence for gay and lesbian young people is reflected in findings of approximately 20 per cent reporting suicide attempts before the age of twenty or twenty-one (e.g. Trenchard and Warren, 1984). A survey of a sample of adolescent psychiatrists in the United States by Kourany (1987) found those who had worked with homosexual adolescents perceived them to be at greater risk of suicide than other adolescents. Hetrick and Martin found the most frequent problems among a group of 300 adolescents concerned isolation and difficulties with family. They suggested 'learning to hide' may be the most important coping strategy adopted by homosexual adolescents and discussed the negative effects this may have. Savin-Williams (1994) suggested that lesbian, gay male and bisexual adolescents may experience verbal or physical abuse from peers and adults, including family. This is very stressful, adversely affects their mental health, and may be associated with school problems, conflict with the law, substance abuse, running away from home, prostitution and suicide.

All the lesbian participants in this study showed evidence of threat to identity occurring during the coming-out process. Women used a variety of coping strategies, varying to some extent with background experience (heterosexual/'always' lesbian) and age/socio-historic period.

As has been seen, for some women, coming out to self may occur during adulthood rather than adolescence. For all lesbians, the issues concerned with coming out to others continue throughout life, and may vary or have different implications for women at different stages of the life-cycle. One issue is that an unmarried lesbian who has not come out is likely to be perceived as a single heterosexual woman, an assumption that is a source of conflict for the lesbian (Gartrell, 1981). Historical period differences need to be taken into account as well as the effects of ageing itself when considering older gay people (Kimmel, 1978). The effects of heterosexism and ageism may be interrelated for older gay men and women, but there are ways in which being homosexual may facilitate adjusting to old age (Friend, 1987). These functional aspects in coping with ageing, suggested by Friend, included gender-role flexibility; 'crisis competence'; and the support of friends and community network.

The family

Family issues include dealing with coming out or not coming out to parents and siblings, as well as possibly husband, children and more distant relatives. We have seen in this study, on the one hand, the wide range of responses that may occur when a lesbian comes out to family, and, on the other hand, the problems experienced where the lesbian has not come out to close family. Greene (1994b) described situations therapists may be confronted with, including families in crisis when an adolescent has disclosed him or herself as gay/lesbian; adolescents concerned with whether or not to tell others about themselves; and adults making decisions about leaving heterosexual marriages to come out. Difficulties with family may be associated with stigmatization (Hammersmith, 1987; Hetrick and Martin, 1987). Rejection is a possible result of coming out to family. For those who have not come out, there is fear of rejection and the associated psychological stress (Hammersmith, 1987).

Strommen (1989) suggested a model of family member response to disclosure of homosexuality. This may be helpful in clarifying what is occurring in coming out to family. The model included three components: the values held by family members; the perceived effect of these values on the relationship between the person disclosing and other family members; and the availability of conflict-resolution mechanisms. Where family reaction was negative, Strommen suggested, two associated processes may be occurring: negative values related to homosexuality are applied to the discloser; and homosexual identity is perceived as negating, or disturbing, the previous family role of the discloser.

Coming out to parents can be a major source of difficulty. Zitter (1987) examined daughters coming out to their mothers from the perspective of intra-psychic considerations, family systems and sociocultural factors. Therapeutic concerns taken into account included that in some cases a decision to come out may not be the best course of action; the possibility of rejection; possible internalized homophobia of both mother and daughter; and the mourning process the mother may go through. Zitter suggested it may be useful to consider coming out in terms of reworking earlier separations from the mother, and that from a family systems viewpoint, a clearer boundary between mother and daughter may develop, and family dynamics change.

Understanding the position of the lesbian mother coming out to her children is of importance too (Kirkpatrick, 1987). A possible approach to easing the process of coming out to one's children has been described by Dunne (1987) in a study of gay men in which role play was used.

Knowledge of availability of social support resources is important as families tend not to approach sources of support they might use in other circumstances, such as friends and general community resources (Neisen, 1987; Hammersmith, 1987).

Feminist perspectives

Conceptualizations of 'internalized homophobia', and of working towards a goal, through therapy, of a positive lesbian identity, require further examination. Certainly, the notion of internalized homophobia remains popular: it has been suggested that it could form a central organizing concept for lesbian and gay affirmative psychology, and be referred to by the more neutral terminology of 'internalized homonegativity' (Shidlo, 1994). However, as Kitzinger (1987) pointed out both the notion of homophobia and that of the 'well-adjusted' lesbian must be seen as liberal humanistic constructions, based on value judgements. The notion of homophobia, Kitzinger argued, depoliticizes the oppression of lesbians, individualizing and personalizing a socio-political phenomenon. Perkins (1991) examined cognitive approaches to therapy with lesbians, and argued that therapy may be seen as anti-feminist and anti-lesbian as it translates oppression into individual pathology. In a development of these ideas, Kitzinger and Perkins (1993) rejected psychological explanations and therapy for lesbians, suggesting these individualize and privatize issues that are political.

The argument that lesbians should not be given therapy, but should be dealt with instead within the lesbian community, must be questioned. Do lesbian communities have the ability, resources and willingness adequately to help women experiencing a highly disturbed state? Sender (1992) expressed doubt on groups of lesbians aiding individuals in crisis and commented on the underlying assumption in Perkins (1991) of a unified lesbian community. Furthermore, Brown (1992) distinguished between therapy with women or lesbians, and feminist therapy. She argued that feminist therapy for lesbians 'is therapy that is clearly political in intent, in which private problems are placed by the therapist in the broader social and cultural framework, and deprivatized' (Brown, 1992, p. 243).

While recognizing the social and political issues involved, the individual should not be neglected. Distress and conflict may be experienced relating both to coming out to self, and coming out to others, and while the aims and underlying assumptions of therapeutic interventions obviously require examination, for some women, counselling or therapy may be vital. It cannot be assumed that lesbian communities are currently able to provide the support necessary for those experiencing extreme distress.

Conclusions

Generally, counselling and therapy for lesbians have reflected specific ideological contexts and theoretical perspectives in determining therapeutic approaches, 'problem' conceptualizations and goals of therapy. Underlying these are different notions of normality and gender. Counselling/therapy of lesbians must recognize the social representations of human nature and gender that form the context for women's experiences as lesbians. Assumptions relating to 'normality' and gender within therapeutic approaches need to be made explicit for evaluation.

10

Summary and conclusions

Coming out to self: a summary

The proposed model

The process of 'coming out to self' is seen as based upon strong emotional feelings directed towards women, together with awareness of lesbianism as an option, and a level of emotional acceptance of lesbianism. These three components lead to possible identification as lesbian.

Emotional basis

Coming out to self takes place within a social context that includes perceptions of people's views of lesbians as negative; a stereotype of lesbians as masculine, abnormal, aggressive and unattractive; and lesbian 'invisibility'. These aspects of the social context are likely to decrease both awareness of lesbianism as an option, and emotional acceptance of homosexuality. This suggests that for identification of self as lesbian to occur, emotional feelings directed towards women would need to be very strong. Indeed, strong emotional feelings for women were found to be central in identification of self as lesbian. Findings supported Wolff's (1973) conceptualization of lesbians as 'homoemotional'.

However, emotion must be viewed as a social construct. In particular, it needs to be understood as reflecting societal representations of gender.

Women's relationship towards men is pertinent. While some women perceived themselves as 'always' having been lesbian, and had had no important relationships with men, others had had relationships with men. Generally, however, it was strong positive emotions towards women and a lack of romantic/sexual interest in men, rather than direct hostility towards males, that formed the basis for identifying as lesbian.

Forming a lesbian identity

For development of a lesbian identity, the emotional basis would generally need to be complemented by some awareness of lesbianism as an option together with emotional acceptance of homosexuality. A variety of factors contribute positively or negatively towards awareness and acceptance. Awareness of lesbianism as an option depends on available social representations of gender and human nature, while a level of emotional acceptance reflects coping with the threat to identity. Available social representations would be specific to historical period. Relevant social representations reflect the stereotyping, perceptions of negative attitudes, and attributions relating to lesbianism found in this study. The negative nature of these would contribute little towards lesbianism being perceived as an option. The majority of lesbian participants had either held a stereotype or mentioned feeling frightened of lesbians before meeting others. Lesbian 'invisibility' also limited awareness of lesbianism as an option.

For some women, involvement with the feminist movement may both heighten awareness of lesbianism as an option and facilitate emotional acceptance, providing an environment in which lesbianism is accepted to a greater extent than it is within society as a whole. Comparatively few women in this study had been directly involved with the feminist movement while coming out to self, although most would have experienced some indirect influence. Where women do come to define themselves as lesbian within a context of direct political involvement with feminism, coming-out-to-self experiences would be different to those of women more isolated from other lesbians. For the more isolated lesbians – the focus of this study – the representations of a largely heterosexual society form the predominant social context.

Emotional acceptance of lesbianism was gradual. Threat to identity (Breakwell, 1986) was evident in all the lesbian participants' accounts. Variation occurred in intensity or type of threat, and in choice of coping strategies. Coping strategies selected may help to determine if/when a woman comes to identify herself as lesbian. Thus, on the intra-psychic level, where women used denial or other deflection strategies, rather than acceptance strategies, there would be delay in coming out to self. Women in the 'always' lesbian group experienced considerable threat during their teenage years and early twenties, but coped mainly through acceptance strategies. Women with a heterosexual background were more likely to report initial repression, suppression or denial. Less group support had been available for older participants. Participants across all groupings mentioned 'being yourself ' as a main benefit of coming out. It is suggested that 'a need for authenticity and integrity' may constitute an additional identity principle guiding the process of coming out.

Women's feelings on coming out to self

There was a long gap of time between first lesbian feelings and identifying self as lesbian for many. Becoming aware of self as lesbian often began with negative or conflicting feelings. A minority of participants mentioned having positive feelings during this time. Current feelings about being lesbian were both positive and negative.

The generally negative or conflicting feelings on initially becoming aware of self as lesbian must be seen as related to the negative attitudes towards homosexuality, stereotyping, attributions, etc. reflected by dominant social representations of gender and human nature.

Becoming aware of self as lesbian may also be considered in terms of social identity theory and salience of social categorization. Conflicting feelings on coming out to self may be viewed as associated with initial perceptions of lesbians as a negatively valued group. Salience of social category is seen as a function of accessibility and fit (Oakes, 1987). This takes into account emotional significance of categorization as well as match between self-perceptions and stereotypical notions. Negative stereotyping of lesbians may decrease perceptions of fit.

Further perspectives

Findings in this study do not lend support to the notion of a linear stage model of coming out to self. Women came to identify themselves as lesbian at widely varying ages, in a variety of different ways, having had very different life experiences.

However, some support was provided for studies that have suggested two types of lesbians (e.g. Ettorre, 1980; Golden, 1987). There were women who perceived their lesbian identity in essentialist terms, as part of their being, something they were 'born' with, or developed into; and secondly, there were those who perceived their lesbian identity as an active choice made during adulthood. However, the distinction between the groups was not always clear, and many women's understanding of their lesbian identity would fall between the two extremes. Although aspects of Kitzinger's notions of lesbian identities (Kitzinger and Stainton Rogers, 1985; Kitzinger, 1987) were evident, clear boundaries between such identities seem unlikely.

Postmodernist/poststructuralist viewpoints have questioned the whole notion of lesbian identity. While this is of theoretical interest, it seems less useful when considering women's experiences and everyday life in our social world. It is through the identities that we construct that we relate to others, and adapt to our social environment. From this perspective, lesbian identity is fundamentally important. To reduce lesbianism to behaviour denies its impact on our sense of self. It would also be likely to make social/political organization more difficult.

'Coming out to self' can only be understood within the social context. Indeed, the 'self' must be seen as developing and being maintained within social interaction (e.g. as suggested by Mead, 1934). A fundamental aspect of the social context concerns the notions of gender that permeate our society and our everyday life. Dominant social representations of gender and human nature may be seen as containing inflexible conceptualizations of gender and sex-role notions, based on heterosexuality, and incorporating power inequalities between women and men, as well as notions of 'normality'. Lesbians in the process of coming out to self require broader, more flexible conceptualizations of gender. The notion of gender boundaries (Condor, 1987) which permit changes in social representations, with boundaries being viewed as negotiable, provides a useful perspective. The process of coming out to self must also be seen as a challenge to male dominance. Within this context, conflict experienced in coming out to self as lesbian may be understood.

Coming out to others: a summary

The main areas of 'coming out to others' examined were coming out to other lesbians; coming out to family and heterosexual friends; and coming out at work. Non-disclosure is as vital to investigate as disclosure: the focus was as much on issues related to decisions not to come out as on coming out itself. Initial circumstances, approaches taken and telling the other person, reactions, and satisfaction with outcome were considered. The findings summarized below reflect the focus here upon more isolated lesbians rather than on political lesbianism. Although political lesbians might confront somewhat similar issues in, for example, coming out to parents, other aspects, such as coming out to other lesbians, would probably vary.

Coming out to others requires viewing from a combination of individual/interpersonal, intergroup and societal perspectives.

'Coming out to others' from an interpersonal perspective

A woman who has not come out to a particular heterosexual person may be seen as coping with threat to identity through 'passing' (Breakwell, 1986); as 'discreditable', with information to manage (Goffman, 1963); as 'markable' (Jones et al., 1984); or as an actor concealing information from the audience (Goffman, 1959). Personal identity rather than social identity would be salient in interaction with the other (Oakes, 1987), although another group membership may be salient. In particular, behaviour may be gender-related (Deaux and Major, 1987). From a self-disclosure perspective, disclosure reciprocity may be inhibited, affecting relationships with others, as well as development of friendship (Jourard, 1971; Chaikin and Derlega, 1976; Miell and Duck, 1986). However, this needs to be balanced against the possible negative effects of disclosure.

Others may assume the woman is heterosexual; or the situation may be more ambiguous with others speculating about her sexuality; having guessed; or feeling uncertain. The lesbian may correctly or incorrectly assume others 'know'. Uncertainty and ambiguity may exist for both lesbian and heterosexual person, affecting the relationship between them.

Differences in lesbian and heterosexual perspectives are fundamental to understanding 'coming out'. Heterosexual participants tended to perceive lesbianism solely in terms of sex, while lesbian participants perceived it as something more than sex, including, for example, love/emotion in their definitions. While lesbian participants' personal views of lesbians tended to be androgynous, over half the heterosexual participants viewed lesbians as masculine. Many heterosexual participants had had little contact with lesbians. These divergent perspectives explain some of the difficulties that occur in coming out.

This study, like previous studies of lesbians and gay men, has indicated varying proportions of the sample 'out' to parents, other family members, heterosexual friends, etc. Thus, for example, 60 per cent of the women had come out to their mothers, but less than 40 per cent to their fathers. Of those who had sisters, two-thirds had come out to one or more of them; and of those with brothers, one-third were out to one or more. However, such figures cannot be seen as representative of lesbians generally. Samples only consist of women and men confident enough about being 'out' to take part in research. Thus, proportions of those who are 'out' may well be inflated.

Initial circumstances contributing towards decisions not to come out included perceptions of negative attitudes towards homosexuality; wishing to protect others from being upset; and feeling it was unnecessary to tell certain people. Contributing towards decisions to come out were need for support, in particular with lesbian relationship problems; feelings of guilt at not being able to speak freely, and being assumed to be heterosexual; and the feeling that the other person would not mind.

The approach taken in telling family or friends that one was lesbian tended to be direct, but sometimes women just assumed others knew, or 'came out' by not hiding being in a relationship. Few women were recorded as 'testing the water' before telling others, although potentially this could be a helpful approach.

When a lesbian tells someone about herself, social identity is made salient rather than personal identity. One possible scenario is that the lesbian has come to perceive her social identity as basically positive. The heterosexual person, however, may perceive lesbian identity as largely negative, and possibly as threatening to the distinctiveness of heterosexuality or gender roles. Attributions made may be based on social category membership.

Positive, neutral and negative reactions to coming out were described. Negative responses ranged from not understanding to rejection. There were some differences in the types of negative reactions mentioned by lesbian and heterosexual participants.

The outcome – lesbian participants' satisfaction or dissatisfaction with coming out – reflected women's perceptions of the reactions of others. Perceived benefits of coming out focused particularly on 'being yourself ', being true to yourself, being a whole person; and secondly, on general relationship to others – being able to stop lying or pretending, being more relaxed, not having to hide, being able to share feelings with friends or family.

The question of coming out at work illuminated some more general issues. First, a lesbian, whether out or not, must also be considered as a woman within the workplace. Second, some participants questioned whether sexuality had any relevance at work, suggesting that personal issues are inappropriate for discussion in the workplace. This view fails to take into account how deeply assumptions of heterosexual relations are woven into everyday life and communication. For the heterosexual woman, saying 'I went to the cinema with my husband/boyfriend on Saturday evening' may not seem of any significance or particularly personal, yet it implies heterosexuality. A parallel statement by a lesbian may be seen as very personal and possibly unacceptable. Such double standards are a reflection of prejudice and discrimination. Overall, this study indicated not only that lesbian participants perceived being out at work as potentially problematic, but also that their concerns were, to some extent, a realistic reflection of heterosexuals' attitudes.

'Coming out to others' from intergroup and societal perspectives

All aspects of 'coming out to others' take place within the social context. Dominant social representations of gender and human nature may be seen as reflecting attitudes, stereotypes, sex-role notions, more general conceptualization of gender, and notions of normality relevant to lesbianism. This study found perceptions of people's attitudes were largely negative, emphasizing 'threat' and 'abnormality'; and a stereotype of lesbians as masculine, aggressive, unattractive and abnormal. Lesbian 'invisibility', including lack of contact of heterosexual participants with lesbians, and low media coverage of lesbian issues, formed a further aspect of the social context. At the most fundamental level, conceptualization of gender, incorporating heterosexual relations and power inequalities between women and men, may be seen as shaping the social context within which coming out takes place.

Coming out into a lesbian community

There was evidence that lesbians were initially perceived as a negatively valued group. This included perceptions of negative associations of the term 'lesbian'; negative feelings on coming out to self; and awareness of a stereotype or feeling frightened of lesbians before coming out to others. The generally negative social context reflected by dominant social representations relating to lesbianism must be seen as contributing towards the difficulties many women experienced in initially making contact with other lesbians.

From the perspective of coping with threatened identity (Breakwell, 1986), group support and/or group action has the potential to facilitate the coming-out process for lesbians. Less group support would have been available for women who first came out during the 1950s or 1960s than for those who came out in later years. The women's movement, in particular, either directly or indirectly, has made coming out, both to self and others, easier. Few women in this sample had been directly involved with feminism when coming out to self. Some ambivalence of feelings towards the women's movement was evident.

Once women have made contact with other lesbians, interdependence and shared threat, as well as depersonalization (Turner, 1984; Turner et al., 1987), may contribute towards positive reinforcement of lesbian identity, group cohesiveness, and emphasis of social identity over personal identity.

Coming out to heterosexual friends or family

As described from the interpersonal perspective, when women come out to heterosexual significant others, social identity is made salient and attributions may be made based on social category membership. Social identity theory provides an intergroup perspective of coming out that allows power relationships between groups to be taken into account. Lesbians need to be viewed as women within a male-dominated society, in addition to being seen as homosexual within a predominantly heterosexual society. Underlying notions of social identity and social attributions are the dominant social representations of gender and human nature. Taking a perspective that incorporates social representations allows consideration of historical period differences with the possibility of the content of dominant representations changing over time.

An area of focus has been the role played by stereotyping in the coming-out process.

Stereotyping

Stereotyping may be considered from both social and individual perspectives. Stereotypes are part of the relevant social representations; and they may affect interpersonal behaviour. The stereotype of the masculine, aggressive, unattractive and abnormal lesbian emerged from the use of three convergent methods: interview questions; a questionnaire of open-ended questions and sentence completion; and sex-role inventories. Sex role was confirmed as an important part of the lesbian stereotype, but other aspects such as abnormality were also evident. Although the notion of sex role may be seen as a limited aspect of gender, and exactly what is being measured is uncertain (e.g. instrumental/expressive qualities), sex role is very clearly a central part of the lesbian stereotype. Of the social functions of stereotyping (Tajfel, 1981), differentiation may be most important for the coming-out process.

It was found that a considerable proportion of women had held stereotypical notions or felt frightened of lesbians before meeting others; and that this had made coming out more difficult or delayed the process for some women.

Interplay of influences

Interaction between coming out to self and others

It has been emphasized that 'coming out to self' and 'coming out to others' need to be seen within the social context, and as interacting. A woman may identify herself as lesbian; be unsure of her sexual orientation; or completely unaware of herself as lesbian. In the first two cases, she may tell a heterosexual significant other about herself. Reinforcement of lesbian identity may occur whether the heterosexual person responds in positive or negative manner. In the third case, although the woman herself is unaware of self as lesbian, another person may perceive her as possibly lesbian. This may have no effect on the woman's perception of her identity, but if the person tells the possibly lesbian woman, modifies behaviour towards her, or perhaps tells others, there is likely to be an impact on the woman's identity. These effects may be positive or negative. An example is denial by the possibly lesbian woman, followed by attempts to prove self heterosexual.

Some influences on coming out

A variety of influences may affect the coming-out process. The interplay of these influences, which range from the cultural or societal to the individual, determine the coming-out process. At the cultural/societal level are the dominant social representations relevant to lesbianism, reflecting stereotypes, attributions, beliefs and attitudes about homosexuality, and notions of gender and normality. The content of these social representations changes over time. Thus the social context is specific to the historical period. Power relations are pertinent too.

Examples of influences include the media, which both reflect dominant social representations, and contribute towards them; and the women's movement.

Further, lesbians' experiences of coming out are affected by their multiple group memberships and the interaction between these. Black lesbians and disabled lesbians, in particular, experience additional oppression within lesbian communities, as within the larger society. While lesbian communities have begun to address these issues, much remains to be done.

On the interpersonal level, a woman's social network and general relationships with others, including, for example, family ties, may influence her coming-out experiences. Individual life events such as career moves, marriage or moving to a different area may facilitate or hinder coming out. These life events and their influence on coming out must be seen within the cultural context of the relevant historical period. A life-span perspective takes into account women's development within the cultural context specific to a particular historical period, interacting with individual life events.

Communication group interviews indicated difficult issues to talk about with family and friends included those relating to identity, relationships and loss. Coming out may involve all of these areas of concern.

Thus, there is an interplay of cultural/societal, intergroup, interpersonal and intra-psychic influences that affects the coming-out process. Coming out to self and others needs to be understood within this complex context.

Methodological issues

Interpretation of the findings of this study must be based on awareness of its methodological limitations. Areas to consider include sampling; interview biases; and interpretation of qualitative data.

The lesbian sample, mainly from one London group, cannot be seen as representative of lesbians generally. Class, race and disability were not investigated. Possibly, women who felt most confident about being 'out' would have been more likely to volunteer to participate in the study than those less confident. The heterosexual sample was also not representative in terms of class, race or disability. Furthermore, heterosexual individuals who felt most uncomfortable about homosexuality would probably have been unlikely to volunteer to take part in the study.

Communication group interviewees were all connected with one academic institution. Like the lesbian and heterosexual groups, participants may have had greater confidence in communication than those who did not volunteer to take part.

Interview material needs to be seen as deriving from interviewee and researcher biases, together with biases arising from interviewee–researcher interaction. It is pertinent that the researcher defines herself as lesbian, most lesbian participants having been aware of this, but most heterosexual participants, unaware. Heterosexual participants may have assumed heterosexuality of interviewer, guessed she was lesbian, or been unsure, with consequent effects on responses.

Orientation of the researcher is also pertinent to the formulation of research questions. A heterosexual researcher might have focused on different issues.

In analysing qualitative material, the researcher structures the framework for analysis, as well as interpreting the material for coding. Bias may occur at both stages. Interview responses may sometimes be ambiguous or contradictory.

Many previous studies and attempts to measure heterosexuals' attitudes towards homosexuals have been methodologically problematic. Their findings must be interpreted with caution, in particular, for example, where constructs were poorly defined, where participant or target sex was not specified, where statistical methods used were questionable, where samples were restricted to student populations, or where social context was neglected. Further, as Kitzinger (1987) emphasized, prejudice may only be understood within the context of particular ideological frameworks.

Implications

Major implications of the findings of this study concern the need for examination of the coming-out process from cultural and intergroup perspectives as well as considering intra-psychic and interpersonal aspects; the importance of notions of gender in understanding coming out for lesbians; and how differences in lesbian and heterosexual perspectives may affect coming out. Further implications relate to practical issues such as education, counselling and therapy; and, on a more fundamental level, potential for facilitation of the coming-out process.

The coming-out process and social-psychological theory

'Coming out' is seen as an essentially social-psychological phenomenon. Analysis within a social-psychological framework provides a basis for description and some explanation of the process, as well as indicating areas where development of theory would be useful. Although coming out needs to be viewed from intra-psychic and interpersonal perspectives, it is only when cultural and intergroup aspects are considered too that a deeper understanding of the process emerges. Social representations of gender and human nature, incorporating notions of gender, stereotypes, attitudes and attributions relating to lesbianism may be seen as underlying the coming-out process.

Two important aspects of the process of coming out are, firstly, its association with historical period; and, secondly, the underlying issues of power. The dynamic nature of social representations allows historical period differences to be taken into account, while social identity theory permits some understanding of power relations between groups. Neither perspective on its own appears to cover both aspects adequately.

While social representations provide a vital cultural perspective, their links with the individual level are less clearly specified. Mead's (1934) notion of self, however, provides a connection between the individual and social, with the self seen as originating and developing within the context of social interaction. Women did tend to perceive their experience of coming out in individual terms, for example, emphasizing 'being yourself' as a main benefit of coming out.

Evidence of coping with threatened identity (Breakwell, 1986) was indicated in lesbian accounts. Identity principles of continuity, distinctiveness and self-esteem, however, were not considered sufficient to describe those guiding the identity processes in coming out. Additional identity principles were required: firstly, a need for authenticity and integrity; and, secondly, a need for affiliation.

Studies on self-disclosure have tended to focus on the individual/interpersonal level. In investigating an issue such as coming out, however, it is essential to consider intergroup and cultural aspects that may affect self-disclosure, and to view the self as social in nature.

Gender issues and coming out

Lesbians need to be considered as women within a male-dominated society, and as homosexual within a predominantly heterosexual society. Taking a social identity perspective contributes towards understanding coming out in terms of group membership and power inequalities between groups. It is argued that coming out as lesbian only becomes an issue within a heterosexist society. Underlying heterosexism are inflexible notions of gender and gender schematic thinking, as well as interest in maintaining the status quo of power relations. For those who aim to maintain the current power imbalance between women and men, lesbianism is seen as a challenge and threat.

How might gender be conceptualized so that heterosexism disappears or diminishes? Although a gender aschematic society (Bem, 1981), or elimination of gender polarization (Bem, 1993), might be the ideal goal, given the base of a biological sex difference, these would seem unlikely to occur. However, a more flexible notion of gender, such as that suggested by the gender boundaries approach (Condor, 1987), and eradication of androcentrism (Bem, 1993), could potentially contribute towards a decrease in heterosexism.

Comparison of lesbian and heterosexual perspectives

It is essential to view coming out both from the perspective of lesbians' perceptions and experiences, and from the perspective of heterosexuals' attitudes. The differences found between lesbian and heterosexual perspectives contribute towards understanding the coming-out process. Fundamentally, definitions of 'lesbian' differed, with heterosexual participants perceiving lesbianism as relating only to sex, and lesbian participants perceiving a broader meaning. This may explain, in part, heterosexuals' negative reactions when a lesbian comes out. They may be comprehending the issue from a limited perspective. Lack of contact with lesbians and general lesbian 'invisibility' make increased understanding less likely. Stereotypical notions of lesbians may then persist: for example, heterosexual participants viewed lesbians as masculine. The coming-out process for lesbians may only be understood within this context of heterosexual attitudes and beliefs about lesbians. This raises the question of the possibility of change in the attitudes and beliefs about lesbianism reflected in dominant social representations.

Education and the media

Could education, for example, contribute towards greater understanding of homosexuality? Some within the lesbian sample suggested that education was of fundamental importance. Heterosexual participants, on the other hand, expressed ambivalence about education relating to homosexuality being provided in schools. Misconceptions about lesbians and lesbianism are reflected in dominant attitudes and beliefs: education could help dispel misunderstandings, but would require a carefully planned approach, sensitive to the many issues involved.

The media provide another potential approach to modifying attitudes and beliefs relating to lesbianism. As with education, there is opportunity both for perpetuation of misrepresentation and misunderstanding, or for an approach that portrays lesbians without stereotypical generalization and misconceptions. Lesbian 'invisibility' does not aid understanding of lesbianism. On the other hand, the approach of the tabloid newspaper may be positively harmful, reinforcing stereotypes and misconceptions. The media have the potential, however, to portray lesbians in a manner that more closely reflects lesbian women's lives.

Lesbian 'invisibility' has to be seen as a problem. It allows misconceptions about lesbians to persist; isolates individuals coming out to self, and makes it more difficult for women to meet other lesbians. Women coming out to self may have no role models, and perhaps only stereotypical notions portrayed by the media. The women will need to take positive action if they are to meet other lesbians. For heterosexual men and women, lesbian 'invisibility' allows perpetuation of stereotypical notions.

Education and the media may provide the means to modify attitudes and beliefs about lesbians. However, fundamental change in attitudes towards lesbians can only be realized through modification of the content of dominant social representations of gender and human nature. Attitudes towards lesbianism cannot simply be modified on a superficial level. What is required is change in thinking, conceptualization, relations and power balance, regarding both gender and notions of normality: fundamental change in our social representations of gender and human nature.

Facilitation of coming out

Facilitation of the coming-out process for lesbians would necessarily involve changes at all levels. Change at intergroup, interpersonal and intra-psychic levels would depend on modification at the societal level. If dominant social representations were to reflect flexible notions of gender that incorporated equality between males and females, and between lesbian/gay and heterosexual persons in our society, then coming out as lesbian would almost certainly cease to be an issue. While notions of gender remain rigid in conceptualization, based on perceptions of differences between the sexes, devaluing characteristics defined as feminine, and maintaining a power imbalance favouring males, coming out as lesbian will continue to be seen in terms of threat and stigma.

Living within the context of a heterosexist society, it is not surprising that a considerable proportion of lesbians seek counselling or therapy at some stage. A potential danger is the individualization of a problem that lies within society, not the individual. On the other hand, counselling or therapy that recognizes the social and societal issues, and implications, may relieve distress and depression, and contribute positively to individual development.

Conclusions

The importance of viewing coming out to self within the social context has been emphasized. Women who come out to self as lesbian may be any age. They may or may not have had a heterosexual past. They may or may not have met other lesbians. What they share is the experience of strong emotional feelings directed towards other women. These emotional feelings when combined with awareness of lesbianism as an option, and a level of emotional acceptance of homosexuality, may lead to identification of self as lesbian (although this outcome is obviously not necessarily the case). Coming out to self was often a gradual process. Coping with threat to identity was usually necessary.

Coming out to others, like coming out to self, needs to be interpreted within the social context. Some women had told certain family members, heterosexual friends or work colleagues about themselves. Others had not. For some the situation was ambiguous: they assumed others 'knew', but had not actually told them verbally. Decisions about whether or not to tell others were based on reasons that included perceptions of others' negative attitudes towards homosexuality; perceived need to protect others; need for support; or the desire to speak freely, and not to be assumed heterosexual. Reactions mentioned were often a mixture of positive, neutral or negative responses.

A main benefit of coming out (to self or others) was perceived as 'being yourself'.

For the lesbian participant, coming out was a major issue that affected her perceptions of self; the way she related to family, friends and work colleagues; and much of everyday life. For the heterosexual participant, lesbians tended to be invisible, rarely thought about, perhaps joked about, and the idea that a family member or friend might be lesbian had usually not been considered. For the lesbian participant, lesbian identity generally meant more than sex.

For the heterosexual participant, lesbianism tended to refer only to sex. Heterosexual participants tended to perceive lesbians as conforming to the masculine stereotype, while lesbian participants perceived lesbians generally as androgynous. However, both lesbian and heterosexual participants viewed the lesbian stereotype as masculine, aggressive, unattractive and abnormal; and perceived most people's perceptions of lesbians as largely negative. These stereotypes and perceptions, are reflected in the dominant social representations of gender and human nature.

The social context has been seen in terms of relevant social representations reflecting stereotypes, beliefs and attitudes; notions of gender, and abnormality; and from a social identity theory perspective, as involving power inequalities between women and men, and further inequality between homosexual and heterosexual groups. In particular, the effect of rigid notions of gender division, with underlying assumptions of heterosexuality, and dominant ideas on human nature and 'normality', have been considered as forming the basis for heterosexism.

The major findings of this study relating to beliefs, attitudes and stereotyping indicate that for any basic change in lesbians' experiences of coming out to occur, there needs to be change at the level of social representations. The most fundamental change required is in conceptualization of gender. Instead of rigid notions of sex categories, a more flexible conceptualization of gender that is not based on division and inequality between women and men, or on assumptions of heterosexuality, is necessary.

Although there will be some similarities between lesbians' and gay men's experiences of coming out, there are also likely to be fundamental differences. It is the power imbalance within our society between men and women that lies at the heart of these differences. Lesbianism poses a challenge to our largely heterosexual, male-dominated society that is different from that of male homosexuality.

Coming out has been considered from intra-psychic, interpersonal, intergroup and societal perspectives. A social-psychological framework that acknowledges and incorporates a perspective of the cultural/ideological level of analysis, an analysis of power issues between groups, and an understanding of the self as originating and developing within social interaction, provides a basis for considering coming out. Social representations, social identity theory, and Mead's notion of self, together, provide a social-psychological perspective that takes into account social/collective issues, and incorporates a focus on power inequalities between groups.

Although the social context has been emphasized, the approach taken in investigation has been largely individual (i.e. individual depth interviews). Individuals may be seen as the product of social interaction and the social context, as reflecting the social context and interacting with it, and as creating the social context. For a comprehensive perspective of social phenomena, examination at both the social/societal and the individual/interpersonal levels is necessary. The individual level should not be neglected. It provides one way of accessing the social level, and one of the ways in which a picture of the social may be made more complete. Thus, this study has attempted to look at the individual within the social context, taking into account issues of power.

Methodological limitations of this study indicate that results must be interpreted with caution. The methodology used, however, may be seen as having permitted some part, at least, of the richness and complexity of issues involved in coming out to have emerged, and be reflected in the findings.

The study indicates a number of possible directions for future study of coming out. Although potentially problematic in design and practicality, the ideal way to investigate 'coming out to self ' would be a longitudinal study, beginning in early childhood, and following through into later childhood, adolescence, young adulthood, and the main adult years. One difficulty would be the large initial sample required as the proportion of those who later identify as lesbian is likely to be small. 'Coming out to others' could be investigated further by interviewing heterosexual women and men who have had close friends or relatives come out to them as lesbian. A more social perspective of coming out could be investigated using group interviews and/or media content analysis. Studies that consider class, race and disability are also necessary. Taking a social identity perspective, the relative importance of lesbian identity in comparison with other group memberships might be examined.

In summary, the major issues that structure the coming-out experiences of individual lesbians are to a large extent located within the social context: the content of dominant social representations of gender and human nature; and power inequalities between women and men. It is modifications at the level of social representations that need to occur if coming out is to become an easier process. Most fundamentally, it is suggested that conceptualization of gender must change.

This book began with a look at an imaginary lesbian going through the process of coming out to herself, meeting other lesbians for the first time, considering whether to come out to family and friends, and dealing with the consequences of being out, or not, to different people. This imaginary character's experiences may now be viewed with greater understanding. She reflected in particular the perceptions of women who perceive themselves as 'always' having been lesbian. While her experiences related especially to women growing up in Britain during the 1950s and 1960s, many aspects of her coming out were common to older and younger women. She experienced the process of coming out to herself isolated from contact with other lesbians. Does pressure to conform to heterosexuality, from family, peers, school and society in general, still lead to the same isolation for young lesbians? Although today's society may be comparatively more open, the evidence of this study indicates such experiences continue to arise. The imaginary lesbian illustrated one pathway through the coming-out process. The main study has demonstrated more of the complexities and ambiguities involved, and focused attention on the social context.

My vision for the future is of a society with fundamentally modified social representations of gender and human nature. There would be a flexible reconceptualization of gender that was not based only/predominantly on heterosexual relations. This would include a blurring of gender division; and an emphasis on human qualities rather than on masculinity and femininity. Lesbianism would be perceived as part of the 'normal' diversity of human relations. There would be recognition, acceptance and encouragement of diversity. In such a context, coming out as lesbian would no longer be a major issue.

References

Abrams, D., Carter, J. and Hogg, M.A. (1989) Perceptions of male homosexuality: an application of social identity theory. *Social Behaviour*, 4, 253–64.

Adelman, M. (1990) Stigma, gay lifestyles, and adjustment to aging: a study of later-life gay men and lesbians. *Journal of Homosexuality*, 20(3/4), 7–32.

Aguero, J.E., Bloch, L. and Byrne, D. (1984) The relationship among sexual beliefs, attitudes, experience and homophobia. In J.P. De Cecco (ed.) (1985) *Bashers, Baiters and Bigots*, pp. 95–107. New York: Harrington Park Press.

Allport, G.W. (1954) *The Nature of Prejudice*. Cambridge, MA: Addison-Wesley.

American Psychiatric Association (1987) *Diagnostic and Statistical Manual of Mental Disorders*. Third edition, revised. Washington, DC: American Psychiatric Association.

American Psychiatric Association (1993) Position statement on homosexuality. *American Journal of Psychiatry*, 150(4), 686.

Appleby, Y. (1994) Out in the margins. *Disability and Society*, 9(1), 19–32.

Ardill, S. and O'Sullivan, S. (1990) Butch/femme obsessions. *Feminist Review*, 34, 79–85.

Armitage, G., Dickey, J. and Sharples, S. (1987) *Out of the Gutter: A Survey of the Treatment of Homosexuality by the Press*. London: Campaign for Press and Broadcasting Freedom.

Averill, J.R. (1985) The social construction of emotion: with special reference to love. In K.J. Gergen and K.E. Davis (eds) *The Social Construction of the Person*, pp. 89–109. New York: Springer-Verlag.

Baetz, R. (1984) The coming-out process: violence against lesbians. In T. Darty and S. Potter (eds) *Women-Identified Women*, pp. 45–50. Palo Alto, CA: Mayfield.

Bancroft, J. (1994) Homosexual orientation: the search for a biological basis. *British Journal of Psychiatry*, 164, 437–40.

Bell, A.P., Weinberg, M.S. and Hammersmith, S.K. (1981) *Sexual Preference: Its Development in Men and Women*. Kinsey Institute for Sex Research, Bloomington: Indiana University Press.

Bem, S.L. (1974) The measurement of psychological androgyny. *Journal of Consulting and Clinical Psychology*, 42(2), 155–62.

Bem, S.L. (1981) Gender schema theory: a cognitive account of sex typing. *Psychological Review*, 88, 354–64.

Bem, S.L. (1993) *The Lenses of Gender: Transforming the Debate on Sexual Inequality*. New Haven and London: Yale University Press.

Berg, J.H. and Derlega, V.J. (1987) Themes in the study of self-disclosure. In V.J. Derlega and J.H. Berg (eds) *Self-Disclosure: Theory, Research and Therapy*, pp. 1–8. New York and London: Plenum Press.

Berger, C.R. and Kellermann, K. (1989) Personal opacity and social information gathering: explorations in strategic communication. *Communication Research*, 16, 314–51.

Berger, G., Hank, L., Rauzi, T. and Simkins, L. (1987) Detection of sexual orientation by heterosexuals and homosexuals. *Journal of Homosexuality*, 13(4), 83–100.

Berger, R.M. (1984) Realities of gay and lesbian aging. *Social Work*, 29(1), 57–62.

Berlant, L. and Freeman, E. (1993) Queer nationality. In M. Warner (ed.) *Fear of a Queer Planet: Queer Politics and Social Theory*, pp. 193–229. Minneapolis and London: University of Minnesota Press.

Black, K.N. and Stevenson, M.R. (1984) The relationship of self-reported sex-role characteristics and attitudes toward homosexuality. In J.P. De Cecco (ed.) (1985) *Bashers, Baiters and Bigots*, pp. 83–93. New York: Harrington Park Press.

Blumstein, P. and Schwartz, P. (1990) Intimate relationships and the creation of sexuality. In D.P. McWhirter, S.A. Sanders and J.M. Reinisch (eds) *Homosexuality/Heterosexuality: Concepts of Sexual Orientation*, pp. 307–20. New York and Oxford: Oxford University Press.

Bradford, J., Ryan, C. and Rothblum, E.D. (1994) National Lesbian Health Care Survey: implications for mental health care. *Journal of Consulting and Clinical Psychology*, 62(2), 228–42.

Breakwell, G.M. (1986) *Coping with Threatened Identities*. London and New York: Methuen.

Breakwell, G.M. (1990) Social beliefs about gender differences. In C. Fraser and G. Gaskell (eds) *The Social Psychological Study of Widespread Beliefs*, pp. 210–25. Oxford: Clarendon Press.

Breakwell, G.M. (1994) Review of *In a Different Voice* by Carol Gilligan. *Feminism and Psychology*, 4(3), 404–6.

Brooks, V.R. (1981) *Minority Stress and Lesbian Women*. Lexington, MA: Lexington Books, D.C. Heath.

Broverman, I.K., Broverman, D.M., Clarkson, F.E., Rosenkrantz, P.S. and Vogel, S.R. (1970) Sex-role stereotypes and clinical judgments of mental health. *Journal of Consulting and Clinical Psychology*, 34(1), 1–7.

Brown, L.M. and Gilligan, C. (1992) *Meeting at the Crossroads: Women's Psychology and Girls' Development*. Cambridge, MA and London: Harvard University Press.

Brown, L.S. (1992) While waiting for the revolution: the case for a lesbian feminist psychotherapy. *Feminism and Psychology*, 2(2), 239–53.

Brown, L.S. (1995) Lesbian identities: concepts and issues. In A.R. D'Augelli and C.J. Patterson (eds) *Lesbian, Gay, and Bisexual Identities over the*

Lifespan: Psychological Perspectives, pp. 3–23. New York and Oxford: Oxford University Press.

Browning, C. (1982) Changing theories of lesbianism: challenging the stereotypes. In T. Darty and S. Potter (eds) (1984) *Women-Identified Women*, pp. 11–30. Palo Alto, CA: Mayfield.

Browning, C. (1987) Therapeutic issues and intervention strategies with young adult lesbian clients: a developmental approach. *Journal of Homosexuality*, 14(1/2), 45–52.

Bruner, J.S. (1957) On perceptual readiness. *Psychological Review*, 64(2), 123–52.

Buhrke, R.A. (1989) Incorporating lesbian and gay issues into counselor training: a resource guide. *Journal of Counseling and Development*, 68(1), 77–80.

Burke, M.E. (1993) *Coming Out of the Blue: British Police Officers Talk about their Lives in 'The Job' as Lesbians, Gays and Bisexuals*. London: Cassell.

Burns, R.B. (1979) *The Self Concept*. New York: Longman.

Buss, D.M. (1995) Psychological sex differences: origins through sexual selection. *American Psychologist*, 50(3), 164–8.

Butler, J. (1991) Imitation and gender insubordination. In D. Fuss (ed.) *Inside/Out: Lesbian Theories, Gay Theories*, pp. 13–31. New York and London: Routledge.

Buxton, A.P. (1994) *The Other Side of the Closet: The Coming-Out Crisis for Straight Spouses and Families*. Revised edition. New York: Wiley.

Card, C. (1995) *Lesbian Choices*. New York: Columbia University Press.

Cass, V.C. (1979) Homosexual identity formation: a theoretical model. *Journal of Homosexuality*, 4(3), 219–35.

Cass, V.C. (1990) The implications of homosexual identity formation for the Kinsey Model and Scale of Sexual Preference. In D.P. McWhirter, S.A. Sanders and J.M. Reinisch (eds) *Homosexuality/Heterosexuality: Concepts of Sexual Orientation*, pp. 239–66. New York and Oxford: Oxford University Press.

Cassell, C. and Walsh, S. (1993) Being seen but not heard: barriers to women's equality in the workplace. *The Psychologist*, 6(3), 110–14.

Cavin, S. (1985) *Lesbian Origins*. San Francisco: Ism Press.

De Cecco, J.P. (1990) Sex and more sex: a critique of the Kinsey conception of human sexuality. In D.P. McWhirter, S.A. Sanders and J.M. Reinisch (eds) *Homosexuality/Heterosexuality: Concepts of Sexual Orientation*, pp. 367–86. New York and Oxford: Oxford University Press.

Chaikin, A.L. and Derlega, V.J. (1976) Self-disclosure. In J.W. Thibaut, J.T. Spence and R.C. Carson (eds) *Contemporary Topics in Social Psychology*, pp. 177–210. Morristown, NJ: General Learning Press.

Chan, C.S. (1995) Issues of sexual identity in an ethnic minority: the case of Chinese American lesbians, gay men, and bisexual people. In A.R. D'Augelli and C.J. Patterson (eds) *Lesbian, Gay, and Bisexual Identities over the Lifespan: Psychological Perspectives*, pp. 87–101. New York and Oxford: Oxford University Press.

Chapman, B.E. and Brannock, J.C. (1987) Proposed model of lesbian identity development: an empirical examination. *Journal of Homosexuality*, 14(3/4), 69–80.

Cohn, N. (1976) *Europe's Inner Demons*. St Albans: Paladin.

Coleman, E. (1987) Introduction. *Journal of Homosexuality*, 14(1/2), 1–8.

Coleman, E. (1990) Toward a synthetic understanding of sexual orientation. In D.P. McWhirter, S.A. Sanders and J.M. Reinisch (eds) *Homosexuality/Heterosexuality: Concepts of Sexual Orientation*, pp. 267–76. New York and Oxford: Oxford University Press.

Coleman, E. and Remafedi, G. (1989) Gay, lesbian, and bisexual adolescents: a critical challenge to counselors. *Journal of Counseling and Development*, 68(1), 36–40.

Coleman, P. (1980) *Christian Attitudes to Homosexuality*. London: SPCK.

Comely, L. (1991) Lesbian and gay teenagers at school: how can educational psychologists help? Paper presented at the annual conference of the British Psychological Society.

Condor, S. (1987) From sex categories to gender boundaries: reconsidering sex as a 'stimulus variable' in social psychological research. British Psychological Society, *Social Psychology Section Newsletter*, 17.

Condor, S. (1989) 'Biting into the future': social change and the social identity of women. In S. Skevington and D. Baker (eds) *The Social Identity of Women*, pp. 15–39. London: Sage.

Cozby, P.C. (1973) Self-disclosure: a literature review. *Psychological Bulletin*, 79(2).

Crawford, J., Kippax, S., Onyx, J., Gault, U. and Benton, P. (1992) *Emotion and Gender: Constructing Meaning from Memory*. London: Sage.

Cruikshank, M. (1990) Lavender and gray: a brief survey of lesbian and gay aging studies. *Journal of Homosexuality*, 20(3/4), 77–87.

Dank, B.M. (1971) Coming out in the gay world. *Psychiatry*, 34 (May), 180–97.

Davison, G.C. and Neale, J.M. (1982) *Abnormal Psychology*. Third edition. New York: Wiley.

Davison, G.C. and Neale, J.M. (1994) *Abnormal Psychology*. Sixth edition. New York: Wiley.

Deaux, K. (1985) Sex and gender. *Annual Review of Psychology*, 36, 49–81.

Deaux, K. and Major, B. (1987) Putting gender into context: an interactive model of gender-related behavior. *Psychological Review*, 94(3), 369–89.

Denman, F. (1993) Prejudice and homosexuality. *British Journal of Psychotherapy*, 9(3), 346–58.

Derlega, V.J. and Berg, J.H. (eds) (1987) *Self-Disclosure: Theory, Research and Therapy*. New York and London: Plenum Press.

Derlega, V.J., Metts, S., Petronio, S. and Margulis, S.T. (1993) *Self-Disclosure*. Newbury Park, CA and London: Sage.

Deschamps, J.-C. (1983) Social attribution. In J. Jaspars, F.D. Fincham and M. Hewstone (eds) *Attribution Theory and Research: Conceptual, Developmental and Social Dimensions*, pp. 223–40. Academic Press, London, European Monographs in Social Psychology 32.

DiLapi, E.M. (1989) Lesbian mothers and the motherhood hierarchy. *Journal of Homosexuality*, 18(1/2), 101–21.

Doise, W. (1984) Social representations, inter-group experiments and levels of analysis. In R.M. Farr and S. Moscovici (eds) *Social Representations*, pp. 255–68. Cambridge: Cambridge University Press.

Dollimore, J. (1988) Different desires: subjectivity and transgression in Wilde and Gide. In H. Abelove, M.A. Barale and D.M. Halperin (eds) (1993) *The Lesbian and Gay Studies Reader*, pp. 626–41. New York and London: Routledge.

Duberman, M.B., Vicinus, M. and Chauncey, G. Jr (eds) (1989) *Hidden From History: Reclaiming the Gay and Lesbian Past*. Harmondsworth: Penguin.

Dunne, E.J. (1987) Helping gay fathers come out to their children. *Journal of Homosexuality*, 14(1/2), 213–22.

Durell, A. (1983) At home. In B. Galloway (ed.) *Prejudice and Pride*, pp. 1–18. London: Routledge & Kegan Paul.

Duveen, G. and Lloyd, B. (1986) The significance of social identities. *British Journal of Social Psychology*, 25, 219–30.

Duveen, G. and Lloyd, B. (1987) On gender as a social representation. Paper presented to the symposium on developmental reconstructions of social representations at the annual conference of the British Psychological Society, University of Sussex.

Dworkin, S.H. and Gutierrez, F. (1989) Introduction to Special Issue. Counselors be aware: clients come in every size, shape, color, and sexual orientation. *Journal of Counseling and Development*, 68(1), 6–8.

Eagly, A.H. and Chaiken, S. (1993) *The Psychology of Attitudes*. San Diego, CA: Harcourt Brace Janovich.

Eagly, A.H. (1995) The science and politics of comparing women and men. *American Psychologist*, 50(3), 145–58.

Elliott, P.E. (1985) Theory and research on lesbian identity formation. *International Journal of Women's Studies*, 8(1), 64–71.

D'Emilio, J. (1983) Capitalism and gay identity. In H. Abelove, M.A. Barale and D.M. Halperin (eds) (1993) *The Lesbian and Gay Studies Reader*, pp. 467–76. New York and London: Routledge.

Epstein, D. (ed.) (1994) *Challenging Lesbian and Gay Inequalities in Education*. Buckingham and Philadelphia: Open University Press.

Ernulf, K.E., Innala, S.M. and Whitam, F.L. (1989) Biological explanation, psychological explanation, and tolerance of homosexuals: a cross-national analysis of beliefs and attitudes. *Psychological Reports*, 65, 1003–10.

Ettorre, E.M. (1980) *Lesbians, Women and Society*. London: Routledge & Kegan Paul.

Faderman, L. (1981) *Surpassing the Love of Men*. London: Junction Books.

Farina, A., Allen, J.G. and Saul, B.B. (1968) The role of the stigmatized person in affecting social relationships. *Journal of Personality*, 36(2), 169–82.

Farr, R. (1982) Interviewing: the social psychology of the interview. In F. Fransella (ed.) *Psychology for Occupational Therapists*, pp. 151–70. London: Macmillan and BPS.

Fassinger, R.E. (1993) And gladly teach: lesbian and gay issues in education. In L. Diamant (ed.) *Homosexual Issues in the Workplace*, pp. 119–42. Washington and London: Taylor & Francis.

Fine, R. (1987) Psychoanalytic theory. In L. Diamant (ed.) *Male and Female Homosexuality: Psychological Approaches*. Washington: Hemisphere.

Firth-Cozens, J. and West, M.A. (eds) (1991) *Women at Work: Psychological and Organizational Perspectives*. Milton Keynes and Philadelphia: Open University Press.

Forstein, M. (1988) Homophobia: an overview. *Psychiatric Annals*, 18(1), 33–6.

Foucault, M. (1979) *The History of Sexuality: An Introduction*. Harmondsworth: Penguin.

Franke, R. and Leary, M.R. (1991) Disclosure of sexual orientation by lesbians and gay men: a comparison of private and public processes. *Journal of Social and Clinical Psychology*, 10(3), 262–9.

Franklin, S. and Stacey, J. (1988) Dyke-tactics for difficult times. In C. McEwen and S. O'Sullivan (eds) *Out the Other Side: Contemporary Lesbian Writing*, pp. 220–32. London: Virago.

Freud, S. (1905) Three essays on the theory of sexuality. In the Pelican Freud Library, vol. 7, *On Sexuality* (1977). Harmondsworth: Penguin.

Freud, S. (1917) Introductory lectures on psychoanalysis. In the Pelican Freud Library, vol. 1, *Introductory Lectures on Psychoanalysis* (1973). Harmondsworth: Penguin.

Friend, R.A. (1987) The individual and social psychology of aging: clinical implications for lesbians and gay men. *Journal of Homosexuality*, 14(1/2), 307–31.

Friend, R.A. (1990) Older lesbian and gay people: a theory of successful aging. *Journal of Homosexuality*, 20(3/4), 99–118.

Frieze, I.H., Parsons, J.E., Johnson, P.B., Ruble, D.N. and Zellman, G.L. (1978) *Women and Sex Roles: A Social Psychological Perspective*. New York and London: W.W. Norton.

Galloway, B. (ed.) (1983) *Prejudice and Pride*. London: Routledge & Kegan Paul.

Garnets, L., Hancock, K.A., Cochran, S.D., Goodchilds, J. and Peplau, L.A. (1991) Issues in psychotherapy with lesbians and gay men: a survey of psychologists. *American Psychologist*, 46(9), 964–72.

Gartrell, N. (1981) The lesbian as a 'single' woman. In M.R. Walsh (ed.) *The Psychology of Women: Ongoing Debates*, pp. 412–20. New Haven and London: Yale University Press.

Gay Teachers' Group (1987) *School's Out: Lesbian and Gay Rights in Education*. London.

Gentry, C.S. (1987) Social distance regarding male and female homosexuals. *Journal of Social Psychology*, 127(2), 199–208.

Gershman, H. (1983) The stress of coming out. *American Journal of Psychoanalysis*, 43(2), 129–38.

Gerson, J.M. and Peiss, K. (1985) Boundaries, negotiation, consciousness: reconceptualizing gender relations. *Social Problems*, 32(4), 317–31.

Giddens, A. (1992) *The Transformation of Intimacy: Sexuality, Love and Eroticism in Modern Societies*. Cambridge: Polity.

Gilligan, C. (1982) *In a Different Voice: Psychological Theory and Women's Development*. Cambridge, MA and London: Harvard University Press.

Goffman, E. (1959) *The Presentation of Self in Everyday Life*. Harmondsworth: Penguin.

Goffman, E. (1963) *Stigma*. Harmondsworth: Penguin.

Golden, C. (1987) Diversity and variability in women's sexual identities. In

Boston Lesbian Psychologies Collective (eds) *Lesbian Psychologies: Explorations and Challenges*, pp. 19–34. Urbana and Chicago: University of Illinois Press.

Golombok, S. and Fivush, R. (1994) *Gender Development*. Cambridge: Cambridge University Press.

Gonsiorek, J.C. and Rudolph, J.R. (1991) Homosexual identity: coming out and other developmental events. In J.C. Gonsiorek and J.D. Weinrich (eds) *Homosexuality: Research Implications for Public Policy*, pp. 161–76. Newbury Park, CA and London: Sage.

Gove, W.R. (1980) Mental illness and psychiatric treatment among women. In M.R. Walsh (ed.) (1987) *The Psychology of Women: Ongoing Debates*, pp. 102–18. New Haven and London: Yale University Press.

Graddol, D. and Swann, J. (1989) *Gender Voices*. Oxford: Basil Blackwell.

Gramick, J. (1984) Developing a lesbian identity. In T. Darty and S. Potter (eds) *Women-Identified Women*, pp. 31–44. Palo Alto, CA: Mayfield.

Green, G.D. and Bozett, F.W. (1991) Lesbian mothers and gay fathers. In J.C. Gonsiorek and J.D. Weinrich (eds) *Homosexuality: Research Implications for Public Policy*, pp. 197–214. Newbury Park, CA and London: Sage.

Green, R. (1987) *The 'Sissy Boy Syndrome' and the Development of Homosexuality*. New Haven and London: Yale University Press.

Greene, B. (1994a) Ethnic-minority lesbians and gay men: mental health and treatment issues. *Journal of Consulting and Clinical Psychology*, 62(2), 243–51.

Greene, B. (1994b) Lesbian and gay sexual orientations: implications for clinical training, practice, and research. In B. Greene and G.M. Herek (eds) *Psychological Perspectives on Lesbian and Gay Issues*, vol. 1, *Lesbian and Gay Psychology: Theory, Research, and Clinical Applications*, pp. 1–24. Thousand Oaks, CA and London: Sage.

Griffin, C. (1985) *Typical Girls? Young Women from School to the Job Market*. London: Routledge & Kegan Paul.

Griffin, C. and Zukas, M. (eds) (1993) Coming out in psychology: lesbian psychologists talk. *Feminism and Psychology*, 3(1), 111–33.

Gross, L. (1993) *Contested Closets: The Politics and Ethics of Outing*. Minneapolis and London: University of Minnesota Press.

Gross, M.J. (1978) Changing attitudes toward homosexuality – or are they? *Perspectives in Psychiatric Care*, 16(2), 70–5.

Hall Carpenter Archives, Lesbian Oral History Group (1989) *Inventing Ourselves: Lesbian Life Stories*. London and New York: Routledge.

Hall, M. (1985) *The Lavender Couch: A Consumer's Guide to Psychotherapy for Lesbians and Gay Men*. Boston: Alyson.

Hall, M. (1989) Private experiences in the public domain: lesbians in organizations. In J. Hearn, D.L. Sheppard, P. Tancred-Sheriff and G. Burrell (eds) *The Sexuality of Organization*, pp. 125–38. London: Sage.

Halperin, D.M. (1989) Is there a history of sexuality? In H. Abelove, M.A. Barale and D.M. Halperin (eds) (1993) *The Lesbian and Gay Studies Reader*, pp. 416–31. New York and London: Routledge.

Hamer, D. with Ashbrook, P. (1994) *Out*: reflections on British television's first lesbian and gay magazine series. In D. Hamer and B. Budge (eds) *The Good, the Bad and the Gorgeous: Popular Culture's Romance with Lesbianism*, pp. 166–71. London: Pandora.

Hammersmith, S.K. (1987) A sociological approach to counseling homosexual clients and their families. *Journal of Homosexuality*, 14(1/2), 173–90.

Hancock, K.A. (1995) Psychotherapy with lesbians and gay men. In A.R. D'Augelli and C.J. Patterson (eds) *Lesbian, Gay, and Bisexual Identities over the Lifespan: Psychological Perspectives*, pp. 398–432. New York and Oxford: Oxford University Press.

Hanley-Hackenbruck, P. (1988) 'Coming out' and psychotherapy. *Psychiatric Annals*, 18(1), 29–32.

Hansard, House of Commons, Official Report, Parliamentary Debates, vol. 124, no. 65, 15 December 1987; vol. 129, no. 111, 9 March 1988.

Hansard, House of Lords, vol. 493, no. 77, 16 February 1988; vol. 493, no. 78, 17 February 1988.

Hanscombe, G.E. and Forster, J. (1982) *Rocking the Cradle: Lesbian Mothers*. Sheba Feminist Publishers.

Hare-Mustin, R.T. and Marecek, J. (eds) (1990) *Making a Difference: Psychology and the Construction of Gender*. New Haven and London: Yale University Press.

Harris, S. (1990) *Lesbian and Gay Issues in the English Classroom: The Importance of Being Honest*. Milton Keynes and Philadelphia: Open University Press.

Haste, H. (1993) *The Sexual Metaphor*. London: Harvester Wheatsheaf.

Haste, H. (1994) 'You've come a long way, babe': a catalyst of feminist conflicts. *Feminism and Psychology*, 4(3), 399–403.

Heath, A. and McMahon, D. (1991) Consensus and dissensus. In R. Jowell, L. Brook, and B. Taylor (eds) *British Social Attitudes: The 8th Report*, pp. 1–21. Aldershot: Dartmouth and SCPR.

Heider, F. (1958) *The Psychology of Interpersonal Relations*. New York: John Wiley.

Herdt, G. (1989) Introduction: gay and lesbian youth, emergent identities, and cultural scenes at home and abroad. *Journal of Homosexuality*, 17(1/2), 1–42.

Herek, G.M. (1984a) Attitudes toward lesbians and gay men: a factor-analytic study. In J.P. De Cecco (ed.) (1985) *Bashers, Baiters and Bigots*, pp. 39–51. New York: Harrington Park Press.

Herek, G.M. (1984b) Beyond 'homophobia': a social psychological perspective on attitudes toward lesbians and gay men. In J.P. De Cecco (ed.) (1985) *Bashers, Baiters and Bigots*, pp. 1–21. New York: Harrington Park Press.

Herek, G.M. (1988) Heterosexuals' attitudes toward lesbians and gay men: correlates and gender differences. *Journal of Sex Research*, 25(4), 451–77.

Herek, G.M. (1991) Stigma, prejudice, and violence against lesbians and gay men. In J.C. Gonsiorek and J.D. Weinrich (eds) *Homosexuality: Research Implications for Public Policy*, pp. 60–80. Newbury Park, CA and London: Sage.

Herek, G.M. (1994) Assessing heterosexuals' attitudes toward lesbians and gay men: a review of empirical research with the ATLG scale. In B. Greene and G.M. Herek (eds) *Psychological Perspectives on Lesbian and Gay Issues*, vol.

1, *Lesbian and Gay Psychology: Theory, Research, and Clinical Applications*, pp. 206–28. Thousand Oaks, CA and London: Sage.

Hetrick, E.S. and Martin, A.D. (1987) Developmental issues and their resolution for gay and lesbian adolescents. *Journal of Homosexuality*, 14(1/2), 25–43.

Hewstone, M. (1983) Attribution theory and common-sense explanations: an introductory overview. In M. Hewstone (ed.) *Attribution Theory: Social and Functional Extensions*, pp. 1–26. Oxford: Basil Blackwell.

Hewstone, M. (1989a) *Causal Attribution: From Cognitive Processes to Collective Beliefs*. Oxford: Basil Blackwell.

Hewstone, M. (1989b) Changing stereotypes with disconfirming information. In D. Bar-Tal, C.F. Graumann, A.W. Kruglanski and W. Stroebe (eds) *Stereotyping and Prejudice: Changing Conceptions*, pp. 207–23, Springer Series in Social Psychology, New York, Springer-Verlag.

Hewstone, M. and Jaspars, J.M.F. (1982) Intergroup relations and attribution processes. In H. Tajfel (ed.) *Social Identity and Intergroup Relations*, pp. 99–133. Cambridge: Cambridge University Press.

Hill, C.T. and Stull, D.E. (1987) Gender and self-disclosure: strategies for exploring the issues. In V.J. Derlega and J.H. Berg (eds) *Self-Disclosure: Theory, Research and Therapy*, pp. 81–100. New York and London: Plenum Press.

Hoagland, S.L. and Penelope, J. (1988) *For Lesbians Only: A Separatist Anthology*. London: Onlywomen Press.

Hodges, A. and Hutter, D. (1977) *With Downcast Gays*. Ontario, Canada: Pink Triangle Press.

Hogg, M.A. and Abrams, D. (1988) *Social Identifications: A Social Psychology of Intergroup Relations and Group Processes*. London and New York: Routledge.

Hollway, W. (1989) *Subjectivity and Method in Psychology: Gender, Meaning and Science*. London: Sage.

Holmes, S. (ed.) (1988) *Testimonies: A Collection of Lesbian Coming Out Stories*. Boston, MA: Alyson.

Hooper, C.A. (1992) *Mothers Surviving Child Sexual Abuse*. London and New York: Tavistock/Routledge.

Horney, K. (1926) The flight from womanhood: the masculinity complex in women as viewed by men and by women. In J.B. Miller (ed.) (1974) *Psychoanalysis and Women*, pp. 5–20. Harmondsworth: Penguin.

Howells, K. (1986) Sex roles and sexual behaviour. In D.J. Hargreaves and A.M. Colley (eds) *The Psychology of Sex Roles*. London: Harper & Row.

Huggins, S.L. (1989) A comparative study of self-esteem of adolescent children of divorced lesbian mothers and divorced heterosexual mothers. *Journal of Homosexuality*, 18(1–2), 123–35.

Hyde, J.S. and Plant, E.A. (1995) Magnitude of psychological gender differences: another side to the story. *American Psychologist*, 50(3), 159–61.

Iasenza, S. (1989) Some challenges of integrating sexual orientations into counselor training and research. *Journal of Counseling and Development*, 68(1), 73–6.

Jaspars, J. and Fraser, C. (1984) Attitudes and social representations. In R.M.

Farr and S. Moscovici (eds) *Social Representations*, pp. 101–23. Cambridge: Cambridge University Press.

Jeffreys, S. (1985) *The Spinster and her Enemies: Feminism and Sexuality 1890–1930*. London: Pandora.

Jeffreys, S. (1989) Butch and femme: now and then. In Lesbian History Group, *Not a Passing Phase*. London: The Women's Press.

Jeffreys, S. (1990) *Anticlimax: A Feminist Perspective on the Sexual Revolution*. London: The Women's Press.

Jeffreys, S. (1993) *The Lesbian Heresy: A Feminist Perspective on the Lesbian Sexual Revolution*. London: The Women's Press.

Jenks, R.J. (1986) Perceptions of two deviant and two non-deviant groups. *Journal of Social Psychology*, 126(6), 783–90.

Jensen, L., Gambles, D. and Olsen, J. (1988) Attitudes toward homosexuality: a cross cultural analysis of predictors. *International Journal of Social Psychiatry*, 34(1), 47–57.

Johnson, M. (1980) Mental illness and psychiatric treatment among women: a response. In M.R. Walsh (ed.) (1987) *The Psychology of Women: Ongoing Debates*, pp. 119–26. New Haven and London: Yale University Press.

Jones, E.E. and Davis, K.E. (1965) From acts to dispositions: the attribution process in person perception. In L. Berkowitz (ed.) *Advances in Experimental Social Psychology*, vol. 2. pp. 219–66. New York and London: Academic Press.

Jones, E.E. and Nisbett, R.E. (1972) The actor and the observer: divergent perceptions of the causes of behavior. In E.E. Jones, D.E. Kanouse, H.H. Kelley, R.E. Nisbett, S. Valins and B. Weiner (eds) *Attribution: Perceiving the Causes of Behavior*, pp. 79–94. Morristown, NJ: General Learning Press.

Jones, E.E., Farina, A., Hastorf, A.H., Markus, H., Miller, D.T. and Scott, R.A. (1984) *Social Stigma: The Psychology of Marked Relationships*. New York: W.H. Freeman.

Jourard, S.M. (1971) *The Transparent Self*. New York: Van Nostrand Reinhold.

Jowell, R., Witherspoon, S. and Brook, L. with Taylor, B. (eds) (1990) *British Social Attitudes: The 7th Report*. Aldershot: Gower, Social and Community Planning Research.

Kahn, M.J. (1991) Factors affecting the coming out process for lesbians. *Journal of Homosexuality*, 21(3), 47–70.

Kehoe, M. (1986) Lesbians over 65: a triply invisible minority. *Journal of Homosexuality*, 12(3/4), 139–52.

Kelley, H.H. (1967) Attribution theory in social psychology. In D. Levine (ed.) *Nebraska Symposium on Motivation. Current Theory and Research in Motivation*, vol. XV, pp. 192–240, University of Nebraska Press.

Kelvin, P. (1973) A social-psychological examination of privacy. *British Journal of Social and Clinical Psychology*, 12(3), 248–61.

Kerlinger, F.N. (1986) *Foundations of Behavioral Research*. Third Edition. New York: Holt, Rinehart and Winston.

Kimmel, D.C. (1978) Adult development and aging: a gay perspective. *Journal of Social Issues*, 34(3), 113–30.

Kinsey, A.C., Pomeroy, W.B., Martin, C.E. and Gebhard, P.H. (1953) *Sexual Behavior in the Human Female*. Philadelphia and London: W.B. Saunders.

Kirkpatrick, M. (1987) Clinical implications of lesbian mother studies. *Journal of Homosexuality*, 14(1/2), 201–11.

Kirsch, J.A.W. and Weinrich, J.D. (1991) Homosexuality, nature, and biology: is homosexuality natural? Does it matter? In J.C. Gonsiorek and J.D. Weinrich (eds) *Homosexuality: Research Implications for Public Policy*, pp. 13–31. Newbury Park, CA and London: Sage.

Kite, M.E. (1984) Sex differences in attitudes toward homosexuals: a meta-analytic review. In J.P. De Cecco (ed.) (1985) *Bashers, Baiters and Bigots*, pp. 69–81. New York: Harrington Park Press.

Kite, M.E. (1992) Individual differences in males' reactions to gay males and lesbians. *Journal of Applied Social Psychology*, 22, 1222–39.

Kite, M.E. (1994) When perceptions meet reality: individual differences in reactions to lesbians and gay men. In B. Greene and G.M. Herek (eds) *Psychological Perspectives on Lesbian and Gay Issues*, vol. 1, *Lesbian and Gay Psychology: Theory, Research, and Clinical Applications*, pp. 25–53. Thousand Oaks, CA and London: Sage.

Kite, M.E. and Deaux, K. (1986) Attitudes toward homosexuality: assessment and behavioral consequences. *Basic and Applied Social Psychology*, 7(2), 137–62.

Kite, M.E. and Deaux, K. (1987) Gender belief systems: homosexuality and implicit inversion theory. *Psychology of Women Quarterly*, 11, 83–96.

Kitzinger, C. (1987) *The Social Construction of Lesbianism*. London: Sage.

Kitzinger, C. (ed.) (1994) Sex differences research: feminist perspectives. *Feminism and Psychology*, 4(4), 501–6.

Kitzinger, C. (1995) Social constructionism: implications for lesbian and gay psychology. In A.R. D'Augelli and C.J. Patterson (eds) *Lesbian, Gay, and Bisexual Identities over the Lifespan: Psychological Perspectives*, pp. 136–61. New York and Oxford: Oxford University Press.

Kitzinger, C. and Stainton Rogers, R. (1985) A Q-methodological study of lesbian identities. *European Journal of Social Psychology*, 15, 167–87.

Kitzinger, C. and Perkins, R. (1993) *Changing our Minds: Lesbian Feminism and Psychology*. London: Onlywomen Press.

Klein, F. (1990) The need to view sexual orientation as a multivariable dynamic process: a theoretical perspective. In D.P. McWhirter, S.A. Sanders and J.M. Reinisch (eds) *Homosexuality/Heterosexuality: Concepts of Sexual Orientation*, pp. 277–82. New York and Oxford: Oxford University Press.

Kourany, R.F.C. (1987) Suicide among homosexual adolescents. *Journal of Homosexuality*, 13(4), 111–17.

Krieger, S. (1982) Lesbian identity and community: recent social science literature. *Signs*, 8(1), 91–108.

Krikler, B. (1988) Homosexuality in the eighties. *Journal of the British Association of Psychotherapists*, 19, 23–42.

Krippendorff, K. (1980) *Content Analysis: An Introduction to its Methodology*, vol. 5, The Sage Commtext Series. London and Beverly Hills: Sage.

Kristiansen, C.M. (1990) The symbolic/value-expressive function of outgroup attitudes among homosexuals. *Journal of Social Psychology*, 130(1), 61–9.

Kubler-Ross, E. (1969) *On Death and Dying*. New York: Macmillan.

LaFrance, M. and Banaji, M. (1992) Toward a reconsideration of the gender–

emotion relationship. In M.S. Clark (ed.) *Emotion and Social Behavior, Review of Personality and Social Psychology*, 14. London: Sage.

Laner, M.R. and Laner, R.H. (1980) Sexual preference or personal style? Why lesbians are disliked. *Journal of Homosexuality*, 5(4), 339–56.

Larsen, K.S., Reed, M. and Hoffman, S. (1980) Attitudes of heterosexuals toward homosexuality: a Likert-type scale and construct validity. *Journal of Sex Research*, 16(3), 245–57.

Leitner, L.M. and Cado, S. (1982) Personal constructs and homosexual stress. *Journal of Personality and Social Psychology*, 43(4), 869–72.

Lesbian History Group (1989) *Not A Passing Phase: Reclaiming Lesbians in History 1840–1985*. London: The Women's Press.

Levine, M.P. and Leonard, R. (1984) Discrimination against lesbians in the work force. In E.B. Freedman, B.C. Gelpi, S.L. Johnson and K.M. Weston (eds) (1985) *The Lesbian Issue. Essays from SIGNS*, pp. 187–97. Chicago and London: University of Chicago Press.

Lewis, J. (1992) *Women in Britain since 1945: Women, Family, Work and the State in the Post-War Years*. Oxford: Basil Blackwell.

Lewis, L.A. (1984) The coming-out process for lesbians: integrating a stable identity. *Social Work*, 29(5), 464–9.

Lloyd, B. and Duveen, G. (1992) *Gender Identities and Education: The Impact of Starting School*. London: Harvester Wheatsheaf.

Lonsdale, S. (1992) Patterns of paid work. In C. Glendinning and J. Millar (eds) *Women and Poverty in Britain: The 1990s*, pp. 95–109. Hemel Hempstead: Harvester Wheatsheaf.

McDermott, D., Tyndall, L. and Lichtenberg, J.W. (1989) Factors related to counselor preference among gays and lesbians. *Journal of Counseling and Development*, 68(1), 31–5.

MacDonald, A.P., Jr and Games, R.G. (1974) Some characteristics of those who hold positive and negative attitudes towards homosexuals. *Journal of Homosexuality*, 1, 9–27.

MacDonald, A.P., Jr, Huggins, J., Young, S. and Swanson, R.A. (1973) Attitudes toward homosexuality: preservation of sex morality or the double standard? *Journal of Consulting and Clinical Psychology*, 40(1), 161.

McIntosh, M. (1968) The homosexual role. *Social Problems*, 16(2), 182–92.

McIntosh, M. (1993) Queer theory and the war of the sexes. In J. Bristow and A.R. Wilson (eds) *Activating Theory: Lesbian, Gay and Bisexual Politics*, pp. 30–52. London: Lawrence & Wishart.

MacKinnon, C.A. (1979) *Sexual Harassment of Working Women: A Case of Sex Discrimination*. New Haven, CT: Yale University Press.

Margolies, L., Becker, M. and Jackson-Brewer, K. (1987) Internalized homophobia: identifying and treating the oppressor within. In Boston Lesbian Psychologies Collective (eds) *Lesbian Psychologies: Explorations and Challenges*, pp. 229–41. Urbana and Chicago: University of Illinois Press.

Markowe, L.A. (1985) Lesbians' perceptions of 'coming out'. Unpublished project report submitted in partial fulfilment of MSc degree at the London School of Economics.

Markowe, L.A. (1992) The 'coming out' process for lesbians: a comparison of lesbian and heterosexual perspectives. University of London, PhD thesis.

Martin, A.D. and Hetrick, E.S. (1988) The stigmatization of the gay and lesbian adolescent. *Journal of Homosexuality*, 15(1/2), 163–83.

Mason-John, V. (ed.) (1995) *Talking Black: Lesbians of African and Asian Descent Speak Out*. London: Cassell.

Mason-John, V. and Khambatta, A. (1993) *Lesbians Talk: Making Black Waves*. London: Scarlet Press.

Mead, G.H. (1934) *Mind, Self and Society: From the Standpoint of a Social Behaviorist*. C.W. Morris (ed.). Chicago: University of Chicago Press.

Michael, R.T., Gagnon, J.H., Laumann, E.O. and Kolata, G. (1994) *Sex in America: A Definitive Survey*. London: Little Brown.

Miell, D. and Duck, S. (1986) Strategies in developing friendships. In V.J. Derlega and B.A. Winstead (eds) *Friendship and Social Interaction*, pp. 129–43. New York: Springer-Verlag.

Mihalik, G.J. (1988) Sexuality and gender: an evolutionary perspective. *Psychiatric Annals*, 18(1), 40–2.

Miller, J.B. (1986) *Toward a New Psychology of Women*. Second edition. Harmondsworth: Penguin.

Miller, L.C. and Read, S.J. (1987) Why am I telling you this?: self-disclosure in a goal-based model of personality. In V.J. Derlega and J.H. Berg (eds) *Self-Disclosure: Theory, Research and Therapy*, pp. 35–58. New York and London: Plenum Press.

Miller, L.C., Berg, J.H. and Archer, R.L. (1983) Openers: individuals who elicit intimate self-disclosure. *Journal of Personality and Social Psychology*, 44(6), 1234–44.

Millham, J., San Miguel, C.L. and Kellogg, R. (1976) A factor-analytic conceptualization of attitudes toward male and female homosexuals. *Journal of Homosexuality*, 2(1), 3–10.

Mitchell, J. (1974) *Psychoanalysis and Feminism*. Harmondsworth: Penguin.

Mohr, R.D. (1992) *Gay Ideas: Outing and Other Controversies*. Boston: Beacon Press.

Money, J. (1987) Sin, sickness or status? Homosexual gender identity and psychoneuroendocrinology. *American Psychologist*, 42(4), 384–99.

Money, J. (1988) *Gay, Straight and In-between: The Sexology of Erotic Orientation*. New York and Oxford: Oxford University Press.

De Monteflores, C. and Schultz, S.J. (1978) Coming out: similarities and differences for lesbians and gay men. *Journal of Social Issues*, 34(3), 59–72.

Morgan, K.S. and Eliason, M.J. (1992) The role of psychotherapy in Caucasian lesbians' lives. *Women and Therapy*, 13(4), 27–52.

Moscovici, S. (1984) The phenomenon of social representations. In R.M. Farr and S. Moscovici (eds) *Social Representations*, pp. 3–69. Cambridge: Cambridge University Press.

Moscovici, S. and Hewstone, M. (1983) Social representations and social explanations: from the 'naive' to the 'amateur' scientist. In M. Hewstone (ed.) *Attribution Theory: Social and Functional Extensions*. Oxford: Basil Blackwell.

Moses, A.E. (1978) *Identity Management in Lesbian Women*. New York: Praeger.

Moses, A.E. and Hawkins, R.O. (1982) *Counseling Lesbian Women and Gay Men*. St Louis, MO: C.V. Mosby.

Muller, A. (1987) *Parents Matter: Parents' Relationships with Lesbian Daughters and Gay Sons*. Tallahassee, FL: Naiad.

Nadler, R.D. (1990) Homosexual behavior in nonhuman primates. In D.P. McWhirter, S.A. Sanders and J.M Reinisch (eds) *Homosexuality/Heterosexuality: Concepts of Sexual Orientation*, pp. 138–70. New York and Oxford: Oxford University Press.

Neild, S. and Pearson, R. (1992) *Women Like Us*. London: The Women's Press.

Neisen, J.H. (1987) Resources for families with a gay/lesbian member. *Journal of Homosexuality*, 14(1/2), 239–51.

Newman, B.S. (1989) The relative importance of gender role attitudes to male and female attitudes toward lesbians. *Sex Roles*, 21, 451–65.

Nicolson, P. (1993) The psychology of women. *The Psychologist*, 6(3), 101.

Oakes, P. (1987) The salience of social categories. In J.C. Turner et al. (eds) *Rediscovering the Social Group*, pp. 117–41. Oxford and New York: Basil Blackwell.

Oakes, P.J., Haslam, S.A. and Turner, J.C. (1994) *Stereotyping and Social Reality*. Oxford: Basil Blackwell.

Oakley, A. (1981a) Interviewing women: a contradiction in terms. In H. Roberts (ed.) *Doing Feminist Research*. London: Routledge & Kegan Paul.

Oakley, A. (1981b) *Subject Women*. London: Fontana Press.

Oliver, M.B. and Hyde, J.S. (1993) Gender differences in sexuality: a meta-analysis. *Psychological Bulletin*, 114(1), 29–51.

Oliver, M.B. and Hyde, J.S. (1995) Gender differences in attitudes toward homosexuality: a reply to Whitley and Kite. *Psychological Bulletin*, 117(1), 155–8.

Olson, M.R. (1987) A study of gay and lesbian teachers. *Journal of Homosexuality*, 13(4), 73–81.

Olson, J.M and Zanna, M.P. (1993) Attitudes and attitude change. *Annual Review of Psychology*, 44, 117–54.

Onlywomen Press (eds) (1981) *Love your Enemy? The Debate between Heterosexual Feminism and Political Lesbianism*. London: Onlywomen Press.

Oppenheim, A.N. (1992) *Questionnaire Design, Interviewing and Attitude Measurement*. London: Pinter.

Page, S. and Yee, M. (1985) Conception of male and female homosexual stereotypes among university undergraduates. *Journal of Homosexuality*, 12(1), 109–18.

Patterson, C.J. (1994) Children of the lesbian baby boom: behavioral adjustment, self-concepts, and sex role identity. In B. Greene and G.M. Herek (eds) *Psychological Perspectives on Lesbian and Gay Issues*, vol. 1, *Lesbian and Gay Psychology: Theory, Research, and Clinical Applications*, pp. 156–75. Thousand Oaks, CA and London: Sage.

Penelope, J. and Wolfe, S.J. (eds) (1989) *The Original Coming Out Stories*. Second edition. Freedom, CA: The Crossing Press.

Perkins, R. (1991) Therapy for lesbians? The case against. *Feminism and Psychology*, 1(3), 325–38.

Petronio, S. and Bantz, C. (1991) Controlling the ramifications of disclosure:

'Don't tell anybody but . . .' *Journal of Language and Social Psychology*, 10(4), 263–9.

Phelan, S. (1993) (Be)coming out: lesbian identity and politics. *Signs*, 18(4), 765–90.

Pilgrim, D. (1991) Psychotherapy and social blinkers. *The Psychologist*, 14(2), 52–5.

Plasek, J.W. and Allard, J. (1984) Misconceptions of homophobia. In J.P. De Cecco (ed.) (1985) *Bashers, Baiters and Bigots*, pp. 23–37. New York: Harrington Park Press.

Plummer, K. (1981) Going gay: identities, life cycles and lifestyles in the male gay world. In J. Hart and D. Richardson (eds) *The Theory and Practice of Homosexuality*, pp. 93–110. London: Routledge & Kegan Paul.

Plummer, K. (1983) *Documents of Life*. London: George Allen and Unwin.

Plummer, K. (1989) Lesbian and gay youth in England. *Journal of Homosexuality*, 17(3/4), 195–223.

Ponse, B. (1978) *Identities in the Lesbian World*. Westport, CT and London: Greenwood Press.

Puddephatt, A. (1991) Private lives and public oppression. *Guardian*, 31 July 1991, 17.

Purkhardt, S.C. (1993) *Transforming Social Representations: A Social Psychology of Common Sense and Science*. London and New York: Routledge/LSE.

Raphael, S. and Robinson, M. (1980) The older lesbian: love relationships and friendship patterns. In T. Darty and S. Potter (eds) (1984) *Women-Identified Women*, pp. 67–82. Palo Alto, CA: Mayfield.

Reinhold, S. (1994) Through the Parliamentary looking glass: 'real' and 'pretend' families in contemporary British politics. *Feminist Review*, 48, 61–79.

Reynolds, M. (ed.) (1993) *The Penguin Book of Lesbian Short Stories*. London: Viking.

Rich, A. (1981) *Compulsory Heterosexuality and Lesbian Existence*. London: Onlywomen Press.

Richardson, D. (1981a) Lesbian identities. In J. Hart and D. Richardson (eds) *The Theory and Practice of Homosexuality*, pp. 111–24. London: Routledge & Kegan Paul.

Richardson, D. (1981b) Theoretical perspectives on homosexuality. In J. Hart and D. Richardson (eds) *The Theory and Practice of Homosexuality*, pp. 5–37. London: Routledge & Kegan Paul.

Richardson, D. (1987a) Recent challenges to traditional assumptions about homosexuality: some implications for practice. *Journal of Homosexuality*, 13(4), 1–12.

Richardson, D. (1987b) *Women and the AIDS Crisis*. London: Pandora.

Richardson, D. and Hart, J. (1981) The development and maintenance of a homosexual identity. In J. Hart and D. Richardson (eds) *The Theory and Practice of Homosexuality*, pp. 73–92. London: Routledge & Kegan Paul.

Risman, B. and Schwartz, P. (1988) Sociological research on male and female homosexuality. *Annual Review of Sociology*, 14, 125–47.

Robinson, B.E., Walters, L.H. and Skeen, P. (1989) Response of parents to learning that their child is homosexual and concern over AIDS: a national study. *Journal of Homosexuality*, 18(1/2), 59–80.

Rose, L. (1994) Homophobia among doctors. *British Medical Journal*, 308, 586–7.

Rosenberg, M. (1979) *Conceiving the Self*. New York: Basic Books.

Rosenblum, L.A. (1990) Primates, homo sapiens, and homosexuality. In D.P. McWhirter, S.A. Sanders and J.M Reinisch (eds) *Homosexuality/Heterosexuality: Concepts of Sexual Orientation*, pp. 171–4. New York and Oxford: Oxford University Press.

Ross, L. (1977) The intuitive psychologist and his shortcomings: distortions in the attribution process. In L. Berkowitz (ed.) *Advances in Experimental Social Psychology*, vol. 10, pp. 174–220. New York and London: Academic Press.

Ross, M.W. (1983) Homosexuality and social sex roles: a re-evaluation. In M.W. Ross (ed.) *Homosexuality and Social Sex Roles*, pp. 1–6. New York: Haworth Press.

Rothblum, E.D. (1990) Depression among lesbians: an invisible and unresearched phenomenon. *Journal of Gay and Lesbian Psychotherapy*, 1(3), 67–87.

Rothblum, E.D. (1994) 'I only read about myself on bathroom walls': The need for research on the mental health of lesbians and gay men. *Journal of Consulting and Clinical Psychology*, 62(2), 213–20.

Rothblum, E.D. and Brehony, K.A. (1993) *Boston Marriages: Romantic but Asexual Relationships among Contemporary Lesbians*. Amherst: University of Massachusetts Press.

Ruse, M. (1988) *Homosexuality: A Philosophical Inquiry*. Oxford: Basil Blackwell.

Rust, P.C. (1993) 'Coming out' in the age of social constructionism: sexual identity formation among lesbian and bisexual women. *Gender and Society*, 7(1), 50–77.

Salmon, P. (ed.) (1991) Psychotherapy and the wider world. *The Psychologist*, 14(2), 50–1.

Sanders, S.A., Reinisch, J.M. and McWhirter, D.P. (1990) Homosexuality/heterosexuality: an overview. In D.P. McWhirter, S.A. Sanders and J.M. Reinisch (eds) *Homosexuality/Heterosexuality: Concepts of Sexual Orientation*, pp. xix–xxvii. New York and Oxford: Oxford University Press.

Savin-Williams, R.C. (1989) Parental influences on the self-esteem of gay and lesbian youths: a reflected appraisals model. *Journal of Homosexuality*, 17(1/2), 93–109.

Savin-Williams, R.C. (1994) Verbal and physical abuse as stressors in the lives of lesbian, gay male, and bisexual youths: associations with school problems, running away, substance abuse, prostitution, and suicide. *Journal of Consulting and Clinical Psychology*, 62(2), 261–9.

Schippers, J. (1989) Homosexual identity: essentialism and constructionism. In D. Altman et al. (eds) *Which Homosexuality?* pp. 139–48. London: GMP.

Schneider, B.E. (1986) Coming out at work: bridging the private/public gap. *Work and Occupations*, 13(4), 463–87.

Schneider, M. (1989) Sappho was a right-on adolescent: growing up lesbian. *Journal of Homosexuality*, 17(1/2), 111–30.

Secord, P.F. and Backman, C.W. (1964) *Social Psychology*. New York: McGraw-Hill.

Sedgwick, E.K. (1990) Epistemology of the closet. In H. Abelove, M.A. Barale and D.M. Halperin (eds) (1993) *The Lesbian and Gay Studies Reader*, pp. 45–61. New York and London: Routledge.

Seidman, S. (1993) Identity and politics in a 'postmodern' gay culture: some historical and conceptual notes. In M. Warner (ed.) *Fear of a Queer Planet: Queer Politics and Social Theory*, pp. 105–42. Minneapolis and London: University of Minnesota Press.

Sender, K. (1992) Lesbians, therapy and politics: inclusion and diversity. *Feminism and Psychology*, 2(2), 255–7.

Shidlo, A. (1994) Internalized homophobia: conceptual and empirical issues in measurement. In B. Greene and G.M. Herek (eds) *Psychological Perspectives on Lesbian and Gay Issues*, vol. 1, *Lesbian and Gay Psychology: Theory, Research, and Clinical Applications*, pp. 176–205. Thousand Oaks, CA and London: Sage.

Shields, S.A. (1987) Women, men, and the dilemma of emotion. In P. Shaver and C. Hendrick (eds) *Sex and Gender*. London: Sage.

Simmons, J.L. (1965) Public stereotypes of deviants. *Social Problems*, 13(2), 223–32.

Skevington, S. (1989) A place for emotion in social identity theory. In S. Skevington and D. Baker (eds) *The Social Identity of Women*, pp. 40–58. London: Sage.

Skevington, S. and Baker, D. (eds) (1989) *The Social Identity of Women*. London: Sage.

Smail, D. (1991) Towards a radical environmentalist psychology of help. *The Psychologist*, 14(2), 61–4.

Smyth, C. (1992) *Lesbians Talk Queer Notions*. London: Scarlet Press.

Snyder, M. and Uranowitz, S.W. (1978) Reconstructing the past: some cognitive consequences of person perception. *Journal of Personality and Social Psychology*, 36(9), 941–50.

Snyder, M., Tanke, E.D. and Berscheid, E. (1977) Social perception and interpersonal behavior: on the self-fulfilling nature of social stereotypes. *Journal of Personality and Social Psychology*, 35(9), 656–66.

Socarides, C.W. (1981) Psychoanalytic perspectives on female homosexuality: a discussion of 'The Lesbian as a "Single" Woman'. In M.R. Walsh (ed.) (1987) *The Psychology of Women: Ongoing Debates*. New Haven and London: Yale University Press, 1987.

Sontag, S. (1979) The double standard of aging. In J.H. Williams (ed.) *Psychology of Women: Selected Readings*. New York and London: W.W. Norton.

Sophie, J. (1985) A critical examination of stage theories of lesbian identity development. *Journal of Homosexuality*, 12(2), 39–51.

Sophie, J. (1987) Internalized homophobia and lesbian identity. *Journal of Homosexuality*, 14(1/2), 53–65.

Spence, J.T. (1993) Women, men and society: plus ça change, plus c'est la même chose. In S. Oskamp and M. Costanzo (eds) *Gender Issues in Contemporary*

Society. The Claremont Symposium on Applied Social Psychology, pp. 3–17. Newbury Park, CA and London: Sage.

Spence, J.T. and Sawin, L.L. (1985) Images of masculinity and femininity: a reconceptualization. In V.E. O'Leary, R.K. Unger and B.S. Wallston (eds) *Women, Gender and Social Psychology*, pp. 35–66. Hillsdale, NJ and London: Lawrence Erlbaum.

Spence, J.T., Helmreich, R. and Stapp, J. (1974) The Personal Attributes Questionnaire: a measure of sex role stereotypes and masculinity–femininity. *Journal Supplement Abstract Service Catalog of Selected Documents in Psychology*, 4(43), Ms. no. 617.

Spence, J.T., Helmreich, R. and Stapp. J. (1975) Ratings of self and peers on sex role attributes and their relation to self-esteem and conceptions of masculinity and femininity. *Journal of Personality and Social Psychology*, 32(1), 29–39.

Spender, D. and Sarah, E. (eds) (1988) *Learning to Lose: Sexism and Education*. Second edition. London: The Women's Press.

Stanley, J.P. and Wolfe, S.J. (eds) (1980) *The Coming Out Stories*. Watertown, MA: Persephone Press.

Sternlicht, M. (1987) The neo-Freudians. In L. Diamant (ed.) *Male and Female Homosexuality: Psychological Approaches*, pp. 97–107. Washington: Hemisphere.

Stevenson, M.R. (1988) Promoting tolerance for homosexuality: an evaluation of intervention strategies. *Journal of Sex Research*, 25(4), 500–11.

Stewart-Park, A. and Cassidy, J. (1977) *We're Here: Conversations with Lesbian Women*. London: Quartet.

Stockdale, J.E. (1991) Sexual harassment at work. In J. Firth-Cozens and M.A. West (eds) *Women at Work: Psychological and Organizational Perspectives*, pp. 53–65. Milton Keynes: Open University Press.

Stoller, R.J. (1975) *The Transsexual Experiment* (Sex and Gender, vol. II). London: Hogarth Press.

Strommen, E.F. (1989) You're a what? Family member reactions to the disclosure of homosexuality. *Journal of Homosexuality*, 18(1/2), 37–58.

Sudman, S. and Bradburn, N.M. (1982) *Asking Questions*. San Francisco and London: Jossey-Bass.

Tajfel, H. (1981) *Human Groups and Social Categories*. Cambridge: Cambridge University Press.

Tajfel, H. (1982a) Social psychology of intergroup relations. *Annual Review of Psychology*, 33, 1–39.

Tajfel, H. (1982b) Instrumentality, identity and social comparisons. In H. Tajfel (ed.) *Social Identity and Intergroup Relations*, pp. 483–507. Cambridge: Cambridge University Press.

Tatchell, P. (1990) *Out in Europe: A Guide to Lesbian and Gay Rights in 30 European Countries*. London: Channel 4 Television.

Taylor, A. (1983) Conceptions of masculinity and femininity as a basis for stereotypes of male and female homosexuals. In M.W. Ross (ed.) *Homosexuality and Social Sex Roles*. New York: Haworth Press.

Taylor, N. (ed.) (1986) *All in a Day's Work*. London: Lesbian Employment Rights.

Trenchard, L. and Warren, H. (1984) *Something to Tell You*. London Gay Teenage Group, London: Trojan Press.

Troiden, R.R. (1989) The formation of homosexual identities. *Journal of Homosexuality*, 17(1/2), 43–73.

Turner, J.C. (1982) Towards a cognitive redefinition of the social group. In H. Tajfel (ed.) *Social Identity and Intergroup Relations*, pp. 15–40. Cambridge: Cambridge University Press.

Turner, J.C. (1984) Social identification and psychological group formation. In H. Tajfel (ed.) *The Social Dimension*, vol. 2, pp. 518–38.

Turner, J.C., Hogg, M.A., Oakes, P.J., Reicher, S.D. and Wetherell, M.S. (1987) *Rediscovering the Social Group: A Self-Categorization Theory*. Oxford and New York: Basil Blackwell.

Tyler, P.A. (1984) Homosexual behaviour in animals. In K. Howell (ed.) *The Psychology of Sexual Diversity*, pp. 42–62. Oxford: Basil Blackwell.

Uleman, J.S. and Weston, M. (1986) Does the BSRI inventory sex roles? *Sex Roles*, 15(1/2), 43–62.

Ussher, J.M. (1991) *Women's Madness: Misogyny or Mental Illness?* London: Harvester Wheatsheaf.

Vance, C.S. (1989) Social construction theory: problems in the history of sexuality. In D. Altman et al. (eds) *Which Homosexuality?*, pp. 13–34. London: GMP.

Viss, D.C. and Burn, S.M. (1992) Divergent perceptions of lesbians: a comparison of lesbian self-perceptions and heterosexual perceptions. *Journal of Social Psychology*, 132(2), 169–77.

Ward, R.A. (1979) Typifications of homosexuals. *The Sociological Quarterly*, 20, pp. 411–23.

Weber, R.P. (1985) *Basic Content Analysis*. (Series: Quantitative Applications in the Social Sciences). Beverly Hills, CA and London: Sage.

Weedon, C. (1987) *Feminist Practice and Poststructuralist Theory*. Oxford: Basil Blackwell.

Weeks, J. (1977) *Coming Out: Homosexual Politics in Britain from the Nineteenth Century to the Present*. London: Quartet.

Weeks, J. (1986) *Sexuality*. Chichester: Ellis Horwood. London and New York: Tavistock.

Weeks, J. (1989) Against nature. In D. Altman et al. (eds) *Which Homosexuality?*, pp. 199–213. London: GMP.

Weinberger, L.E. and Millham, J. (1979) Attitudinal homophobia and support of traditional sex roles. *Journal of Homosexuality*, 4(3), 237–46.

Weitz, R. (1984) From accommodation to rebellion: the politicization of lesbianism. In T. Darty and S. Potter (eds) *Women-Identified Women*. Palo Alto, CA: Mayfield.

Weitz, R. (1989) What price independence? Social reactions to lesbians, spinsters, widows and nuns. In J. Freeman (ed.) *Women: A Feminist Perspective*. Fourth edition. Palo Alto, CA: Mayfield.

Wellings, K. and Wadsworth, J. (1990) AIDS and the moral climate. In R. Jowell, S. Witherspoon and L. Brook with B. Taylor (eds) *British Social Attitudes: The 7th Report*, pp. 109–26. Aldershot: Gower and Social and Community Planning Research.

Wellings, K., Field, J., Johnson, A.M. and Wadsworth, J. (1994) *Sexual Behaviour in Britain: The National Survey of Sexual Attitudes and Lifestyles*. Harmondsworth: Penguin.

West, D.J. (1977) *Homosexuality Re-examined*. London: Duckworth.

West, D.J. (1983) Homosexuality and lesbianism. *The British Journal of Psychiatry*, 143, 221–6.

Whitley, B.E. Jr (1987) The relationship of sex-role orientation to heterosexuals' attitudes toward homosexuals. *Sex Roles*, 17(1/2), 103–13.

Whitley, B.E. Jr (1988) Sex differences in heterosexuals' attitudes toward homosexuals: it depends upon what you ask. *Journal of Sex Research*, 24, 287–91.

Whitley, B.E. Jr and Kite, M.E. (1995) Sex differences in attitudes toward homosexuality: a comment on Oliver and Hyde (1993). *Psychological Bulletin*, 117(1), 146–54.

Wilkinson, S. (ed.) (1986) *Feminist Social Psychology: Developing Theory and Practice*. Milton Keynes: Open University Press.

Wilkinson, S. and Kitzinger, C. (eds) (1993) *Heterosexuality: A Feminism and Psychology Reader*. London: Sage.

Williams, J.A. (1984) Gender and intergroup behaviour: towards an integration. *British Journal of Social Psychology*, 23, 311–16.

Williams, J.H. (1987) *Psychology of Women: Behavior in a Biosocial Context*. Third edition. New York and London: W.W. Norton.

Wilson, M. (ed.) (1991) *Girls and Young Women in Education: A European Perspective*. Oxford: Pergamon Press.

Wittig, M. (1992) One is not born a woman. In H. Abelove, M.A. Barale and D.M. Halperin (eds) (1993) *The Lesbian and Gay Studies Reader*, pp. 103–9. New York and London: Routledge.

Wolff, C. (1973) *Love between Women*. London: Duckworth.

Woodman, N.J. and Lenna, H.R. (1980) *Counseling with Gay Men and Women*. San Francisco and London: Jossey-Bass.

World Health Organization (1992) *The ICD-10 Classification of Mental and Behavioural Disorders: Clinical Descriptions and Diagnostic Guidelines*. Geneva: World Health Organization.

Zanna, M.P. and Pack, S. (1975) On the self-fulfilling nature of apparent sex differences in behavior. *Journal of Experimental Social Psychology*, 11, 583–91.

Zitter, S. (1987) Coming out to Mom: theoretical aspects of the mother–daughter process. In Boston Lesbian Psychologies Collective (eds) *Lesbian Psychologies: Explorations and Challenges*. Urbana and Chicago: University of Illinois Press.

Subject index

Author index